Who Killed Jill Dando?

The case of Barry George
A shocking miscarriage of justice

S. C. Lomax

www.kemptonmarks.com

A Kempton Marks Book
An Authors OnLine Ltd Company

Copyright © Kempton Marks 2005

Text Copyright © S C Lomax 2005

Cover design by Sandra Davis ©
Back cover picture by kind permission of Mike Bourke

The Rights of S C Lomax to be identified as the author of this work have been asserted in accordance with sections 77 and 78 of the Copyright Designs and Patents Act 1988.

All rights reserved. No part of this publication may be reproduced, stored in a retrieval system, or transmitted in any form or by any means, electronic, mechanical, photocopy, recording or otherwise, without prior written permission of the copyright owner. Nor can it be circulated in any form of binding or cover other than that in which it is published and without similar condition including this condition being imposed on a subsequent purchaser.

ISBN 0 7552 0503 0

Kempton Marks
40 Castle Street
Hertford SG14 1HR
England

This book is also available in e-book format, details of which are available at www.authorsonline.co.uk

I dedicate this book to Barry George and Jill Dando:
May the truth out and justice finally prevail.

Contents

Glossary	vi
Foreword	xi
Chapter 1: A background to the crime	1
Chapter 2: Monday 26 April 1999	9
Chapter 3: Clues and the police investigation before George became a suspect	15
3.1: The police investigation is launched	15
3.2: The scene of the crime	17
3.3: The statements from witnesses	21
3.4: The post mortem examination	22
3.5: Early actions in the investigation	25
3.6: The motive of the killer	28
3.7: Discovery and elimination of suspects	38
Chapter 4: The police investigate George	49
4.1: How George came to be investigated	49
4.2: George is questioned	52
4.3: George's personality	56
4.4: Motive	58
4.5: Searches of George's flat	59
4.6: Further investigations into the suspect through covert operations	62
4.7: George's criminal record	63
4.8: The police decide whether or not George should be charged	63
Chapter 5: The evidence against George	67
5.1: Obsessions	68
5.2: Loner	70
5.3: George's interest in firearms	70
5.4: Witnesses and identification	72
5.5: George's actions on the day of the crime and his suspicious actions two days later	77
5.6: The particle	80

People

Susan Bicknell – a member of staff at Hafad, who has always been adamant that George was with her at 11:50 on the day of Dando's murder.

Janet Bolton – a witness who saw a man running down Gowan Avenue between 11:35 and 11:40 on the day of the shooting.

Barry Bulsara – one of George's aliases used to pay homage to the late Freddie Mercury, lead singer of the rock group 'Queen', whose real surname was Bulsara.

Police Constable Cain – an officer who was present at one of the searches of George's flat, and handled George's Cecil Gee jacket.

Detective Chief Inspector Hamish Campbell – the Senior Investigating Officer (SIO) in the Oxborough investigation.

Robert Charig – A friend of George for over twenty years.

Susan Coombe – a resident of a Bed and Breakfast establishment where George lived in the 1980's. She was a prosecution witness called to give evidence of George's interest in guns.

Charlotte de Rosnay – a witness who saw a man jogging down Gowan Avenue approximately two hours before Dando's murder.

Stella de Rosnay – a witness who saw a man jogging down Gowan Avenue approximately two hours before Dando's murder; the mother-in-law of Charlotte de Rosnay.

Michelle Diskin – George's sister.

David Dobbins – a former friend of George who the prosecution called to provide evidence at trial of George's interest in guns.

Helen Doble – a friend of Dando, who found Dando's body slumped outside 29 Gowan Avenue.

Marilyn Etienne – George's solicitor at the time of his arrest, trial and appeal.

Alan Farthing – Dando's fiancé at the time of her death.

Mr Justice Gage – the judge who presided over George's trial.

Detective Constable John Gallagher – the officer who first questioned George in connection with the murder.

Terry Griffin – a postman who saw a man stood near Dando's house one and a half hours before the shooting.

Professor Gisli Gudjonsson – an expert psychologist who believes George is incapable of planning an efficient act of execution.

The Reverend John Hale – a witness who claims to have seen armed police officers enter George's flat during one of their searches.

John Hole – a man known to have stalked Dando until approximately one year before her death.

Detective Inspector Horrocks – the officer who suggested, in February 2000, that a review should be made of the earliest information provided to the police.

Richard Hughes – Dando's next-door neighbour, who saw the gunman leave the scene of the crime.

Elaine Hutton – a member of staff from Hafad who testified at trial that George was present at the centre at *"around midday"* on the day of the shooting.

Mr Robin Keeley – a prosecution expert witness who believed that Firearms Discharge Residue from the scene of the crime matched alleged residue from a jacket belonging to George.

Doctor John Lloyd – a defence expert witness who believes that the alleged particle of Firearms Discharge Residue, found in a jacket belonging to George, does not relate to the crime.

Steve Majors – one of George's former aliases, which he used whilst being interested in stunts.

Michael Mansfield QC – The defence barrister at the trial and appeal hearings.

Susan Mayes – the main prosecution witness who claimed to have seen George near Dando's home four and a half hours before the murder. Without her evidence it is almost certain that George would not have been convicted.

Major Peter Mead – a ballistics expert, called by the defence, who believed that Dando's murderer committed the crime in a *"near perfect"* manner.

Julia Moorhouse – a witness who claims to have been with George at 12:30 on the day of the murder, near Hafad.

Theresa (Terry) Normanton – a witness who allegedly saw a man on Gowan Avenue at 09:50 on the day of Dando's murder.

Susan Oddie – a woman who informed the police that George owned air rifles and was mentally unstable.

Thomas Palmer – One of George's aliases during the 1980's taken from a former member of the SAS.

Ramesh Paul – a member of staff from Traffic Cars who was confronted by an agitated George on the day of the murder and two days later.

Orlando Pownall QC – the Senior Treasury Counsel (Barrister) who led the prosecution at the trial and appeal hearings.

Joseph Sappleton – a witness who provided a description of a man the police originally believed could have been Dando's killer. It was Sappleton who helped produce the E-fit.

Helen Scott – a witness who saw a man near Dando's home on the evening before the murder.

Detective Inspector Snowden – the officer who interviewed George at Hammersmith Police Station.

Leslie Symes – a member of staff at Hafad who told the police that George was at the centre at 11:00 on the day of Dando's murder, but later said the visit was made after lunch.

Rosario Torres - a member of staff from Hafad who believed George was at the centre between 12:30 and 13:00 on the day of the murder.

Geoffrey Upfill-Brown – a neighbour of Dando who saw the gunman make his escape.

Mark Webster – a defence expert witness who claimed at trial that the fibre found on Dando's raincoat was insignificant evidence.

Doctor Susan Young – a psychologist who believes that George could not commit a murder and maintains his innocence.

Foreword

During the afternoon of 26 April 1999 news began to spread of a horrific incident that had taken place in Fulham, south-west London. A woman had been shot in the head outside her home. A woman being shot in the daytime in a suburban street in Britain is shocking. Such crimes make us realise the dangers that exist in our society. This was not just any woman though; in this instance the victim of the crime was the television presenter Jill Dando.

More than two years later, on 2 July 2001, a forty one year old man named Barry Michael George was convicted at the Old Bailey, by a majority of ten to one, of murdering Dando. Only eleven jurors decided upon the verdict at George's trial, as a member of the jury had been released due to a family bereavement. Millions sighed in relief, believing that justice had prevailed. However, the case of Barry George has proven to be one of the most controversial in recent British criminal history. Although George has launched two unsuccessful appeals he has an ever-growing number of supporters, including Members of Parliament, who believe he was not the man responsible for shooting the television presenter.

Who Killed Jill Dando? argues that the mystery surrounding Dando's murder has still not been resolved, with an innocent man serving a life sentence for a crime he did not commit. Although George hopes to have his case once again referred to the Court of Appeal his struggle is tremendous. Public opinion towards him has been adversely affected by the huge attention of the media who have frequently gained pleasure from demonising him. The adverse publicity to his case began before he entered any courtroom and continues to this day.

Prior to being charged with the murder of Dando, newspapers informed the public that Barry Bulsara, an unemployed, disabled man who lived alone in a flat on Crookham Road, Fulham and had served in the Territorial Army had been arrested in connection with the murder of Jill Dando.[1] Barry Bulsara claimed to be a cousin of Freddie Mercury. The potential consequences of this information

---

[1] *The Guardian*, 26 May 2000.

entering the public domain, if George had been released without charge when the public knew the identity and address of the main suspect, is unthinkable. Such exposure of information without doubt had an effect which cannot be fully appreciated upon the future of George.

A series of articles and photographs were published, along with what the judge who presided over George's trial, Mr Justice Gage, termed *"lurid headlines"*. The public was informed of details such as that George had altered his appearance. This was irrelevant although people could infer incorrect theories from such information.

It was articles like these that the future jurors were exposed to before the trial had begun. Such stories were covered in newspapers, on television and the radio. The public could not avoid exposure to such 'news' pieces. In addition to what had been told before he was charged, the public had a large amount of information about the defendant that could be interpreted as suggesting he was guilty. The majority of this information was in the public domain *before* a jury had been selected. The jurors heard the media's attempts of presenting the case for the prosecution before the trial had begun. Very few, if any, media publications or programmes prior to, and during the trial gave a balanced view. The jury must have been swayed when reading such information. The judge had told them to forget all they had heard, but this is appreciably difficult. What ever happened to the maxim 'innocent until proven guilty'?

Justice, more often than not, responds indirectly to public opinion. As a result of the media's coverage of the case the public opinion was, on the whole, firmly against George. In such cases true justice is challenged, particularly as the jury without doubt heard defamatory stories of the defendant.

As a result of the derogatory nature of the media's reportage, it is imperative that a full discussion of George's case should be presented to the public. This book attempts to offer the facts that can be used to demonstrate George's innocence.

I first began to have doubts regarding the case on the evening of George's conviction whilst watching a televised reconstruction of part of the trial. Up until this point in time my knowledge was confined to what had been presented by the media. The reconstruction highlighted the weaknesses of the prosecution and inspired me to write a piece of fiction based upon the murder of Jill Dando and the subsequent events.

However, when George's appeals were dismissed I felt compelled to involve myself in the campaign by writing a factual account to draw attention to what the Justice For Barry campaign call *'a mockery of justice'* that should be *'rectified as a matter of urgency.'* My research left no doubts in my mind that Barry George is the victim of one of the most shocking miscarriages of justice this country has seen in recent years. *Who Killed Jill Dando?* is the culmination of my research.

Who Killed Jill Dando? is an updated edition of my debut book *The Case of Barry George*. This new edition contains discussion of an alleged confession made by Barry George, reported by a recently released sex offender who, upon leaving prison, approached a national tabloid newspaper to sell his story. The new evidence, used by George's legal team to argue that his conviction should be quashed, is also discussed.

I would like to apologise to the family and friends of Jill Dando for discussing what must be a very painful subject. However, when they believed they saw a milestone when George was convicted in 2001, they really saw an illusion.

This book was written independently of the official Justice For Barry campaign, although I have occasionally referred to points raised by the campaign and by Barry George himself. The views and beliefs expressed in *Who Killed Jill Dando?* are my own, and are not necessarily shared by JFB.

It is hoped this book provides the relevant facts and will demonstrate that the evidence against George is not as convincing as many would like to believe, even if it does not convince readers that George is innocent.

S. C. Lomax

sclomax@kemptonmarks.com

March 2005

Chapter 1:

A background to the crime

"I am totally devastated and unable to comprehend what has happened. Jill was respected for her professional ability, admired by all who met her and adored by anyone who got to know her." [2]

The above words were echoed by many members of the public on hearing the news of the murder of Jill Dando. The majority of people in this country were shocked to hear that a woman could be shot just outside her home in broad daylight. On the evening of her death *The Six O'clock News* was extended to pay a lengthy tribute to the presenter. When they heard of the crime large numbers of members of the public paid their own tributes either by posting messages on the BBC website or by laying flowers outside Dando's home.

This book is not intended to form a biography of either Jill Dando or Barry George; there are plenty of accounts of the lives of both of these individuals. It is the sole purpose of this book to prove George's innocence, but in order to do this we need to understand the crime and have at least some background information about the victim. To take a glimpse into Dando's life is important if we are to understand for what reason, or reasons, her life was untimely ended.

The motiveless crime is a figment of the imagination. There is always a reason why someone would wish to carry out any sort of illegal activity, even if the reasoning is complex, and the shooting which occurred outside 29 Gowan Avenue is no exception. There may exist in her background a clue as to why such an act should be committed. Could it be the case that the past is the key to the present?

For whatever reason Dando was killed, it is important the reader

---

[2] The words of Alan Farthing, Jill Dando's fiancé, following the shooting.

is made aware of the background to this crime so that information discussed later in this book can be fully understood.

Jill Dando was born on 9 November 1961 in the town of Weston-Super-Mare on the coastline of north Somerset. It was in this town that Dando would spend her childhood years and the early years of her adult life. In 1965, aged just three, she had undergone major heart surgery and there had been fears she would not survive. Of course she did survive, and despite the surgery she grew to have a normal childhood.

Dando was the daughter of a compositor who worked for the local newspaper, *The Weston Mercury*, and her older brother became a reporter for the same newspaper when he began his working life. Dando too decided to apply for a job working for the *Mercury* when she left school in 1980. In order to be successful in her application, she was required to write a five hundred word essay detailing her thoughts on the year 2000. The editor was satisfied with her writing skills, and offered her a job with the company. Dando had now stepped off the ground and on to the first step of the staircase to fame.

Weston-Super-Mare is not exactly the most exciting of places to live, and so being a journalist writing about current affairs within the town unsurprisingly does not meet up to glamorous expectations by a long shot. For this reason, presumably, Dando looked towards a more fulfilling job. Maybe she had an ambition from a young age, and a long-term career strategy made out in her mind, or maybe working for *The Weston Mercury* just did not provide her with the stimulation a young journalist needs. After all, her brother had moved on from the newspaper. While she remained working for *The Weston Mercury* her talent was being confined. However, she knew that to cease working for this newspaper which had created the foundation of her career would mean that she, like her brother, would have to leave her childhood town and her family home. She was therefore reluctant to seek employment elsewhere.

During the five years which Dando had spent working for this local newspaper, she had also worked for a hospital radio station. This experience would provide her with a taste for a different form of media from writing. She had enjoyed the work, and so in 1985 when she found an advertisement for a position at BBC Radio Devon, she decided to apply. After a successful interview (Dando was to prove very successful in interviews, which is not surprising when you consider her future career) at the age of 23 Dando began working in radio.

Radio Devon provided her with the opportunity to achieve greater fulfilment, and it would only be a short period of time before Dando was co-presenting the station's breakfast show. Even so, her ambition made her want greater things; she wished to gain employment in as high a position as her ability allowed. Dando would always question her ability to perform certain roles. She was modest about her potential despite the fact that she had tremendous abilities and the personality which makes it possible for a person to reach their potential. In a tribute to Dando following her death, Judi Kiseil, the managing editor of *The Weston Mercury*, wrote,

> "No one doubted she had potential to go far. The wonder was she ever doubted it herself ... It was soon obvious she had the personality to reach the top of her profession ..."[3]

In 1987, Dando applied for a job at *Television South West*. Once again, she charmed her way through another successful interview to be given the job of a television reporter. Dando would now be in the form of media for which she is best known. Again, her employment for the regional television station was short. After a few months Dando was asked to go to London to discuss the possibility of working on the newly-improved *BBC Breakfast Time*. This would mean that if she accepted, Dando would be making a huge leap forward from regional television to national television. Her natural radiance and ability was evident to those interviewing her, and after that first meeting she was offered the job. Although she would have some doubts later on, she accepted. It would be in the BBC that Jill Dando would dedicate the rest of her working life.

During the period of time in which she worked for the BBC in London, Dando was involved in a large number of projects. Here only a small number, that are relevant to the case, will be discussed.

In 1992 Dando began presenting the television programme *Holiday* which is the BBC's version of *Wish You Were Here...?* Tied in with this show were the later spin-off shows based upon this programme, to make what had been a show which was aired during the period when most people book their holidays into an almost year long series.

---

[3] *The Weston Mercury*.

The role of presenting *Holiday* undoubtedly appeared on the surface very glamorous to many viewers with its bonus of travel to many destinations across the globe. However, due to the amount of travel required Dando found the job to be very demanding. As she was involved in other work with the BBC the frequent travel meant she was often physically worn out and had very little time for herself. She did not see her friends or family as often as she would have liked, which must have been a strain upon relationships. It was for this reason that in 1999 she announced she was leaving the programme. This had been considered on many occasions in the past, but her impending marriage meant the many visits abroad were not possible. Dando's announcement came soon before her death; Dando told *The Radio Times* that she was *"determined... to move away from all those holiday programmes"*. The issue featuring the interview was still on sale on the day Dando was killed.

Dando displayed a tremendous amount of talent when presenting *Holiday* and the programmes related to this travel series. As a result of her ability to interest the viewers she acquired many fans. However a television programme which shows a female presenter who often appears in summer wear can ultimately result in a person or people acquiring a fixation. It is indisputable that many people became attracted to Dando because of her appearances on *Holiday*.

As a result of the time taken up by *Holiday*, from 1994 onwards Dando could no longer continue to co-present *BBC Breakfast Time*. Instead she decided to present *The Six O'clock News* when her schedule made it possible for her to do so.

The role of newsreader is one that generally requires formality in order to ensure serious news stories are conveyed in the most appropriate manner. In order to achieve the desired effect, many newsreaders appear too formal. Dando carried out this role professionally, and although she maintained a sufficient degree of formality in her work when reading the news, as well as when presenting the other television programmes she worked upon, Dando gave a more informal and natural performance. This made her a woman who the viewers could see to be an ordinary person; people could relate to her. Dando's warm personality radiated and was apparent to all her viewers. This was one reason for her success, but unfortunately it could have been one of the ultimate reasons for her death.

In 1999 Dando announced she had also resigned from reading the news to enable her to enjoy more of a personal life.

5.7: Other forensic evidence   81
5.8: George's lies to the police   82
5.9: Any other evidence   83
5.10: George's criminal record   84

Chapter 6: Arguments to suggest George is innocent
6.1: Obsessions   86
6.2: Loner   92
6.3: George's interest in firearms   93
6.4: Witnesses and identification   99
6.5: George's actions on the day of the crime and his suspicious actions two days later   118
6.6: The particle   130
6.7: Other forensic evidence   136
6.8: George's lies to the police   139
6.9: Any other evidence   142
6.10: George's criminal record   144
6.11: Any other arguments in George's defence   145

Chapter 7: Further discussion of the evidence   149

Chapter 8: A false confession?   157

Chapter 9: Reason to doubt?   164

Chapter 10: The man who murdered Jill Dando   175

Chapter 11: Conclusions   181

Bibliography   202

Appendix   185

Glossary of Terms, Places and Names

Terms

Firearms Discharge Residue – microscopic particles of firearms discharge residue (FDR) are released from a gun when it has been fired.

HOLMES – the computerised database system used by the police to collate information. It is an acronym for Home Office Large Major Enquiry System.

Operation Oxborough – the name of the police investigation into the murder of Jill Dando.

Places

29 Gowan Avenue – the Fulham home of Jill Dando and the scene of the crime.

2b Crookham Road – the home of Barry George.

Hafad – Hammersmith and Fulham Action for Disability (an advice centre located approximately half a mile from the scene of the crime where George visited on the day of the murder and two days later).

Traffic Cars – a taxi company located near the scene of the crime where George visited on the day of the murder and two days later.

It was undoubtedly in her role as co-presenter of the television programme *Crimewatch UK* that Dando was best known. After her death the irony that she had been involved in the fight against crime and had died as a result of crime was frequently highlighted. This meant inevitably most people remember her as *'the woman who presented Crimewatch'* despite the fact she had worked on other programmes more frequently and over a longer period of time.

The first episode of *Crimewatch,* which Dando co-presented alongside Nick Ross, was screened in September 1995, and so Dando only worked on the programme for just over three and a half years. Crime was an issue Dando was very much interested in and Nick Ross would claim after her death that Dando was passionate about *Crimewatch.* The fact that episodes were shown once a month meant that the role of co-presenter for this programme was ideal for her. Far less time was demanded working for this programme than for any of the other projects in which she was involved. Also, Dando did not write the scripts (a task which her predecessor had always carried out along with Nick Ross). Dando was due to finish working for *The Six O'clock News* and *Holiday* but there was no doubt she intended to continue her involvement with *Crimewatch.*

One of the final projects undertaken by Dando before her death was a new series involving something that has become increasingly popular in recent years, antiques.

Dando had enjoyed filming *The Antiques Inspectors* partly because it was filmed in Britain, which meant that it was a less demanding programme than *Holiday.* It is likely that (had she lived longer) when she ceased to continue presenting *The Six O'clock News* and *Holiday* she would continue presenting this programme.

The first episode of *The Antiques Inspectors* was aired on the evening before the fatal shooting incident. Dando believed it had been very successful; ratings were high and many had praised her for what was an enjoyable programme. As a mark of respect no further episodes of the series, which had been recorded in advance, were ever shown.

To advertise this new series on the BBC *The Radio Times* featured an interview with Dando and a discussion of the new programme. On the magazine's front cover there was a photograph of Dando dressed in leather and some newspapers were to claim this was the reason Dando was murdered. On the back cover of the magazine there was an advertisement offering crime books. At the top of the page it read, *'Couldn't you just murder?'* When the magazine was laid flat, with the cover facing up, it read *'Couldn't you just murder? Jill Dando'*

Additional projects included a televised appeal, which was made to help the people of Kosovo. The Milosevic regime's attempt to enforce its policy of ethnic cleansing had resulted in the displacement of large numbers of Kosovan refugees. Dando had made a public appeal for funds to be raised so help could be given to those people forced out of their homes. This is very relevant to the case, and some have argued that this appeal for financial assistance in order to help the people of the war torn country was directly responsible for Dando's murder.

Dando was in the running for presenting the BBC's coverage of the new millennium and she was due to commentate on the wedding of Prince Edward and Sophie Rhys-Jones. The importance of both of these events for many is a reflection of how valued she was by the BBC and just how good she was at her job. It is rather ironic that writing about the year 2000 was to begin Dando's media career, and by 1999 she was popular enough to be in the running for presenting the BBC's year 2000 celebrations.

Dando would also continue presenting *Crimewatch*, *The Antiques Inspectors* and many other one off projects including a two-part *Panorama* special discussing organ transplants and an eight-part special about the police and crime.

In the final months of her life, when Dando was not filming television programmes or preparing for them, she was often being interviewed for magazines and newspapers or participating in charity events. It is, therefore, clear that Jill Dando was very busy as a result of her career.

It is tempting to concentrate upon the professional and public face of a celebrity. All too often we hear stories of fans, of television soaps in particular, approaching members of the cast and insulting them because the characters they play have done wrong in the television programme. Most people concentrate solely upon what they see on the television screens, neglecting to consider that these people are essentially ordinary, with private lives. What they see on the screen is an act, with even newsreaders often displaying a false charm. Let us now consider some aspects of the private life of Jill Dando. Some detectives would later state that it would be here the solution to the murder would lie.

Between 1980 and 1999 Dando had emerged from a small

newspaper and risen to become one of the BBC's leading television presenters. In 1997 she had been named the BBC Personality of the Year at a prestigious ceremony and would later be referred to as the face of the BBC, although in life she was not quite a celebrity in the true definition of the word. Along the way during this period she had helped charities, locally and nationally, and had tried to continue her family life with her parents and brother. The mother she was very close to died in 1986.

It is not particularly surprising then that during this period of time she had not married and had children. She had relationships but, prior to meeting Alan Farthing, these had not resulted in engagements let alone weddings. David James Smith, in his book *All About Jill: The Life and Death of Jill Dando*, provides a detailed and interesting account of Dando's love life. It is clear from this account and the police investigations that Dando's relationships often overlapped one another. With her often seeing more than one man at a time, the reality of her personality can be said to be in conflict with the image she portrayed publicly. Dando was a real woman living in the modern world and had the lifestyle to match.

Dando was often the partner who ended the relationships she was involved in. David James Smith shows that on more than one occasion the relationship was ended just as the man was wishing for more commitment. Dando informed one man she did not believe she was capable of deep love, she told others she did not have the time for serious relationships.

Perhaps one, or more than one, of the presenter's former lovers could have been angered when Dando announced her engagement to Farthing, thus showing the men, who had in some cases hoped to marry the presenter themselves, she was indeed capable of deep love.

Dando would never be happier than when she was with her future fiancé Alan Farthing. She met Farthing, a gynaecologist, in 1997. The couple had much in common and over time the relationship became increasingly serious. During Dando's memorial service on 28 September 1999 Sir John Birt, Director-General of the BBC, discussed in his speech how happy Dando was when she was with Alan:

"Jill was a happy person - and she had never been happier than during her time with Alan. She confided to friends that he was clever and kind and made her laugh. She couldn't believe her luck."

By the end of January 1999 they had publicly announced their engagement. Their wedding was due to take place in September.

Dando had placed her home, 29 Gowan Avenue in Fulham, onto the property market prior to her murder. She had moved into Alan Farthing's home in Chiswick, West London, and only used her own home occasionally for work purposes. The couple were planning to buy a home together once they had married. By 26 April 1999, Dando had not sold her house although a relative of Dando's next-door neighbour, Richard Hughes, had made an offer. It must always be remembered when reading the following chapters, that Dando's visits to 29 Gowan Avenue were becoming increasingly rare and there was no pattern as to when these visits occurred.

Despite the fact she was no longer to present the *Six O'clock News* or *Holiday*, she was happy. Dando had fame and the lifestyle that came with it, and more importantly she had love and her wedding and future to look forward to. Things were certainly looking good, and it was a tragedy her life should be ended just as she was at her happiest.

Towards the end of her life fears had appeared in Dando's mind. Dando worried she had acquired a stalker. She had good reason to believe this, for in 1998 an obsessed man had harassed her with frightening telephone calls and letters. Due to her warm personality Dando gained many fans. However, she had also gained the attention of more than her fair share of hard-core fanatics who had become fixated with the celebrity. By the beginning of 1999 Dando had told colleagues she seriously feared for her safety. Her fears were later to be justified in an incident that would end her life and shock the nation.

Dando never presented the BBC millennium programme and she was never to see the new millennium. Her prediction, which initiated her media career, that by the year 2000 she would be married with two children, was proven to be very wrong. A single bullet ended her hopes and dreams and it stole a unique woman from the lives of many. That bullet was fired on Monday 26 April 1999.

Chapter 2:

Monday 26 April 1999

"There are some sick people out there. The programme [Crimewatch UK] has made me more aware of personal safety ... I also know that crimes are very rare. I always tell myself: don't have nightmares, do sleep well."[4]

For the reasons described in the last chapter Jill Dando was very happy when she woke up on the morning of Monday 26 April 1999. On Saturday 24 April she had attended a Royal Legion dinner party at the Natural History Museum. This charity event had proven to be both successful and enjoyable. On the Sunday Dando had received a telephone call from Alan Farthing's father congratulating her on her performance on *The Antiques Inspectors*. This had delighted her, as had their discussion regarding the plans for her wedding to Farthing.

The alarm clock at Farthing's home went off at 06:45 that morning and, if Dando was not already awake, it was at this time her final day was to begin. The weather that morning was typical for April. It was a grey, dull and miserable start to the day. For much of the morning it was overcast, with clouds and rain in the form of drizzle.

According to information provided during the trial by Farthing, he went to have a shower and when he had finished he found Dando had made breakfast for him and had returned to bed. Dando was not working on this particular day, although she was due to attend a charity event at lunchtime. The couple chatted while Farthing ate. Farthing left at 07:25 and he was never to see his fiancé alive again. The next time he would see her face would be when he was identifying her body at Charing Cross Hospital.

---

[4] Jill Dando speaking in an interview for BBC Online, as reported in *The Guardian*, 3 July 2001.

There is not a lot of information available to show what Dando did before she left Farthing's home that morning. It is known a few telephone calls were made; a significant number of her final hours were spent on the phone to various people. At 08:00 Farthing's mother phoned and at some point before 10:00 Dando's best friend called from work for a chat. It does not appear that any of her activities at the home of Alan Farthing can enlighten us upon the reason for her death. It is known Dando left the house in Chiswick, West London, at around 10:00.

Dando was aware she needed to do some shopping. On the Saturday of that week (two days before the fateful day) she had visited her home in Gowan Avenue and had discovered her fax machine cartridge needed to be changed. For this reason she intended to go to Hammersmith Mall to buy a replacement so that she would not miss any more faxes which were sent to 29 Gowan Avenue. She only planned to make a brief visit to the shopping centre, to buy paper and a cartridge, before making an even briefer visit to her own home in order to replace the cartridge and fill her fax machine with a supply of plain paper. Few people will have known that Dando had planned to visit her own home.

On her way to the mall, she stopped at a BP petrol station in order to fill her blue BMW 320i convertible with petrol. She also bought a pint of milk from the shop at 10:23 am. During this journey numerous telephone calls were made and received. None are directly relevant to the crime and so these will not be discussed fully. One important call was received at 10:30. Dando's agent phoned to enquire if Dando had received the faxes that had been sent to her. Of course, Dando had not because the fax cartridge needed to be replaced. Dando told her agent she intended to visit 29 Gowan Avenue after shopping.

Prior to visiting the mall, at around 10:40, Dando went to King Street, which is in close proximity to the indoor shopping centre. Whilst at King Street Dando purchased some paper for her fax machine from Ryeman's stationery shop. The receipt showed her purchase was made at 10:46. She then went to the mall, though her time of arrival is not known for certain. However, the last images which were ever to be recorded of the woman who had spent a significant part of her life in front of the camera were captured on CCTV in and around this indoor shopping centre. At 10:55 she was seen entering Dixon's Link shop where she hoped to buy a cartridge for the fax machine. The footage shows how she browsed through the cartridges but was unable to find what she was looking for. She left the shop without making a purchase.

After the visit to this shop there are few images of Dando other than those of her car as she headed towards her Fulham home. It is known that soon after leaving Dixon's shop, she began her journey to Gowan Avenue. Despite having been unable to find a cartridge suitable for her fax machine, Dando had decided to make a brief visit to her own home. She knew she had to go to the charity event and so she decided to leave the milk in her own fridge rather than travel all the way back to Chiswick. Dando also intended to buy some fish for the evening meal, so she would also put this in the fridge at her own home. She intended to collect these items on her way back from the event, which was closer to Fulham than it was to Chiswick, as a matter of convenience.

It is known Dando received a phone call on her mobile phone at around 11:00. Following the murder the police studied CCTV footage and found frames showing what was assumed to be Dando's BMW heading towards Fulham shortly after 11:00. Also around this time another driver saw her stuck in traffic as she headed towards Fulham.

It is known that Dando bought two filleted Dover soles at around 11:20. These were purchased at Copes Seafood Company, which is located on Fulham Road close to the corner of Munster Road, approximately 500 yards from Gowan Avenue. After visiting this shop Dando made the final leg of the journey to her home.

At 11:30 Dando arrived at Gowan Avenue and immediately parked her car outside her home, which is unusual as Gowan Avenue has many cars parked on the road, even at 11:30 on a Monday. However, another motorist had recently driven away and therefore vacated this parking space. Dando locked her car and activated the alarm. The distinctive sound which could be heard when the car was locked informed neighbours the celebrity was making a visit to her home.

Dando, carrying the fish and milk which she intended to put in her fridge and collect later, turned towards her home and presumably opened the gate before heading up the path towards her door. Her car keys were in her hand, as was a bag of shopping. Her handbag was on her shoulder. The handbag was later found unzipped, and it is believed she was about to take her house keys from it. The car keys and house keys were kept separately. Given a few seconds, she would have been able to unlock her front door and enter the house. Time, however, was against her.

It would appear that the killer passed through the gate after Dando. He could not have been lying in wait planning to ambush his victim. Dando had walked up her path, and she would not have made this short walk if she had seen anybody there. There is nowhere to hide in front of the house as it is only a small area. There was a bay tree and a small wall, but this was not sufficient cover to remain unseen for a long period of time. The gate was not a complete barrier to vision. The killer would therefore have been unable to stay there for very long. If he did then it increased the chances of him being caught, as anyone walking past could see and the police would be alerted.

Very soon after she began to walk the very short distance up her path Dando's next-door neighbour, Richard Hughes, heard a scream. He later described the scream as *"distinctive ... she sounded quite surprised"*. Hughes also explained how he thought she must be sharing a joke with her fiancé and he thought nothing of it. However, he was surprised and curious when he heard his neighbour scream a second time. He described the scream as quite lengthy.

The killer did not waste time. After following his victim he grabbed her by her right arm, forcing her to the ground. Presumably he did this so anyone who happened to look in that direction would be unable to see what was happening. With his left hand he held the gun as he crouched behind his victim, holding her tightly so she could not escape. She was unable to put up much resistance; the fact she had bags in her hands would not have helped her. Perhaps she attempted to get her keys so she could quickly get inside her house, but she had insufficient time.

It is likely that the first scream was her reaction to seeing the man, and possibly the gun. Her second scream presumably occurred immediately prior to the bullet being fired. The killer had pressed his gun into the side of Dando's head, causing her to scream. Dando's head was horizontally positioned, just above the doorstep, and her body was possibly parallel with the door (the reasoning behind this is discussed in the next chapter). When the killer pulled the trigger few people heard the shot due to the close proximity of the barrel to the victim's head, which smothered the explosive sound.

On hearing the second scream, Richard Hughes looked out of his shutters from the upstairs room in which he was sitting, to see a respectable-looking man whom he at first believed could have been a friend of the television presenter. The man was seen to close the gate behind him as he left, and he turned left down Gowan Avenue towards the busier Fulham Palace Road. Hughes described the man's manner to the police as calm. He commented on how he walked *"very calmly away"*. It must be noted that the period of time from Dando locking her car to being shot, and Hughes seeing the man walk *"very calmly away"* lasted only seconds. It is believed that no more than thirty or forty seconds could have elapsed. Presumably, the killer made his entrance only seconds before the first scream. This would mean that there was no time for a conversation or any form of exchange. Hughes believed it was one minute. As will be demonstrated later, overestimating time is a recurring problem in many cases, including this one.

At some time just after 11:30 a telephone call was made to Dando's mobile phone, but no one answered. Had this call been made just before she was shot, while the killer was holding her against the ground? Or did the phone ring after he left the scene? Either way none of the neighbours heard the ringing, and Dando was unable to answer.

Around ten to fifteen minutes after the gun was fired Helen Doble, who had often spoken to the television star, was walking past 29 Gowan Avenue. It was at this point it was realised a crime had occurred, when Jill Dando's body was seen slumped on the ground. At George's trial Doble described the horrific experience of how she discovered the body:

"It is just incredible that with one step everything changed. I was going about my business and anticipating the possibility of seeing Jill. To suddenly encounter such a violent scene was completely horrific. It took me a few seconds to realise it was Jill because of the way she looked. It was clear to me that she was dead."

It was Doble who made the call to the emergency services before seeking help from a neighbour she knew. On arriving at the crime scene and seeing the state of Dando the neighbour, a Ms Saunders who was at the home of Charlotte de Rosnay when Doble found her, went to the doctor's surgery which was only a few doors away. The doctor had left for lunch, but the receptionist came to see if she could help. The noise these three women made caused Richard Hughes, the man who was apparently suspicious on seeing the man walking away following two screams, to wonder what had happened. This was approximately ten to fifteen minutes after the murder. After seeing the man who presumably was the killer he went to use the bathroom and got dressed, believing nothing untoward had happened to his neighbour. The call for the emergency services was made at 11:47, and therefore it was quite some time between the shooting and the body being discovered. The body was outside, but the hedge and gate obstructed the view. The body could only really be seen from close range. The fifteen-minute delay shows that the killer was able to murder a woman in broad daylight, on a London street, without arousing suspicion.

Dando was lying on the ground with her head on the doorstep. The neighbours noticed her car keys were in her hand. She was unconscious and bleeding. The wound was clearly very serious, but none of the neighbours were aware it was caused by a bullet which had been fired at close range. For this reason, and also because no one as yet had commented on how they heard a gunshot, it was initially believed Dando had been stabbed in the head. During the phone call to the emergency services, Doble told how Dando turned blue and was not breathing. The neighbours feared she had died.

At around 11:53 a police immediate response vehicle arrived on the scene. Two ambulances soon followed, before a helicopter landed nearby bringing a doctor to the scene of the incident so that the paramedics could be assisted. At 12:20. Dando was taken to Charing Cross Hospital where she arrived at 12:30. By this time an hour had elapsed. Even if a much shorter period had passed the injury would have proved to be a major problem. The medical staff would have had a difficult challenge in keeping their patient alive. Realistically they were aware that nothing could be done to save Dando's life. However, in spite of the nature of the injuries sustained the staff attempted to revive their patient. Despite their efforts Dando died from her injuries. She was pronounced dead at 13:03.

Chapter 3:

Clues and the police investigation before George became a suspect

'Detection is, or ought to be, an exact science and should be treated in the same cold and unemotional manner.'[5]

3.1: The police investigation is launched

As stated in the last chapter the call to the emergency services was made at around 11:47, and within six minutes a police car arrived outside 29 Gowan Avenue.

Scotland Yard began an investigation into what they believed to be an incident in which the television star Jill Dando had been stabbed in the head. Later, the investigation would be named Operation Oxborough, the name being selected randomly with Oxborough being the name of a village in Norfolk. It was Detective Chief Inspector Hamish Campbell who assumed the role of Senior Investigating Officer (SIO) and in doing so became the man responsible for one of Britain's largest, most expensive and in some ways most controversial murder investigations.

As in most investigations incredibly little was known in the early hours of the investigation. This is demonstrated by the fact the police originally believed they were dealing with a stabbing incident and it would not be until later that it would be determined the cause of death was a bullet fired into the head. Presumably soon after 13:03 that terrible day, the police were informed their assault had become a murder investigation. At this moment in time a formal identification had not been made but there was little doubt as to the identity of the victim. The identification was merely a formality.

---

[5] Sherlock Holmes speaking in *The Sign of Four*.

The police were fully aware of the pressure they would face when investigating the murder. In all high profile cases the police are under immense public pressure to capture those responsible, and this is particularly the case when a celebrity or some other high profile member of society is killed. We expect the police to capture the guilty one(s), and we expect nothing less than the police to meet this demand. As Dando had been the co-presenter of *Crimewatch*, the public doubly expected her murder to be solved. She was, as far as many were concerned, a much loved celebrity, and the police were soon to discover how well respected she was when the terrible news was released to the public, stating at first, Dando had been attacked with a knife, but later she had been murdered. However, the criminal mind can often be ingenious and it is hardly surprising to anyone who understands this, that the police sometimes fail to meet public expectation.

At the time of the Dando shooting, the Metropolitan Police Force already had other high profile cases to investigate which were receiving mounting criticism. A series of nail bombings, in which members of ethnic minorities and homosexuals were targeted, needed to be resolved. Also, bitter feelings were still held against Scotland Yard regarding the murder of Stephen Lawrence. The Macpherson Report, which had investigated the handling of the Lawrence murder, had found the Met had made monumental blunders during their enquiries, they had failed to perform their duty and that they were guilty of *'institutional racism.'* Unsurprisingly public confidence in the Metropolitan Police was greatly reduced.

The Macpherson Report not only criticised the Metropolitan Police for their poor performance in the Stephen Lawrence case. When the report was published in February 1999 (only two months prior to Dando's death) it strongly criticised the way in which the Met handled murder investigations. It showed that on average ninety-two percent of all murders in Britain were solved. However, the report severely criticised the Met who were, it said, only capable of solving eighty-four percent of murders in the area it policed. Clearly they were significantly behind the national average and needed to catch up.

When Jill Dando was shot only two months after the report was published, the police, understandably, would have recognised the immense importance of solving this high-profile case. Up to fifty detectives were immediately assigned to the investigation on a full-time basis, although the number reduced slightly as the months passed by. With so many detectives working solely on a single murder hunt other cases suffered; vital resources were being diverted from other investigations solely for the Jill Dando inquiry. For example the investigation into the killing of Katerina Koneva stopped in 1999 as a direct result of Hamish Campbell (who had headed the hunt for the killer) being given full-time responsibility for Operation Oxborough. Koneva's mother would later talk about how angry she became when the police stopped making telephone calls to her because they were too busy on the Dando investigation. *"Equal justice was not being done."*, she would say. Fortunately Koneva's killer has since been convicted, but the postponement of active investigations could have realistically resulted in her death remaining unsolved.

Concentrating on one case was not likely to enable the Metropolitan Police to catch up with the ninety-two percent average of successfully solved murders. The shooting of Jill Dando had to be solved as quickly as possible so that work on other cases could continue. Someone had to be held to account to satisfy statistics and reduce public criticism. The investigation into the murder of Jill Dando was therefore, at least to a certain extent, a political issue and one that needed to be resolved. To restore confidence in the police, and more importantly the Metropolitan Police, the person or people responsible for Dando's death needed to be caught ... regardless of the price. This then, was the pressure DCI Campbell and the rest of the murder squad found themselves under, and the pressure would increase as time passed by. It is important to realise how badly the police needed to catch the killer, as such an understanding could explain why the investigation was conducted in the way it was.

3.2: The scene of the crime

As is routine in any criminal investigation where forensic evidence is sought to be a means of assistance, the scene of the crime was cordoned off. Access to Gowan Avenue was prevented also. By the time the officers from the Scenes of Crime Branch had arrived however, a number of people had been outside 29 Gowan Avenue; Helen Doble, Ms Saunders, and the receptionist from the doctor's surgery, Richard Hughes, Hughes' sister-in-law, the paramedics and police officers. These people may have destroyed some evidence left by the killer, but this will never be known.

It has been presumed Dando's killer did not steal anything from his victim. She had her purse and handbag with her although her handbag was open. This was probably because she had opened it to take her house keys out and put her car keys in at the same time. This indicates the killer's need for speed and him not wanting to leave clues. This point will be discussed further in a later section within this chapter.

Identification Officers from the Scenes of Crime Branch of Scotland Yard arrived at 29 Gowan Avenue soon after Dando's body was removed. In 1988 The Metropolitan Police Force began to phase out the Scenes of Crime Officers (SOCO) believing these officers provided unsatisfactory results. Every time a Scenes of Crime Officer retired, he or she was replaced with an Identification Officer who is primarily qualified in the locating, lifting and identification of fingerprints although they are capable of working with other pieces of forensic evidence. The garden was covered with a large tarpaulin to prevent evidence being destroyed while a fingertip search was conducted.

The front door of Dando's house, and the gate at the end of her path, were removed for analysis in the hope that some evidence would be found. Inspection of the door later revealed a small dent towards the bottom from where the bullet had hit the door after passing through the victim's head. Although it was not important to the neighbours to remember the position of the body, their primary concern was to help her in any way which would prevent death. Their statements revealed information which in conjunction with the dent on the door and the post mortem findings which will be discussed later, proved Dando had her head close to, if not touching, the ground when the gun was fired.

The gate provided no information of relevance to the investigation. Fingerprints were lifted and these were compared to the fingerprints of all who had reason to touch the gate. However, no anomalous fingerprints were found, which Oxborough investigators took to be a sign that the killer's fingerprints were not present.

Oxborough were unfortunate in terms of the amount of forensic evidence yielded outside 29 Gowan Avenue. No DNA, from anyone other than the victim, was located at the scene. None of the killer's hairs were found on the victim or near her. The footprints in the garden could not be dated and they could have been anyone's prints as it was likely they had been there for some time. These were tested with sophisticated technology having been used to estimate the weight of the individual(s) who made the prints. No significant handprints were found anywhere at the scene. Examination of the victim and her clothing would later find microscopic particles of firearm's residue as well as a fibre that possibly came to be on Dando's raincoat when her killer's clothing came into contact with her. In essence no evidence was found at the scene, which could later be used to link a suspect with the murder, with certainty.

The person responsible did not leave any personal effects, which could be useful in assisting the detectives in their attempts to determine the identity of the man responsible.

A bullet and cartridge were discovered close to Dando's body. This indicates the killer wished to act quickly, as it would have been wiser to take the time to retrieve at least the cartridge. The bullet was a 9 mm calibre and therefore it was determined the gun used to fire the fatal bullet had been a 9 mm calibre firearm.

Upon the cartridge, the makers' mark was clearly visible on the head-stamp. The mark read 'R-P .380 auto'. This showed an American firearms' manufacturer known as Remington Arms Co., Inc had produced the cartridge (the R-P stood for Remington Peters). The .380 round showed that the weapon used was a 'short' as opposed to a 'parabellum'. Studies of the cartridge in conjunction with the bullet suggested the firearm used in the crime was a 9 mm calibre semi-automatic short handgun.

The gunman could have attempted to remove the writing from the cartridge, through gouging, grinding or scraping, in a bid to make the task of identifying the ammunition and type of weapon used more difficult. Many will inevitably ask why he did not do this. He could fairly easily have removed the text from the cartridge by etching away the lettering. However, he probably knew that experts would be able to temporarily produce an image of the figures. This is achieved through grinding, sanding and polishing the metal casing to a level deeper than the deepest gouge before adding acid and copper salts to restore, for a few minutes, the figures removed by the criminal.[6]

---

[6] (Houde. 1999: 168).

Usually a spent cartridge will have marks upon its surface that have been produced by the extractor and the ejector within the firearm. The bullet too would usually have marks upon its surface created when it was fired and passed down the barrel. These are known as rifling marks and are left on any bullet when a rifled weapon is used. Rifled weapons, unlike smooth-bored guns such as shotguns, have a spirally scored barrel interior composed of lands (raised spiralling) and grooves (indented spiralling). When the trigger is pulled rifling causes the bullet to rotate on its axis, thus preventing it from diverting from a stable course.

When these marks are present it is possible, through studies by ballistics experts, to match a bullet with a particular gun, for each weapon has a unique series of lands and grooves. However, the bullet and cartridge found outside 29 Gowan Avenue did not have such marks. This indicated that the weapon used had been converted in some way to make it smooth-bored. Studies showed the firearm used to kill Dando must have been a reactivated-deactivated handgun. This was either a former blank firing handgun which had been converted to allow live rounds to be fired, or a handgun with a smooth barrel which had once been over twenty four inches in length and had been shortened. In the first two cases the barrel would have been drilled and replaced with smooth tubing during the conversion process, thereby creating a barrel that had no rifling within.

There were, however, six curious indentations upon the cartridge. These marks were created through crimping. Many people crimp spent cartridges so they may be used again. Crimping tightens the cartridge round a bullet. However, the cartridge used in the murder of Jill Dando had never been used before. It was also curious, the crimping marks on the cartridge were clearly indicative of manual crimping. This was clear through the irregularity of the spacing of the indentations on the cartridge and their varying appearance. Usually a tool is used which leaves fewer marks identical in appearance. The marks on the cartridge, found outside 29 Gowan Avenue, varied suggesting that someone had manually tapped the cartridge. A nail, a pin of some sort, possibly a drawing pin, or some other small, pointed implement capable of making such puncture marks, was used.

The police have never seen such marks. Experts consulted, from across the world, have never seen or heard of these type of marks.

Of all the criminal activities carried out across the globe since the creation of the cartridge loaded firearm there are no records of these marks ever having been encountered. They were, and still are completely unexplainable as far as the police are concerned.

These indentations could have been made in order to assist the gunman in performing his act of execution indicating whoever made the marks had specialist knowledge of firearms; a knowledge which enabled him to create marks no one else could understand.

3.3: The statements from witnesses

The police received information from the public relating to a large number of sightings of men acting suspiciously, and also reports of vehicles seen close to the scene of the crime whose movements were considered to be relevant to the incident.

Many of the sightings reported to the police are discussed in the appendix starting on page 185. The sightings themselves are referred to throughout this book and these can all be found in the appendix.

It must be noted that in many criminal investigations, especially high-profile cases, large numbers of people will come forward to offer information about suspicious people they have seen. In the case of the Jill Dando murder, which of course took place in daylight, many sightings were inevitably reported as a consequence of the daily appeals for information and the emotions of the public at the time. Many innocent actions can be interpreted as being suspicious. People unconnected to any criminal activity could be construed as being involved in a crime, merely for being in the locality of where the offence was committed.

Although the sightings are fully discussed in the appendix of this book, it is important to mention here the only two sightings that almost certainly refer to the killer. Richard Hughes lived at 31 Gowan Avenue (next door to Jill Dando). After hearing his neighbour scream for the second time he looked out of his window to see a white man aged in his mid to late thirties, who was taller than 5'7" in height, of medium build with thick black, collar length hair, which was brushed back. The man was clean-shaven and was not wearing glasses. He was wearing a dark wax or Barbour style jacket. A man living opposite from Dando's home also saw the gunman leave Dando's garden at the same time as Hughes' observation. Geoffrey Upfill-Brown described the murderer as being aged between thirty and forty, around 5'10" in height, of medium build with a mop of thick, black, straight hair, which was collar length and could have been a wig. He was wearing very dark, tending to black, baggy clothing with a jacket reaching down to his knees.

The man, who was certainly Dando's killer, turned left having closed the gate. Although other witnesses reported a man who matched the description provided by these two witnesses, it can only be known for certain that Jill Dando's killer was last seen quickly walking and running, down Gowan Avenue, towards Fulham Palace Road.

3.4: The post mortem examination

A post mortem was conducted in the afternoon of April 26. DCI Campbell already knew Dando had received a gunshot wound; the doctors who had tried in vain to save the victim's life had informed him of this. However, he was unwilling to share this information until it had been confirmed.

The post mortem examination confirmed Dando had died from the injuries sustained when a single bullet was fired into the side of her head. The entry wound of the bullet was just above the victim's left ear and the exit wound was located just above her right ear. Examination of the entry wound revealed an impression in Dando's skin, which had been caused by the barrel of the gun having been pressed hard into the side of the head. Dando was shot in what is known as a 'hard contact kill' (a murder where the gun is pressed into the victim's head when the trigger is fired). Examination of the mark showed a silencer had not been used. The explosive sound was reduced by the hard contact of the barrel with the victim's head when the bullet was fired.

The entry wound, along with the location of the mark left on the house door as a result of the impact from the bullet, indicated Dando's head had been parallel, or almost parallel, to the door and had been in a low position when the trigger was pulled.

Particles of Firearms Discharge Residue (FDR) were found in the hair of the victim and on her clothing. Residue is released from a gun when it has been fired. Such residue cannot inform us of the weapon used in the attack.

Examination of the scrapings of Dando's fingernails did not reveal any skin cells which could be from the killer. This indicates the victim did not scratch her killer in trying to resist and escape. This is in keeping with the police view of events. The detectives within the murder squad believed the killer had acted so swiftly, his victim had insufficient time to make any valiant attempt to struggle free.

Abrasions on her arm and hands were also discovered. These are consistent with the theory that the victim had been forced to the ground and held in a low position when the trigger was pulled. In addition to these, the post mortem examination found a small bruise upon Dando's right forearm. Although it could not be determined with certainty, it appeared this was an indication of the gunman having grasped the presenter, holding her tightly as he held her in a low position with the gun pressed into her head. And the pressure from this restraining action resulted in the formation of the bruise.

Although the next point does not relate to the victim it is relevant here. It is important we consider the possibility that the victim's blood transferred onto her killer. As has been mentioned previously, the barrel of the gun used in the murder was pressed hard into Dando's head. It is believed this was in order to reduce the sound of the shot so few people would hear the gun being fired (only one or two neighbours did hear the shot; Dando's next door neighbour did not hear it) but also to prevent a large amount of the victim's blood being transferred onto the killer. A man could not easily escape, in broad daylight, having committed a murder if he had blood upon him. Of course, it would have been easier if the killer had fired from a distance, but this would mean he had more chance of being seen and his aim may have been less accurate.

However, it is certain the killer would have had to leave the scene with the victim's blood upon him. Despite the adaptation of the weapon and the closeness of the barrel to the victim's head, the killer would still have the victim's blood upon him when he left the scene of the crime. When asked if the gunman would have had blood transferred onto him Harry J. Bonnell. M.D., of 4n6pathology, Inc., (an American company) stated, *"Most likely yes, there will be at least a small amount of back-splatter."* Asked the same question, Professor Derrick Pounder from Dundee University told that on firing the gun the victim's blood would be transferred onto *"the hand and sleeve of the hand holding the gun."*

As the murderer may have held his victim when the bullet was fired, it is possible blood splattered elsewhere. This cannot be said with certainty, however. Nonetheless, the gunman would have fled from the scene of the crime with blood upon him, even if it was not clearly noticeable.

The police claimed it could not be determined whether the man they sought was right or left handed, but it would seem most likely he was left handed (or ambidextrous). This deduction is based upon marks the killer left on Dando's body.

Dando was shot when she was at her doorstep, and so the killer must have been behind her when he fired the fatal shot. There was no room in front of the victim, and she was found with her head on the doorstep, which proves the gunman was behind her when he pulled the trigger. The post mortem examination showed the gun had been held against the left side of the victim's head. Indeed, it was pressed so hard against the head, the barrel had left a mark upon the skin. The entry point of the bullet was above the left ear. The examination also revealed a bruise upon the right arm of the corpse where he had held her while he fired. This obviously proves that the gun was being held in the killer's left hand.

Of course, it can be argued that just because the gun was held in the left hand of the killer, it does not necessarily prove that the murderer was left handed or ambidextrous. It is possible that a person can fire a gun with their weaker hand, particularly from close range. Richard Hughes' statement did indicate that the criminal was carrying a phone, gun or some other object in his right hand. This does not prove at all that the killer was right handed. This witness saw the gunman close the gate and then walk left down Gowan Avenue. From where Hughes was standing the killer's right hand side would be barely visible except for when the gate was being closed. If it was not at this point that the object was in the gunman's right hand it is difficult to determine how Hughes could have seen it. This is especially the case as Geoffrey Upfill-Brown, who certainly saw the same man Hughes did, never mentioned seeing anything in the man's right hand even though he saw the right hand side of the man (as he was standing on the opposite side of the road to Hughes) and despite the fact that he made a mental note of as many details as he possibly could. It can be assumed that the gunman was seen to be holding the object in his right hand while he was closing the gate; a task that he may naturally have used his stronger left hand to perform. He placed the object in his right hand to close the gate, and may have kept it in that hand briefly as he began to leave the scene of the crime.

It is probable that he was left handed or ambidextrous, or at the very least that he was trying to give the impression that he was left handed, something indicative of planning and intelligence if this is the case.

3.5: Early actions in the investigation

The police began a search of the Fulham area shortly after they arrived on the scene. A police helicopter was sent to over fly the vicinity of the crime scene. Incidentally, an hour after the crime, George was standing chatting to a woman about the helicopters flying overhead. However, the police search of the area revealed nothing. They had hoped they would possibly make a sighting of the killer as he fled. In all probability, due to the time delay between the crime and the police search having been begun, the gunman would have been far away. He would almost certainly have been out of the sight of those searching for him.

As a result of sighting O (See page 191) an area along the bank of the Thames was cordoned off as police searched in the hope that evidence may have been left in this location. As a result of this rumours began to spread that Dando's killer had committed suicide by throwing himself into the river. It was soon found there was no truth at all in this belief.

A man of the same general appearance as Dando's killer, was seen throwing an object into bushes in Bishops Park. This sighting is not included in the appendix because of an unwillingness on the part of the police to divulge further details regarding this man. It would appear that the police ruled this out at a very early stage, almost certainly because of what the object was. A newspaper report stated simply that a man was seen throwing an object into bushes.

The area in which the object was thrown was cordoned off and searched. A knife was recovered. When the knife was found a post mortem had not been carried out and so the cause of death had not been determined with certainty. Only a few detectives knew that the weapon used had been a gun. However, even at this stage the knife was not believed to have been the murder weapon. After only one mention at a press conference on 27 April 1999 references to this weapon disappeared into history along with the sighting of the man who had thrown it into the bushes. However, could the knife have some indirect relevance which up until now, nobody has considered? If it was a knife the man was seen to be throwing into bushes, then could he have been responsible for another crime that took place in Fulham on the morning of Jill Dando's murder? If this is the case then could he have been viewed to be acting in a suspicious manner and consequently his actions wrongly interpreted as those of a man who must have been involved in Dando's murder?

One of the first tasks assigned to detectives in the murder squad was determining Dando's movements and actions before her death. Officers spent a substantial amount of time studying the footage from one hundred and ninety one security cameras from the shops visited by Dando before she made her final visit to Gowan Avenue, and footage showing her car journeys on that day. Studies of the tapes revealed it did not appear that, on the day of the shooting, Dando had been followed by anyone who could have been responsible for her murder.

The presenter's mobile phone calls were studied but these also provided no information; they just created a list of more people who needed to be interviewed and eliminated.

Her actions and movements were reconstructed as much as possible, but no clues as to the identity of the criminal, or the reasons for the murder, were gleaned through such means.

The day after the murder DCI Campbell held a press conference, during which he appealed for witnesses to come forward and provided some general information regarding the shooting. He informed the media that the key sightings they were focussing upon were G, J, K and Q (See pages 188–190). An emphasis was placed on sighting G. This man was later found to have had no involvement in the crime.

Press conferences were held on an almost daily basis during the early weeks of the Oxborough investigation. This was because the media wished to have more information regarding the shooting and the inquiries being made into the crime. The police hoped that extensive media attention would result in the procurement of valuable information.

However, Campbell was aware the provision of details to the

press led to valuable police time being consumed. There was also not the manpower, nor the time available, for Campbell and his team to review and investigate all of the information provided by the public as it was, yet still appeals for further information were all too frequently being made. The incident room was receiving large numbers of calls each day. Messages received on the day of the murder were often not acted upon until nearly a year later. It cannot be denied, the Metropolitan police failed to act upon information despite the large numbers of officers on the murder squad who only worked upon the investigation into Dando's death. Indeed some of the pieces of information were never acted upon. The police had too much information without them asking for more.

Another task, which was considered to be potentially valuable, was tracing and interviewing all of those who had viewed or shown an interest in Dando's home once she had placed it onto the property market. The police believed the murderer may have arranged a viewing in order to gain intelligence that would aid his plan of murder. After tracing and interviewing these people they were all found to be potential purchasers and so this route of enquiry proved, like so many other inquiries, to be fruitless.

On 30 April 1999 police issued an E-fit of the man they believed to be the killer. Joseph Sappleton, who reported sighting Q, assisted the police in compiling the image. He claimed he was ninety percent satisfied with the likeness. This picture was widely displayed in the media. It was frequently given a caption with words to the effect of *'the man who killed Jill Dando.'* There were constant appeals for this man to come forward to be eliminated from the murder squad's enquiries. To this day his identity remains unknown.

On 5 May 1999 the inquest into Dando's death opened. When called to give evidence, Campbell told the inquest that Oxborough's prime suspect was the man reported in sighting Q, the man police referred to as 'Sweating Man'. This is quite strange when it is considered he did not closely resemble the man seen outside the victim's home following the murder, and also this man was observed fifteen to twenty minutes after the crime in the vicinity of the scene of the murder. This man, who was seen to be the prime suspect, was just one of the many who appeared to be suspicious on that particular day.

By May 1999 the police believed they did not have any

significant information. Incidentally by this date several calls referring to Barry George had been received and their details had been recorded in the police database known as HOLMES (an acronym for Home Office Large Major Enquiry System). For this reason detectives turned to the programme co-presented by Dando before her death, *Crimewatch UK*. This was in the hope that a reconstruction of the events of the day, and a fresh appeal for information could result in one or more viewer being able to enlighten Oxborough regarding the solution to the mystery surrounding Dando's murder. The *Crimewatch* studio and the incident room together received five hundred telephone calls as a direct result of this appeal made on 18 May 1999. However, unlike the calls received as a result of many of the appeals featured on this programme, none of the information regarding Dando's murder was considered to have been significant; no arrests or breakthroughs were made.

3.6: The motive of the killer

Dando was murdered in a violent and aggressive fashion. The killer had pressed the barrel of his gun firmly into the victim's head so he could carry out a hard contact kill. As he did so he grasped the victim's right arm so hard a bruise was created. He fired a single bullet through Dando's skull which presumably killed her almost instantly if not instantly. Before carrying out the hard contact kill the gunman had forced his prey to the ground outside her home in a street in which many people lived, at a time when it was possible for anyone to walk past. He had arrived swiftly at the scene, carried out the shooting and then left as quickly as he had arrived. This was a cold and violent murder. The inevitable question is why was it committed?

Dando had worked for *Crimewatch,* and other television programmes, as well as having a private life. Therefore, the police were aware, there were a number of different possibilities. They therefore had a large number of theories to consider as to what the killer's motive could be. The media was heavily interested in the Dando murder investigation with newspaper and magazine articles being written on a daily basis and the television news airing updates and renewing appeals frequently. Each media company tried to provide new information and new stories to the public in an attempt to increase the number of readers, viewers and listeners. As a result of this media attention many theories emerged as to the possible motive of the killer and so police had to investigate more and more theories. This inevitably resulted in attention to certain aspects of the case being insufficiently explored.

One of the first questions to consider in any murder inquiry is, if the victim had a will, who is the main benefactor? Dando did not have a will. Who then would acquire the celebrity's estate, worth over one million pounds? Detectives soon discovered whom, but this did not enlighten Oxborough upon the identity of the killer. This is because it was Dando's father who received his daughter's money. Therefore, the victim was not killed in an attempt to obtain money from her estate.

It appeared nothing had been stolen from the victim when she was murdered. When Dando was found she still had her engagement ring on her finger, her handbag containing her purse and house keys on her shoulder, and her car keys in her hand with her expensive BMW convertible located close by. Dando was about to unlock her house door and enter. However, the murderer did not allow the victim to enter the house and in doing so he did not provide himself with the opportunity to steal anything within the building. It would seem, therefore, the killer was not hoping to gain immediate financial resources through murder. Either that or he panicked and fled upon seeing what he had done. However, he had walked away *"very calmly"*, which suggests he did not immediately panic, or at least exhibit signs of panicking.

It is often the case, when a person is murdered, the assailant had intended to commit a robbery or another relatively minor offence that had gone wrong when the victim failed to comply with the criminal's demands. Or, the criminal had feared the presence of the victim would lead to their arrest. Burglaries, robberies, rapes, kidnappings and other such offences have often ended in a tragic manner. Therefore Oxborough had to consider the crime they were investigating could have been the consequence of a botched attempt of another form of criminal activity.

The circumstances of this homicide seem to suggest such a scenario did not occur. The weapon and ammunition used in the shooting were not those typically employed by the petty criminal. Offenders who do not intend to fire a bullet do not use an adapted weapon, which is difficult to make or obtain. The criminal visited

29 Gowan Avenue for one purpose alone, to murder Dando. Therefore police soon ruled out the possibility of a crime other than murder having been intended.

As Dando was the co-presenter of the television programme *Crimewatch* the police inevitably researched the possibility the presenter could have been killed in an act of revenge. As is shown on each episode of *Crimewatch*, the programme has been responsible for acquiring information that has led to the arrest and conviction of a large number of criminals. It was therefore considered to be a possibility that Dando had been shot by someone seeking revenge for having been imprisoned due to the programme.

Dando first appeared on *Crimewatch* in September 1995, less than four years before her death. Detectives believed therefore, any criminal who had a significant hatred towards Dando because she had been partly responsible for their imprisonment would still be serving their sentence. However, police neglected to consider a friend or a relative of a person serving a prison sentence could have acted on behalf of a convict imprisoned as a result of a *Crimewatch* appeal.

Criminal history has shown many people have sought revenge on behalf of a prisoner. Police officers, witnesses, lawyers and judges have been killed or attempts made upon their lives by those seeking to punish the people responsible for the capture and imprisonment of a friend or loved one.

However, the police were convinced it was too unlikely that *Crimewatch* was the reason why the television presenter had been killed. They therefore ceased to consider it as a route of inquiry.

Oxborough briefly considered the view that Dando was shot by a professional hit man. A hit man could have been hired by an ex-boyfriend or somebody who had grievances against the presenter but who could not, personally for whatever reason, carry out the crime. Detectives found this theory to be an unlikely solution to the mystery surrounding the shooting. They rejected this line of enquiry on the basis the killing did not have the hall mark features of a professionally organised act of execution. Dando was shot only once, whereas typically, a hit man will fire twice to ensure his victim is killed. However, the killer must have known there was no chance Dando could have survived. The paramedics and doctors at Charing Cross hospital attempted to revive her, but realistically she was dead already. Also a hit man will usually shoot his victim in the back of the head as this causes most damage and it reduces the amount of contact he has with the victim. Dando, however, was shot in the side of the head. One final point to make, which suggests the killer was not a hired hit man is, the murderer held Dando, whereas a professional would want as little contact as possible.

It has been suggested, it is possible, the attacker could have been an amateur hit man; a thug hired by someone who disliked the victim and wished her dead. Although this is more possible than the view that a professional was responsible, it is quite unlikely this could have been the case. There had been physical contact and therefore it would seem there was emotion and personal hatred involved within the shooting. A man who had never met the celebrity and who did not personally dislike her or what she represented, would not grasp her tightly and hold her to the ground. The police were almost certainly correct in their view, Dando's killer must have had a strong personal motive in order to kill the presenter, as reflected in the method of conducting the kill. It would therefore be unlikely for the murderer to be acting on behalf of someone who wished the celebrity to be killed. Whoever shot Dando must have hated her personally; a hit man usually only kills for the money, yet the gunman was killing due to hatred.

A popular theory was Dando was murdered by a Serb hit man, in an act of revenge for her attempts to help the people of Kosovo. It should be remembered, when Dando was killed, Britain was at war with Serbia.

Two weeks before Dando's death a similar murder had occurred in Belgrade. The owner of a newspaper, which had criticised Milosevic and his regime, was shot dead outside his home. In making a televised appeal to help the Kosovan refugees Dando may have been perceived, by Serbian militants, to be critical of the Serbs. Is this the reason why Dando was shot dead just outside her own home?

Tony Hall, the Chief Executive of BBC News, was one of the first people to publicly speak of his grief on the day of the murder. As well as showing how shocked he was by the incident, he commented on the need for the protection of celebrities when he said, *"I think we have to think carefully about people in the public eye and what protection, if any, they should have."* The day after Dando's murder, and therefore the day after Tony Hall had spoken of his shock on hearing of his colleague's death, Hall received a death threat from a man who telephoned the BBC in order to lay blame on Britain for the deaths of many innocent people when a television centre in Belgrade was bombed as part of NATO's campaign in Kosovo. The caller showed the possibility that Dando was murdered in an act of revenge,

> *"Yesterday I call you to tell you to add a few numbers to your list. Because your government, and in particular your Prime Minister Blair, murdered, butchered seventeen innocent young people. He butchered, we butcher back. The first you had yesterday. The next one will be Tony Hall."*

Another telephone call, this time to the BBC in Belfast, also contained a claim of responsibility for Dando's murder. The Serbian caller maintained Dando had been murdered because the BBC was the voice of the British Government and so, because innocent Serbians died in the Belgrade bombing, Dando was killed.

Alan Yentob, the director of television at the BBC, described the shooting as *"evil"*. He too received a death threat from someone believed to be Serbian. John Humphrys, the presenter of the Radio Four programme *Today,* also received a death threat from a Serb source. On the *Today* programme Humphrys had discussed the war with Serbia. Martin Bell, a former war correspondent for the BBC, received a death threat just days after Dando's murder. Whoever made these threats must have been paying close attention to the aftermath of Dando's murder.

This claim is further substantiated when it is considered two weeks before Dando's murder she had received a letter from someone who may have been a Serb or at the very least someone who had Serbian leanings. The police confirmed it was from a *'Serb source'*. The letter criticised her appeal to raise funds for Kosovan refugees; an appeal which had been made a fortnight prior to her murder. Incidentally one of George's relatives, who in 2004 publicly expressed his opinion that there are good grounds to believe someone connected to Serbia killed Dando, received an intimidating letter from a Serbian living in Northern Ireland.

Therefore, a compelling argument to suggest the solution to this mystery relates to Serbia can be made. Is it merely a coincidence that Dando should receive a letter in protest and condemnation of her attempts to help the Kosovan refugees and then after her murder someone who at the very least had Serbian leanings should claim responsibility for her murder? And then three of Dando's colleagues at the BBC who had openly spoken out about the murder should then receive death threats?

If a Serb, or someone with connections to Serbia, murdered Dando then it would mean her death was even more tragic than is believed. In that case Dando would have been shot dead for no reason other than her wish to help the lives of others. If this was the case then it would not have simply been a case of murder; it would have been a case of assassination.

The police in time believed this was not the solution to the crime. Oxborough considered this theory for *"a short while"* but disregarded it saying, the theory was *"far fetched"*, *"outlandish"* and there was *"no evidence whatsoever"* to support the view of the presenter being shot by a Serbian hit man. And so, without tracing the person/people who had been responsible for the death threats and who had seemingly claimed responsibility for Dando's murder, the police, in their minds, put this theory behind other possible explanations as to why the television presenter was violently shot dead. Clearly the Serbian line of inquiry was not fully explored and as no one was ever interviewed, there was insufficient reason to cease the investigation into this possible motive for Dando's death.

Certain events that have taken place following George's conviction have shown 'international terrorism' can threaten the world in many different forms. We have the benefit of hindsight and are aware the theory that Dando was killed by a Serb, was not as outlandish as DCI Campbell had believed it to be in 1999 and 2000.

Could it be the case that a sympathiser of the Serbian's had killed Dando in an act of revenge for the British action against the Serbian military campaign against Kosovo? The police concentrated on the view the killer could have been a Serb, who else should a sympathiser and supporter of the Serbian campaign wish to kill than the woman who had publicly appealed for financial help to support the people of Kosovo?

It would seem the gunman wished to humiliate his victim; he left her outside in broad daylight in an undignified position slumped onto the ground. Many killers leave their victims outdoors, but this usually is the case when a crime is committed in the darkness and/or in a secluded location. Dando was left on public display

33

when the killer had the opportunity to perform his task indoors and so prevent any passing member of the public disturbing him or seeing the crime. This suggests he wished to humiliate Dando, which in turn indicates he possessed anger, frustration and hatred towards the celebrity. This was not merely the result of a man venting anger, it was the result of a man who sought revenge; a very different concept. There can be very little doubt that the killer hated his victim, but for what reason could he possibly have to hate Jill Dando?

As Dando had announced her plans to marry Alan Farthing on 31 January 1999, and had said she was to appear less regularly on television, did the murderer feel betrayed by someone he was obsessed with? If the latter is the case, as the police believed it to be until George came into the picture and they could not prove he had an obsession with Dando (this will be discussed in the next chapter), then this would mean the killer was either an obsessed fanatic or an ex boyfriend.

The police considered the possibility that a man who had an obsession resulting in him engaging in stalking Dando was responsible for causing her death. Often when a celebrity is murdered the police consider a stalker could be responsible. This is because celebrities acquire not only fans and admirers, many also acquire individuals who wish to become close to the celebrity and in doing so, often take to writing letters to the celebrity and occasionally making efforts to meet them and follow them.

The view of a stalker having killed Dando was considered mainly because Dando had (as was described in Chapter 1) discussed her fears with colleagues that she had attracted a man who harboured an unhealthy interest in her. This man had visited 29 Gowan Avenue and posted a letter through her door, as well as sending letters to the BBC. This man will be discussed in the next section.

It is possible the killer stalked his victim at some point, possibly when he was acquiring the information required to make the murder possible. However, there is very little evidence to suggest Dando's killer was a stalker. The only evidence to suggest such a theory was possible were the sightings of 'Trilby Man'. As shown in the appendix, Trilby Man was almost certainly uninvolved in the shooting. There is no evidence at all to suggest Dando was being stalked in 1999. If she was, then the person who was carrying out this activity was being incredibly careful to prevent his victim from knowing of his activities. In Chapter 1 it was stated, Dando had fears for her safety. However, these fears had been unfounded with the only basis for such a belief having been her past experience with a stalker and her concerns that her change of image would result in unwanted attention. If Dando was the target of unwanted attention, then her fiancé, Alan Farthing, was oblivious to it. No letters had been posted to her home address and she had not received any frightening phone calls.

Jeremy Dyer, a man convicted of stalking a television news presenter named Sarah Lockett, offered an insight into the mind of a stalker. Dyer sent letters to Lockett, which over time became increasingly worrying. Dyer was obsessed with Lockett, and in one of his letters he referred to the Dando murder. He had been sending letters and suggested attempting to meet Sarah Lockett for some time, but when the news presenter heard of Dando's death and Dyer's comments, she feared for her safety and informed the police. Dyer shared his views about what he believed to be the killer's motive,

'Jill Dando's death seems totally pointless. If I was stalking Jill Dando I would have KIDNAPPED HER OR DONE SOMETHING ELSE TO HER RATHER THAN SHOOTING HER THROUGH THE HEAD. ... How can you enjoy shooting someone in the head? Unless you hate them of course. It seems like a waste of a victim if you ask me.'

The killer was more likely to be a man with an obsession who had become angered with the celebrity due to her engagement and/or her plans to leave *Holiday* and *The Six O'clock News*. As Dyer commented, Dando's killer must have hated his victim. The killer was more likely to have been an obsessed fan, whose interest in the celebrity had grown for some time, only for him to become enraged at the prospect of 'losing' her when she was to marry and reduce her number of appearances on television. Those people who become obsessed with a person in the public eye become attracted by the appearance, personality or beliefs of the individual (or a combination of these factors). When the characteristic(s) which the fan is attracted to is altered, the fan can turn his attention to someone else. Or, as is often the case, they can become angry believing they have been let down or betrayed by the celebrity who in the view of the fan, has undergone a huge change in which they become alienated. Mark Chapman, the man who shot John Lennon dead, believed the former Beatle had altered. He felt John had betrayed him and many other fans by no longer believing in the messages he had conveyed through his music. This made Chapman angry and so he travelled a great distance to Lennon's home in order to kill the singer.

Many fans can believe they are in some form of relationship with the person they see on television. They can feel when a newsreader, presenter and so on, stares into the camera and smiles, the smile is being directed to them alone. Many individuals become obsessed with a celebrity at some point in their life, but only a small proportion take this a stage further than simply thinking of the person they like.

Dando had recently altered her image. She had attempted to adopt a sexier look. It is possible that such an alteration caused an obsessed fan who had become attracted by her former more respectable image, to become angry and feel betrayed.

At first the police believed the murderer may well have been an obsessed fan whether he was a stalker or not. However, this theory was soon considered to be a less likely solution to the enigma because no evidence was found to suggest that an obsessed individual had targeted her. Of course Oxborough were aware, men obsessed with Dando existed, they simply did not believe it was such a man who was responsible for her death.

The personal hatred, reflected in the murder, suggests the possibility that the gunman was someone from Dando's personal life. An ex-boyfriend was a possible candidate for the man who killed Jill Dando; a man from Dando's past who had a grudge of some sort because of a failed relationship. Soon after Dando's murder Professor Capitanchik from Aberdeen University said he believed the killer may well have been an ex-boyfriend, *"... if I was a police man working on the case I would be looking at all her previous boyfriends very closely."*

As mentioned in Chapter 1 there will have been a number of ex-boyfriends who, upon hearing of her plans to marry Alan Farthing, may have become jealous, hurt and angry. Jealousy can have many effects upon a person's mind and behaviour; one of the common results is violence.

As you will read, Barry George did not have any of the above reasons to kill the victim; he does not fit into any of these categories.

The possibility of a Serbian link cannot be ruled out. The argument that Dando was murdered as a result of the NATO action against the Serbs is far more compelling than the view of a man who appeared to have no interest in the victim could have killed her (i.e. George). Someone with a motive to murder the celebrity claimed responsibility for Dando's murder and so this possibility can never be ruled out until there is sufficient reason to rule out such a theory.

It is also quite possible a feeling of betrayal could have motivated the killer. He may have felt cheated by Dando when he heard she had become engaged and/or she had announced she was going to be appearing less frequently on television; a nightmare scenario for anyone who had acquired a fixation with the celebrity. Therefore an obsessed fanatic could have committed the murder. This is the theory DCI Campbell and his team favoured.

Alternatively, an ex-boyfriend could have become enraged in a fit of jealousy when he heard of Dando's impending marriage to Alan Farthing. He may have felt betrayed and humiliated by the woman he had loved and quite probably still loved. Perhaps he had planned to marry the presenter but the relationship had ended. How could he read in the newspapers and magazines of Dando's engagement and not feel affected? His jealousy made it impossible for him to sit back and watch the woman he loved marry another man. It would not be sufficient for him to kill Alan Farthing for that would leave the betrayer alive. By now his feelings of anger had made him recall the pain he had experienced when the relationship between Dando and he had ended. The gunman could never forgive Dando. He needed her dead, so he would no longer have a reminder of how he had been betrayed every time he saw her on television or in a magazine or newspaper. In a fit of anger he created a plan to seek revenge ... a plan he executed with perfection.

This may sound like mere supposition but it could well be the solution to the mystery surrounding Dando's death. There are a number of ex-boyfriends who it will be shown were not investigated sufficiently; Dando hurt some of these when she ended their relationship. It would be libellous and hypocritical to suggest names or develop this point further.

3.7: Discovery and elimination of suspects

In a criminal investigation suspects should not be eliminated until there is conclusive evidence they were uninvolved in the crime being investigated. However, in the Jill Dando murder inquiry a large number of suspects were eliminated, but were they sufficiently investigated? In the Oxborough investigation many theories of who the killer could be were eliminated without full investigation.

There were numerous theories as to what type of person could have killed Dando. This is inevitable as there were a number of different theories as to the motive of the killer. The tracing of suspects is often easier when the motive of the murder is understood. However, as shown in the preceding section no motive was ever established for why Dando was murdered.

Prior to Gallagher's meeting with Barry George, Oxborough detectives did not consider any of the suspects they had met as being significant. Discussion of these suspects is, however, relevant because if George is innocent it is still quite possible one of the suspects eliminated by the police was the man who murdered Dando.

Due to the number and nature of sightings detectives believed three men had been behind the plot to kill the television presenter. This incorrect belief was the premise of the investigation for a significant amount of time. If more than one man was involved, then it would mean numerous individuals each had a desire for Dando to be killed. It would also mean there was an increased chance the police would discover the identities of those responsible due to the possibility of disagreements and disloyalties within the gang. News that this theory, which had been a dominant part of Oxborough's enquiries had been rejected, came when Campbell told the press,

"If a criminal gang, let's say of three, were at work in Gowan Avenue then there would be three times as many people behind the scenes who would know about it. Yet we've heard nothing from the Underworld."

DCI Campbell made some assumptions that were unwarranted on this, the most unique of cases. He assumed that if a gang was responsible for the murder then the underworld must have known about it. This is not necessarily the case. It is only the case if the British underworld were involved but not, of course, if it involved foreign nationals - yet the theory was dropped. Campbell's reasoning, in this instance, is unsound and indicative of how easily theories were rejected. In 1995 an armed robbery, in which £6.6 million was stolen from a security van, occurred in Salford, Greater Manchester. As in the Oxborough investigation a reward for £250,000 was offered for information. Despite the massive reward no information was provided by the criminal underworld and the crime remains unsolved. However, it is a known fact that at least three armed raiders participated in the well-planned robbery. Therefore Campbell was wrong to assume that Dando could not have been killed by a gang of three criminals simply because a large reward had not tempted a member of the underworld to speak to the police.

It is most probable, however, that Campbell was correct in saying a lone gunman had committed this well executed murder, even though his reasoning for the assumption was flawed. It is a difficult task for one man to escape the arm of the law despite a multimillion pound investigation. It is harder still for two, three or more to escape justice. If more than one person was involved in the plot and execution, then it would mean they each had a personal hatred for Dando and their loyalty towards one another is unwavering even to this day. Of course this is possible, although incredibly unlikely, but only one man pulled the trigger that ended Dando's life.

From the outset of the investigation, and for a significant period of time during the investigation, police focussed upon trying to locate their prime suspect; the man seen at the bus stop described in sighting Q; the man they named 'Sweating Man'.

On 30 April 1999 an E-fit of this suspect was released. Despite extensive media coverage nationally, this man has never been traced. However, the police eliminated him from their enquiries when they began to believe only one man could have been behind the murder. At this point they realised 'Sweating Man' did not match the description of the man seen in sightings J and K, the gunman.

All of Dando's known ex-boyfriends were interviewed in case one of those could have been motivated to kill the presenter out of jealousy or some other similar motive. When questioning all suspects at this time, the police had been told to compare the suspect to the man shown in the E-fit; Sweating Man. These men were interviewed whilst there was a view the man depicted in the E-fit was the killer. Throughout much of the Oxborough investigation there was an over-reliance upon the E-fit of 'Sweating Man'. The police used the E-fit as a means of eliminating suspects. Campbell had created a set of criteria which officers should use when interviewing suspects. One of the main criteria throughout the investigation was how closely the suspect resembled the man depicted in the E-fit; the man who Sappleton had described. The police traced, interviewed and eliminated the ex-boyfriends largely because they did not look like the man who was seen twenty minutes after the murder. The E-fit depicted a man who was not the man seen by Hughes or Upfill-Brown, however, and therefore he almost certainly had no involvement in the murder of Jill Dando.

Of course, ex-boyfriends were not eliminated solely on the premise of how closely they resembled 'Sweating Man', other factors will have been taken into account; did they have an alibi? Did they have a motive? However, criminal history has taught us, partners of killers will often lie about their boyfriends' or husbands' whereabouts. It has been claimed Sonia Sutcliffe did this on many occasions. Therefore, even if an ex-boyfriend looked nothing like the E-fit, and he had an alibi for the time of the shooting, it does not mean he was not Dando's murderer. However, the police were happy to eliminate suspects when there could have been the possibility of the suspect being the gunman. By 9 August 1999 the police had ceased to continue inquiries into the victim's ex-boyfriends, claiming there was no evidence to suggest any of them had been responsible.

In addition to the E-fit the police placed an emphasis upon those who owned a Range Rover during the early stages of their inquiries when Dando's known ex-boyfriends, amongst other suspects, were being interviewed. There was no conclusive evidence to suggest that the gunman escaped in such a vehicle. Despite this, any suspects who did not own a Range Rover and did not look like Sweating Man would have been viewed upon as less likely candidates for Dando's murder.

Her filofax was studied, and all those whose details were within were traced and interviewed, in the hope one of them could be the gunman or someone could shed some light upon what appeared to be an enigma.

The police believed that in contacting the many hundreds of people in Dando's filofax, they had contacted all of her ex-boyfriends and people she knew personally. This may well be true, for Dando was in the habit of recording everyone's number for quick reference. However, it is possible some individuals were unaccounted for by this method. For example, Dando may have made acquaintances with individuals who secretly admired her yet she did not consider them in a way which resulted in their inclusion within her filofax.

Realistically the police cannot say they contacted all of Dando's ex-boyfriends and people who knew her. They claimed there were no secret compartments in her life, but this is not to say Dando did not have hidden depths at some point in her life.

In order to determine if Dando had been murdered as a result of a vendetta because of her work on *Crimewatch,* detectives spoke with criminals in the Underworld. Campbell claimed, during George's trial, those criminals consulted had laughed at his officers when asked if they had any information regarding Dando's murder. They could not understand why anyone would wish to murder a woman who only co-presented a crime programme; such a theory seemed illogical. Such a belief had been strengthened when, despite a substantial reward, no information was provided. On 10 May 1999 *The Daily Mail* newspaper offered a £100,000 reward for information leading to a conviction. At the same time a businessman offered a further £50,000. Despite such a large incentive, detectives received no information they regarded to be significant. On the one hundredth day after the murder, 3 August 1999, *The Sun* newspaper offered another £100,000.

The fact no one came forward to provide information, and claim the reward, suggests the gunman acted entirely alone; the underworld was not in any way involved. Often a criminal will come forward to inform the police about someone. It is worth the risk of being disloyal in order to gain £250,000. It would seem that nobody sold him the adapted gun and cartridge and therefore he must have adapted them himself. If he had been sold such a unique cartridge and distinctive weapon then someone would have informed Oxborough. Alternatively these could have been bought from abroad independent of anyone in Britain. Either way this suggests the killer had extensive knowledge regarding firearms or/and contacts with criminals overseas.

It was not very possible to locate potential suspects to pursue the Serbia line of enquiry, due to the distance between Britain and Serbia and the fact, at the time we were at war with one another. If a suspect had lived abroad and only came to England for 'the kill' then it would be difficult to find the gunman. He would have been unknown to people in England. It would be ideal for him to kill Dando and then return overseas. This could explain why the killer was willing to murder outdoors in a street where anyone could walk past at any time. Did he know he could not be caught because he knew he could be on his way back to Serbia soon after shooting the presenter? However, as was stated in the last section, the police did not believe a Serbian assassin was responsible and did not attempt to trace potential Serb suspects. The source of the threats made against staff at the BBC was never discovered.

In addition to these, other individuals came to be considered in the murder investigation. These people were mainly brought to the attention of officers working on the case by phone calls and other forms of correspondence.

It is often the case in criminal investigations that people who provide information to the police become suspected of committing the crime. Detectives suspected Richard Hughes, Dando's next-door neighbour, for some time. This was largely because of the inconsistent nature of the statements he made following the incident. He could not make up his mind as to what happened when he saw Dando's body, and the media picked up on this, informing the police of their suspicions. Also his behaviour had been viewed as odd, he told the three women, who were with Dando of the man he had seen from his window. The way in which he told the women seemed to be unnatural. It appeared to at least one of them, he was acting in a defensive manner by informing them of the man who must have been the killer in an attempt to divert attention from himself. When his story kept altering many became convinced of his guilt.

It seemed strange that Hughes could hear a scream, and see the killer walking away, yet not appear outside his home for fifteen minutes. He told police he had not suspected anything wrong had occurred, and his attention was only drawn to the situation when he heard the commotion from outside when the three women had gathered around the body. Those who doubted this witness commented on how the fifteen-minute delay provided him with plenty of time to shoot Dando, run away and then enter his house through the back, appearing fifteen minutes later through the front door. He could then pretend he saw a man and provide police with a description of a man who did not look like himself.

Hughes did himself no favours by lying in his statement. He did not, as John McVicar discovered, only see half of the man's face. Instead he saw almost all of the face of the man seen leaving the scene of the crime[7]. He allegedly lied because he believed he too could be killed if the gunman realised that someone could recognise him. Hughes did not change his statement.

Hughes' wife bore a passing resemblance to the victim if viewed from behind. They also drove the same model and colour BMW. It was speculated, and still is speculated by some, that the intended victim of the shooting outside 29 Gowan Avenue was in fact Hughes' wife. In one of his statements, Hughes told officers that when he heard Dando's car alarm being activated he thought it was his wife who had returned. Had Hughes killed Jill Dando by mistake, intending to murder his wife? It was a possibility that had to be considered although detectives were soon satisfied Hughes' wife had not been the intended victim. No one could explain why Hughes, or anyone for that matter, would wish to murder his wife. Although the possibility he wished to kill his wife was rejected, Hughes briefly remained a minor suspect in Dando's murder.

However, Richard Hughes was not the only man who saw the killer making his escape. Upfill-Brown did not recognise the man as his neighbour Richard Hughes. This witness also described seeing a man who was taller than Hughes, who is only 5'7. Eventually the police ceased to consider Hughes as a suspect, they could not find any realistic motive or indeed any evidence connecting him to the crime. He did not murder Jill Dando.

At an early stage in the investigation an informant provided police with the name Steve Savva. Savva was a mechanic working in a London garage. Detectives were persuaded to consider him a suspect when he was named as an Underworld assassin. This information must have been considered potentially great, because he was kept under surveillance for six months before being eliminated from the inquiry in December 1999, when it was learnt

---

[7] (McVicar. 2002: 98).

the informant had provided incorrect details. This, therefore, was a time consuming false lead.

In February 2000 police flew to Australia in pursuit of a potentially valuable suspect. Martyn Gilbert was the man who numerous newspapers claimed had created a shrine to Dando. He regularly communicated with people over the Internet. In his e-mails he frequently discussed Dando in a sexually explicit manner. Oxborough were informed of Gilbert when he stopped e-mailing one woman shortly after the murder. She believed he had a fascination with the presenter and when she stopped receiving messages from the suspect, she contacted the incident room to voice her suspicions.

The police eventually located him; two weeks after the murder he had emigrated to Australia. When he was interviewed the police satisfied themselves he had no involvement in the murder; he had stopped contacting the woman because he was moving.

As was stated in Chapter 1 Dando had been intimidated by an obsessed fan who had infringed the privacy of the target of his affection. John Hole had written letters, sent Valentine's cards and made telephone calls to the BBC television centre. Due to the fact that Dando's address was accessible to the public through the Electoral Register, and through interviews she had participated in, it became known the presenter lived in the Fulham area of south-west London. This meant Hole was able to locate the home of his fantasy woman.

Although he never met her, despite his attempts outside the BBC studios, John Hole did visit 29 Gowan Avenue. How many times he travelled to this home is unknown but he did, on one occasion, post a letter through the victim's letterbox.

The name John Hole was in the public domain before the murder. He had been exposed, via the media, as a stalker long before Dando was killed. He was accused of harassment; an accusation which, despite being true, he believed to be *"a bit unfair"*. Detectives were therefore, aware of this potential suspect who had hoped to have a relationship with the presenter until she had sought assistance to deter his harassment.

The police easily located this man and were satisfied with his claim that he no longer harboured any feelings for, or for that matter had any interest in, Dando. Hole was swiftly eliminated from the investigation.

Partly due to the problems caused by John Hole, Dando was concerned that other men had unhealthy feelings for her. It was for this reason she thought twice about clothing she wore during photo shoots, because she was worried how people would react to her appearance.

The police discovered there had been approximately forty to fifty men who had an obsession with Dando and who had crossed the line by trying to contact her. An even higher number, of over one hundred, had an unhealthy interest in the presenter. However, all of these were traced, interviewed and eliminated from the list of suspects.

Just two days before her death Jill Dando and Alan Farthing had attended a Royal Legion Ball. At this charity event Alan Farthing had become concerned regarding a man who seemed to take an unusual interest in his fiancé. The man, who has been referred to as 'Julian' appeared to know many details regarding Dando's background, including the schools she had attended. Following the murder the police were informed of 'Julian', but after tracing and interviewing him they were happy to eliminate him from their inquiry.

It is a rather curious aspect of society that when crimes are committed there are some individuals who, despite having no involvement in the criminal activity, will claim responsibility for what has occurred.

Soon after Dando's death a funeral director named James Shackleton came forward to inform the police he was the man seen running down Gowan Avenue following the shooting, though he denied having played any role in the murder. He claimed to having been searching through skips for wood to use in the manufacture of coffins, before being chased by a homosexual who wished to rape him. Due to the fact he had the same general appearance as the man seen on Gowan Avenue, and he freely admitted he was there at that time and was seen by the witnesses, the police decided he could have been the man responsible. Police officers raided his home and arrested him in connection with the crime. Shackleton alleges the officers were armed.

It was soon discovered he had a history of claiming responsibility for things he had not done, in a bid to gain attention. This is not to say he did not shoot Dando though. However, he was also taller than the man seen leaving the garden of 29 Gowan Avenue and therefore it was determined he was not the man detectives were hunting. Oxborough eliminated this man from their inquiries.

On 18 May 1999 detectives studied photographs that someone had taken to be developed. The photographs were of Dando and had been taken from a television screen. Oxborough did not read anything into these and so the person who took the pictures was not investigated regarding the possibility that he could have been obsessed with the presenter and therefore, could have been the man they were hunting.

On 27 May 1999 Oxborough arrested a man they believed could have been involved in the shooting. The police, who were informed about the man by a tip-off, did not believe the suspect was the gunman for he did not resemble the E-fit. However, detectives investigating the murder believed he could have been one of the three men they were looking for (at this point in time police still believed there were three men involved in the crime).

The man was interviewed but police did not find sufficient evidence to charge him. They also did not find a significant reason to ask for extensions to detain the suspect for a longer period of time. He was released on bail while enquiries were carried out, in the hope that further information could be used to charge or eliminate him. No information linking him to the murder of Jill Dando was ever discovered.

There is an online resource known as 192.com which has proven to be very useful in finding a person's home address. Upon typing a name into a box on the screen, the programme will search its system and produce a list of people with that name, along with their address, phone number and a map showing the location of their home. It is essentially an online version of directory enquiries. However, even those people who are ex-directory still have their addresses on this site, for it searches through the electoral registers also. What is more, up until recently, those who registered to use the service were able to have several free searches before payment was required.

When Dando was murdered the administrators of 192.com searched their records and soon informed police that a person had searched for Dando's address in November 1998. After exhaustive enquiries the person was traced. He was found to be uninvolved in the murder. He allegedly typed in Dando's name to test the service. He was soon eliminated from the investigation.

During the course of their investigation police revealed that a highly curious series of incidents had taken place, which were of the greatest suspicion and indicated Dando had acquired a stalker who knew a large amount of information about the victim. On 1 February 1999 Dando's gas, electricity and water suppliers each received a telephone call from a man claiming to be the presenter's brother; he called himself James Dando. The man wished to have Dando's bills transferred to his name. He claimed this was more convenient for Dando. The caller knew the presenter's home address and, rather frighteningly, he knew other details including the number of her account.

It should be noted Dando announced her engagement on 31 January 1999, the day before these calls had been made. The police took this to be a sign that the killer may have been an obsessed fan who had become disgruntled by the engagement; a man who wished to accumulate information and have some impact upon his target's life.

It was eventually discovered the person who made these telephone calls was a journalist who seemingly had no involvement in the crime. We can only speculate about the reasons for these bizarre calls because, as always, Scotland Yard have remained tight lipped about the issue. Regardless of his motivations this man was soon eliminated from the investigation.

At a later stage, a few months after 'James Dando' had made the strange telephone calls to the suppliers of Dando's utilities, BT received a phone call. The caller may have been the journalist but the police have remained silent about this issue. Nevertheless the man who phoned British Telecom also wished to have the victim's bills transferred to his name. Again he knew many details about the presenter, such as her home address and her telephone number; her telephone number was ex-directory and therefore not available to the public.

Four months before Dando's death another suspicious phone call had been made although the journalist who made the calls described above was not responsible. In December 1998 a man searched through a residential phone book for J. Dando. He called the number listed, believing it was possible the presenter would answer; he was wrong. Instead a woman with the same initial, who was not related to the victim, picked up the phone. The caller was disappointed but engaged in a conversation lasting ten minutes, with the woman, in which he attempted to extract as much information as he possibly could from her about Dando. J Dando was unable to help him.

It is possible this man was, in some way, involved in the crime.

Alternatively he could have simply been one of the many obsessed fans attracted to Dando. Whatever the reason for the telephone call it was a highly suspicious action carried out by an individual who had an interest of some kind with Dando. The man, whose manner was described as polite and respectful, has never been traced. Could the caller have been Dando's killer?

On 18 November 1999 another suspect was arrested in connection with Dando's death. This suspect was brought to the attention of Oxborough when it emerged he was responsible for one of the sightings of Range Rovers on the day of the shooting. He had stolen the Range Rover, which is why the vehicle was seen to be moving in a suspicious manner.

However, after only a few hours it was determined his only crime on that day was the theft of a Range Rover, with which he was later charged.

Despite a large number of routes of enquiry and a large number of suspects, there had only been a handful of suspects worthy of consideration, with three men having been arrested, and these were soon eliminated.

The public criticisms were increasing in frequency and emotions were running high. Earlier in the course of events certain newspapers had claimed Dando's killer would never be caught. By February, this view had increased in popularity and would continue to do so. People increasingly hoped for a breakthrough to occur as the first anniversary of the murder approached. However, as the anniversary arrived the police had not charged a man in connection with the murder, and they had made another appeal on the *Crimewatch* programme. The police, however, did have a suspect by this time although the public were not aware of this and an arrest had not been made.

In February 2000 Detective Inspector Horrocks had suggested reviewing the early information which was, in his opinion most likely to be fruitful. DCI Campbell agreed and set his detectives the task of reading through those messages in the hope more than one would refer to a suspect who had not yet been questioned. Amongst other names, which had become lost in the system, was the name of a man who lived half a mile from Dando's home. That man was Barry Michael George.

Chapter 4:

The police investigate Barry George

"My feeling is that Barry looked disposable. They thought he could disappear and no one would notice. They thought it was just him and his elderly mum. They didn't realise he had a large family network." [8]

This chapter will discuss the investigation into Barry George. It will not discuss the evidence, for comments regarding evidence will be made in the next two chapters. Where necessary, evidence will be referred to but will not be elaborated upon.

The police had been made aware of George in the first week of the investigation. However, he was not considered to be a suspect worthy of immediate consideration. It was therefore almost a year until it was discovered he could have been involved in the crime. Once George had been traced it was the job of the detectives involved in the Oxborough murder squad to investigate him and then either eliminate him or implicate him. This would mean seeing how George connected to the clues which had been obtained, and if necessary finding new clues to see whether or not he was involved with the murder of Dando.

4.1: How George came to be investigated

As was briefly stated in the last chapter, D.I. Horrocks suggested that the earliest information received should be reviewed. It is a common belief amongst detectives that if a crime is to be solved it is usually the earliest information which proves to be the most useful (often the information received within the first forty-eight hours). In many investigations such information may seem to

---

[8] A comment by Michelle Diskin, the sister of Barry George, in *The Daily Telegraph* on 3 July 2001.

be irrelevant or unimportant, with other pieces taking greater priority. However, the seemingly more important pieces are often shown to be unrelated to the crime and those earlier pieces occasionally become lost. This occurred during the investigation into the murder of Jill Dando. Eight pieces of information which had been received by police within the first few weeks of the investigation related to George. Four pieces of information were provided by staff at Hammersmith and Fulham Action For Disability (Hafad), an advice centre on Greswell Street within close proximity to Gowan Avenue. Two clues were from a member of staff at Traffic Cars, a local taxi firm. One call was made by a woman, named Susan Oddie, who knew George. Vicky Murphy, who had met George on a bus and engaged in conversation with him, provided the final piece of information. These clues had been entered into HOLMES, where they were given a low priority status.

These eight pieces of information together provided what must have been considered to be an important lead. They told how a man named Barry Bulsara (although the first Hafad call did not include his name and Oddie had called him 'Busara'. Also, the Traffic Cars' calls did not provide a name) of Crookham Road, Fulham, had visited both Hafad and Traffic Cars on the day of the murder, and on this day he had been agitated. Two days later he visited both locations demanding information about his earlier visits and he had appeared threatening. One message, the message from Susan Oddie, told how Barry 'Bulsara' was mentally unstable and he owned rifles. The information provided by Vicky Murphy showed that a man claiming to be Freddie Mercury's cousin had informed her he was going to give a reading at Dando's memorial service.

The messages should have been linked together at an earlier stage in Oxborough's inquiries. Gallagher quickly found connections between most of the messages in February 2000, so why were they not connected earlier on? There was sufficient information to link most of them together; DCI Campbell himself had spoken of a *"failure"*.

Campbell used one of the oldest excuses possible when explaining why these messages were not acted upon sooner. He told that Oxborough had been overburdened with large amounts of information and so messages referring to George had become lost. This may have been a valid reason why Peter Sutcliffe evaded justice for so long, but Dando was murdered in 1999, in the age of technology, and not 1969 when the Yorkshire Ripper began creating havoc.

In February 2000 the task of tracing, investigating and eliminating Barry 'Bulsara' was given to Detective Constable John Gallagher.

One of Gallagher's initial actions was to interview staff at Hafad. The women spoken to could not be sure of the time at which George had visited on the day of the murder, providing times between 11:00 and 14:00. Later, when Ramesh Paul from Traffic Cars was interviewed, he told Oxborough detectives that George had got in a taxi at 13:15 on the day of Dando's death. He also informed Gallagher that George had probably arrived at the office fifteen to twenty minutes earlier. This meant George's whereabouts at 11:30 on the day of 26 April 1999 could not be verified.

Staff at both Hafad and Traffic Cars had become suspicious when George made a second visit two days after the crime. He appeared agitated and demanded knowing what time he had visited on the day of the murder and also what clothing he had been wearing. This action seemed to be very odd and so the incident room received several phone calls in the space of a few weeks as a result.

Gallagher carried out further research into George and before long this 'odd' man was considered to be a suspect worthy of careful consideration in Oxborough's investigation into the murder of Dando. On 5 April 2000 Campbell was informed about the suspect.

Gallagher had made attempts to contact George by visiting the suspect's flat. However, he was never found at home. The detective resorted to posting cards through his letterbox asking him to phone the police station. However, George never phoned; he assumed the officer wished to speak to him regarding a bicycle accident he had recently been involved in, and so he passed the cards on to his solicitor, as he did not believe they were important. Unable to gain contact with the suspect through this method, Gallagher decided to wait at the social security office George visited in order to collect the benefits he received due to his disability. On 11 April 2000 DC Gallagher first met Barry George.

4.2: George is questioned

On the day on which successful contact with George was first made, 11 April 2000, Gallagher questioned the suspect in order to determine his actions on the day of the murder.

The Police and Criminal Evidence Act 1984 states that if it is suspected a person to be interviewed has a mental disorder, then they shall be accompanied by a responsible adult during questioning. The responsible person should ideally be a social worker or someone else experienced in working with people who are mentally handicapped or mentally disordered. When the police first asked to question George, a social worker was invited to be present but she refused. For this reason it was decided that the questioning should be conducted at the home of George's elderly mother, Margaret George, to enable her to act as the responsible adult. The interview took place at her home because George did not wish to let the police into his flat due to the mess. Later, when police interviewed George at the police station, a social worker was present.

At his mother's home George informed Gallagher, when making his statement, that on 26 April 1999 he thought he had left his flat at around 12:30 although this was only a guess on his part. He claimed he had at that time made his way to Hafad on foot, which would have taken him between fifteen and twenty minutes. He had walked along Crookham Road, down Fulham Road, along Fulham Palace Road, down one of the small side streets off Fulham Palace Road and along Stevenage Road until he reached Greswell Street on which Hafad is located. George said after his visit to Hafad he walked to Traffic Cars because he needed to travel to a cancer information centre in order to collect some information.

In telling the police he thought he may have left his home at 12:30 he did not provide any explanation as to his whereabouts at 11:30 when Dando was shot; he had provided no alibi. This information, which George signed despite having clearly displayed uncertainty as to the accuracy of the details, was later used against him.

George does not have a very good memory. It should therefore be expected that when asking him to recall what he did on a given date, after almost a year had elapsed, he would not be able to recollect details with accuracy. Robert Charig, who has been friends with George for over twenty years, says his inaccuracy is to be expected:

> "This is somebody with epilepsy, a problem that affects the brain ... It can wipe out short-term memory and may have some effects upon long-term memory. And this was a year ... from the murder. I don't think you could expect somebody under those circumstances to remember things in detail."[9]

George was also asked about his interest in guns and in the victim. He told the detective he had been in the Territorial Army and during his service he had fired rifles whilst under supervision. He claimed he had never heard of Dando before her death and he had only learnt her name after the shooting as a result of the media's attention to the case.

George told Gallagher that on the day of the murder he had been wearing a black suit, white shirt and red tie, or jeans and a t-shirt.

The police created a myth regarding George's ability to recall his actions and what he was wearing on the day of the murder. The public were first informed of this incorrect belief when *The Guardian* newspaper quoted an officer as saying:

> "He was the first person we interviewed who knew precisely where he was and what he was doing without a moment of hesitation. It was as if he had been preparing for the visit."[10]

This myth has continued to exist as a result of journalists and other writers, whose ignorance and inability to research correctly led to this false notion having been recorded on many occasions since that first interview at George's mother's home.

George never made a specific statement of what he was doing, where he was or what he wore. Regarding the clothing, as has been previously stated, he simply commented that he could have been wearing either a suit or casual clothing. This is not at all as precise a description as the police themselves alleged had been provided to them. On several occasions during the police interviews the police commented on how on the day of the murder George had worn a

---

[9] *Cutting Edge*, 2002.
[10] *The Guardian*, 3 July 2001.

suit. Each time George corrected them by stating he wore a suit or casual clothing. The police seemed to ignore the references to casual clothing, as they were not consistent with descriptions provided by witnesses.

If he had been preparing for the visit surely he would have told Gallagher he left his flat before the murder and not afterwards. That way he would have had some sort of explanation as to his movements at the time of the shooting. The fact of the matter is, George could not remember precisely what he wore or what he did on the day of the murder.

It would later be claimed that George altered his alibi, thus indicating he may have been responsible for the crime. Prior to the commencement of the trial Michael Mansfield QC, who was to represent George during the trial, was told the defendant believed he had left his flat on Crookham Road at around 10:50 on the day of the murder and that he had still been in Hafad after 12:30, possibly until just before 13:00. This was in conflict with the statement he had made at his mother's home.

It must be noted George does not wear a watch and it is therefore impossible for him to give specific times. Also he has no sense of time and cannot distinguish between morning and afternoon. During the later police interviews, the suspect stated he thought the time was *"getting on for afternoon"*. When first asked, he could not remember. How could anyone be expected to remember at what time he had visited an advice centre more than one year after the visit had taken place? It is inevitable that, given time, his account would change, particularly when he heard that more than one witness had said he had been at the centre significantly earlier than he had told the police.

On 25 May 2000 George awoke to the sound of someone banging on his door. Opening his door to see what was happening he found four police officers standing outside. George expected they had arrived to carry out a search of his property but their visit this time was for a different purpose. George was arrested, handcuffed and taken to Hammersmith Police station for questioning in connection with the murder of Jill Dando.

Except on a few occasions, where DCI Campbell questioned his prime suspect, it was DI Snowden's responsibility to gain implicating information from George during the formal interviews. Snowden was believed to have the most appropriate interview technique of the detectives available. At 6'6" tall he is also an imposing, if not intimidating, figure.

George, who was always incredibly polite during questioning, was accompanied by a social worker, who acted as the responsible adult, and his solicitor, Marilyn Etienne.

It is the role of the 'responsible adult' to participate in the interviews in order to ensure the suspect understands all that is said, offer advice to the suspect and communicate with the suspect to ensure the interviews are being conducted fairly. The police are not knowledgeable or experienced when it comes to interviewing people with medical and psychological illnesses. Suspects can often become confused and make comments which can be misinterpreted by the listener. For this reason it is essential for the appropriate adult to participate fully in the interview. George made comments which would later be used against him, but the social worker did nothing.

At no point during the police interviews did George confess or provide any incriminating evidence.

During questioning George once again denied having any interest in Jill Dando. Did he even know who Jill Dando was? *"Until after her death, I had no idea until then"*, he claimed. He admitted he had learnt who she was since her death *"because it's been widespread throughout the media."*

Whilst DI Snowden interviewed Barry George, other detectives had the task of questioning everyone listed in his mother's address book, although nothing of any interest was uncovered during this time-consuming activity. A police officer later supplied a copy of the book to a journalist, resulting in many attempts to gain information from relatives and friends of the family. The same journalists besieged Margaret George's home, shining torches through her letterbox at all hours, dropping letters and notes through the door, telephoning her almost constantly and using other means to try and gain contact with the suspect's elderly mother. She had a nervous breakdown as a result. Journalists also travelled to Ireland where they followed another of George's relatives everywhere he went. Both he and George's mother maintain that someone, presumably a journalist, *'interfered'* with their telephones.

Before George was charged he participated in one conventional identity parade, along with eight foils (volunteers), because he had denied he was the man seen by the witnesses on the day of the shooting. None of the witnesses who attended the parade, including some of the witnesses whose evidence will be discussed in the following two chapters, identified George as the man they had seen in the Gowan Avenue area. The witnesses included Joseph Sappleton (the man whose description led to the creation of the E-fit) and a worker from Copes Seafood Company. For this reason George was advised to exercise his legal right by refusing to participate in any further conventional parades. Future parades, which were composed of video images of George's face, along with the faces of eight other men, took place after he was charged.

By law, the police are only permitted to hold a suspect in custody for twenty-four hours before charging or releasing them. The investigating officer can apply for extensions from a magistrate, however, if there are sufficient grounds to do so. The maximum amount of time a person can be held in custody is ninety-six hours. After this period the suspect must be charged or released without charge. As the twenty-four hour period came to an end police realised they had insufficient evidence to charge George. However, it was Campbell's view that George was responsible and therefore he applied for an extension in the hope that further information could be acquired.

Magistrates granted an extension permitting detectives to hold their suspect in custody for an additional twenty-four hours. However, this proved to be insufficient time for them to acquire evidence that the suspect was responsible for the murder and so three further extensions, one for twenty-four hours and two for twelve hours each, were requested as each period came to an end. In total Campbell was provided with the full ninety-six hours to investigate his prime suspect while George was in custody. Of these ninety-six hours only eight would be spent interviewing George.

From the evening of 27 May onwards, despite Campbell's attempts to interview the suspect, under the instructions of his solicitor George exercised his right to silence.

4.3: George's personality

George often used to claim he was the cousin of Freddie Mercury, using the alias Barry Bulsara. Many neighbours were irritated by the fact that he played Queen music at very loud volume. They believed he was odd but most believed him to be harmless. Some of his neighbours, and people who knew him, trusted George with their children. On the whole most believed he was just immature although some believed he was mad and laughed at him when watching his games. He was not seen as a threat.

George is an epileptic who has suffered severe seizures. The police were aware of this and they were also aware he had at least one psychological disorder as well as a low IQ. Psychologists believe that George suffers from Asperger's syndrome, histrionic personality disorder, narcissistic personality disorder and paranoia. He therefore has a number of conditions that leave him with a severe disadvantage in life, but these conditions do not make someone more likely to commit a crime. Indeed it has been suggested by The National Autistic Society that sufferers of Asperger's syndrome are less likely to commit criminal acts because they have a very strong sense of what is right and wrong.

Those who have known George, or have had any contact with him, including myself, claim he is almost always agitated and worried, because of his paranoia. According to a prisoner who served with him in Whitemoor Prison following his conviction, George is *"hard work"* and everyone who speaks to him *"goes away shell-shocked and frustrated."*

Before his arrest George spent most of his time walking the streets, riding on his bicycle and talking to strangers in the hope he could make friends and relationships. The people he approached were usually women he liked the look of and wished to get to know better. The police discovered this through talking to people who knew him.

Many people judge the accuracy of the guilty verdict against George by viewing DCI Campbell's comment on *Crimewatch* on 19 April 2000. On this programme Campbell gave an opinion of the killer's personality, which later, many people would be impressed by. He said:

"... link these things together; the loner, the obsession with Jill Dando, the obsession with firearms ... this interest ... this ability to alter or change them, so a previous gun club member, this interest with guns and perhaps specialist books and magazines".[11]

---

[11] *Crimewatch UK,* 19 April 2000.

The official view of this description is that it was based upon information gained through Campbell having attended a seminar in Birmingham where the possible characteristics of the killer's personality were discussed.

However, it must be realised that this edition of *Crimewatch UK* was broadcast live two days after the search of 2b Crookham Road had begun, and already George was Campbell's prime suspect, with the order having been given for George to be kept under surveillance. By the time of the *Crimewatch* appeal Campbell had a large amount of information about George; he knew the suspect was in possession of gun magazines, that he showed signs of an interest in women and possible indications of an interest in Dando, and that he lived alone. It is highly possible that Campbell saw a man he believed to be a loner with an obsession with guns and an apparent obsession with women, and so he moulded his view of the killer on his suspect. Campbell could not prove that George had an obsession with Dando, but he hoped he would later be able to establish George did have such an obsession. It can be dangerous to discover a suspect from an offender profile. It is more dangerous to base a profile upon a suspect.

4.4: Motive

It is always preferable in a criminal investigation if it can be established that the suspect had a reason to commit the crime they are accused of. Campbell was unable to determine any motive George could possibly have. He could only state, *"He was internally driven, but I cannot say what drove him to kill her."*

This is not sufficient, as the motive of the killer is always necessary in order to understand the crime committed. If it could be proven George had a motive, then it would be easier to understand that he could be responsible for the crime. At no point has any indication of a motive been shown.

It could not be argued that George held any grudge against Dando, or had any motive whatsoever for wishing her dead. It could only be suggested that he allegedly disliked the BBC because he believed they had treated his idol, Freddie Mercury, badly prior to his death. George is believed to have expressed his dislike to a member of staff at the BBC in 1991. Is this sufficient reason for a man to kill? It would seem rather unlikely, with *The Guardian* newspaper being right to call this a *'weak anecdote'*.[12] Between 1991 and 1999 George made no other comment to show he held a grudge against the corporation and George's brief period of work at the BBC appears to be the happiest period of his life. One of George's relatives worked for the BBC for six years. George never mentioned any grievances he had against the corporation to him, only ever speaking of it when he asked whether his relative could obtain free tickets for *Top of the Pops*. If he possessed bad feelings, he never did anything to act upon them, despite making frequent visits to the BBC centre in Wood Lane to collect free newsletters. It is difficult to believe he could wait eight years before enacting revenge on behalf of his hero.

4.5: Searches of George's flat

On the day on which Gallagher had first questioned George at his mother's home, the officer entered 2b Crookham Road for the first time. Gallagher did not have the opportunity to search the contents, as he did not have a warrant and also at the time there was not sufficient reason for George to be considered a significant suspect; he was just one of many. However, he was able to briefly look around. He found George's flat was in a terrible state and was barely habitable. There was rubbish everywhere. When George had informed the police about his flat being untidy when they had asked to question him, he was not lying.

On 17 April 2000, two days after the suspect's fortieth birthday, police officers led by DC Gallagher arrived at 2b Crookham Road, the home of George. They had come to search the premises for any evidence which could connect George to the murder. George was not in at the time so the officers let themselves in by forcing the lock.

The search was conducted by a POLSA team. POLSA is an acronym for Police Search Advisor, which means there was a trained search adviser present. POLSA trained officers are allegedly *'expert at making systematic searches using methods and equipment unique to this branch of police work'*.[13] However, as you will read in Chapter 6 the searches were not conducted in a way that reflected any degree of expertise.

---

[12] *The Guardian*, 3 July 2001.
[13] (Fleming and Miller. 1995: 251).

Photographs of the flat were taken and later a video camera would be used. This was to enable DCI Campbell, and other members of the murder squad who had not visited Crookham Road to see for themselves what the suspect's home was like; it must have sounded unbelievable when Gallagher had described it.

The Police and Criminal Evidence Act 1984 states that search of a suspect's belongings or property should be conducted with care and consideration for the property and privacy of the suspect. It is known George was deeply upset by the fact that his home and a flat owned by his mother were searched. On one occasion George was found sitting on the street outside his flat while officers were searching inside.

The search which began on 17 April 2000 was the most fruitful of the three searches conducted at the suspect's home, as far as the police were concerned. The search was not confined to one day and so George had to temporarily move while the police looked through his belongings and removed items for more detailed inspection and examination. This search was the most fruitful partly because the period of time the search team had available to them was greater than is usually available and so they were able to recover a large amount of material. Their task was still difficult, however, due to George's untidy habits.

Officers had a list of items to recover if they could be found. However, this search and the second search only scratched the surface. It was clear a more detailed search was required.

Many newspapers and magazines, some of the magazines relating to firearms, were removed. These will be discussed in the next two chapters along with the other evidence recovered during searches. Curiously police discovered in the flat a large number of rolls of undeveloped photographic film. These were removed so they could be developed.

The main reason for this search being fruitful was that a Cecil Gee coat belonging to George was removed for examination along with other items of clothing. Within a pocket of this coat a particle was found, which without doubt is the most famous and controversial particle of British criminal history. One officer would later claim that once the particle had been found, *"We knew that we had enough evidence to arrest him."*

The particle was discovered and compared with the FDR found on Dando at the beginning of May 2000 by the scientific support.

Campbell was informed about the fact that the particle was a compositional match on 5 May 2000. However, George was not arrested until 25 May 2000 and so this particle, which became a major part of the prosecution's case against George, was not seen to be sufficient evidence for an arrest to be made. It was not, as would be later admitted, considered significant.

Campbell believed a second search was needed. The 17 April search had recovered some items suggesting George had an interest in firearms and a possible interest in the victim, but none of this constituted evidence of his involvement in the crime. George was now considered to be the prime suspect in the investigation and evidence had to be found in order to confirm Campbell's opinion.

On 11 May 2000, after a second warrant had been obtained, Gallagher once again led a search team to Crookham Road. George answered his door this time, and so a forced entry was not required. Gallagher admitted pushing George out of the way as he entered the flat.

This search recovered more of what had been discovered in the first search; newspapers, magazines, photographic film, handwritten documents and other such items were seized. Together, these would further show George had an interest in firearms and a possible interest in the victim. Essentially no proof of George's involvement could be found during this search. No weapons or ammunition, or anything that could be used to show George was a killer, were found.

Once George had been arrested nothing could prevent Campbell from ordering the largest scale search of George's flat which could possibly take place. Every single item from inside the flat was placed in crates, which were then placed in a lorry to be taken away for analysis. This task alone was lengthy due to the fact that George was a hoarder of many items collected over the years.

When the flat was empty a fingertip search began, with forensic teams searching for evidence, mainly of firearms usage. They were hoping to find more particles of FDR. Floorboards were lifted and all hollow walls had cameras inserted within them in the hope something would be found hidden within those out-of-sight locations. There was nothing hidden.

4.6: Further investigations into the suspect through covert operations

As part of the investigation into George, Oxborough detectives positioned a static camera which constantly recorded George's flat. What could the police possibly hope to achieve through this? What knowledge and evidence could they acquire through this expensive method of surveillance? The camera could only record footage of George entering and leaving his flat. It recorded nothing else at all. All that was shown was that George left his flat on many occasions during the day. This information was already known. It was an ascertained fact, George spent his time walking around the streets of Fulham engaging in conversation with strangers and people he knew who worked in local shops and businesses.

After a year had elapsed this could not realistically have provided Oxborough detectives with any additional information to what they already had at their disposal. Did they expect to see George walk out of his flat with a gun in his hand? If they did, then they would have been disappointed. This means of investigation provided the investigating officers with no proof whatsoever regarding George's involvement in the murder of Dando.

After the first search had been conducted at Crookham Road, George was kept under surveillance every day until he was arrested, between 07:00 and midnight. There was no evidence at all to suggest George had any interest in guns. At one point George realised he was being kept under surveillance and for this reason he panicked and told people he knew the police believed he had killed Dando. Some of them incorrectly took this to be a sign that he was feeling guilty whereas in reality he was worried about being watched.

When studying the chronology, it is understandable George became distressed when he discovered he was being followed. On 11 April 2000 he was interviewed in connection with the murder of Jill Dando. 15 April was his fortieth birthday. On 17 April he returned home from a walk to find the police had forced open the door of his flat and a team of police officers, some of whom were armed (this will be discussed in Chapter 6) were searching through his belongings. On this day George was told he would have to move out of his home, something that deeply upset him, as did the search of his mother's home. On 19 April the crime was once again discussed on *Crimewatch*, but on this occasion DCI Campbell's description of the killer uncannily matched George. On 18 or 19 April the police began to follow the suspect during the daytime, everywhere he went. It is understandable George was upset when he discovered he was being followed.

Campbell ordered a policewoman to attempt to befriend the suspect and gain his confidence in order to try and extract information from him. This was a very risky action as trials have collapsed as a result of this method of operation. Colin Stagg, who was accused of murdering Rachel Nickell, was acquitted when it was learnt that an undercover policewoman had befriended him in an attempt to obtain information. For this reason the policewoman was not supposed to ask George any leading questions. However, she did ask him an indirect question about his interest in guns, to which George responded, *"Don't talk to me about guns."* The officer, who only attempted to speak to George on one occasion in an Internet café, learnt absolutely nothing to suggest the suspect was a murderer. George did not follow the officer and he did not show any interest in her at all.

4.7: George's criminal record

As is to be expected the police looked at George's criminal record. This of course could not be expected to amount to any degree of proof of guilt and would be inadmissible as evidence in court. However, the police discovered, amongst other offences, George had been sentenced to thirty-three months in prison for attempted rape. George confessed to the attempted rape and his involvement in this offence, which took place almost two decades before Dando's murder, does not mean that he shot the presenter. George's record did contribute to the belief that he was the man Oxborough were hunting. His criminal record will be discussed further in the following two chapters.

4.8: The police decide whether or not George should be charged

As the ninety-six hour deadline fast approached, the Oxborough team reviewed the evidence they had acquired against their prime suspect.

And what evidence did they have? It amounted to precious little. They only had supposition that George was obsessed with firearms, women and the victim; the evidence from staff at Hafad (who partially substantiated George's alibi) and Traffic Cars; the particle and some other minor pieces of evidence. Of course, only the particle could be classed as evidence that possibly linked George to the crime.

It is not unfair to speculate that the particle's importance to the police increased as it was realised they had failed to acquire more significant evidence. George had only been interviewed regarding the presence of the particle on Saturday 27 May 2000; the day before he was charged and after extensions had been granted. Etienne had not been informed of its presence (as George's solicitor she should have been informed as she had specifically asked on a prior occasion to be told of any forensic evidence to enable her to discuss this with her client) until the subject arose during questioning. If the particle was considered to be significant it would have been asked about before the first twenty-four hours had elapsed.

Campbell's only hope of charging his suspect, in the absence of significant evidence, now lay predominantly upon the famous particle, the piece of evidence which had previously been viewed as not being particularly important. The police hoped that with George remanded in prison they would be able to acquire information and further evidence during the interim period between George being charged and the trial.

The police were incredibly fortunate that this was a lengthy delay, further prolonged through legal arguments. The evidence of Julia Moorhouse only came to their attention, via HOLMES, just days before the trial was due to begin, and almost one year after George was charged. It was also only four months after George was charged that a witness, named Susan Mayes, identified George as the man she believed she had seen in Gowan Avenue on the morning of Dando's murder. It is important to stress that if the police had not acquired this positive identification there is no doubt the case would have collapsed.

There were serious doubts as to whether or not George should be charged. Frequent discussions occurred between Campbell and a senior official from the Crown Prosecution Service, Alison Saunders, during which it was decided whether or not the evidence against George was sufficiently strong to survive the scrutiny of a defence counsel in court. When deciding whether a case should be referred to a court, the Crown Prosecution Service tests the evidence. If, in the opinion of the CPS, the evidence is more likely than not to lead to a conviction then the recommendation to charge the suspect is given. Can it be said that the evidence Oxborough had in May 2000 was sufficient to result in a conviction? Following the first appeal hearing at the Court of Appeal, the CPS issued a press release in which Saunders said, *"I have always maintained that the evidence provided a compelling picture of Barry George's guilt."*[14]

Is it not possible Saunders was influenced by the view that George matched the characteristics the killer was believed to have? This profile, unknown to Saunders, was quite conceivably based upon George and so, understandably, she must have taken this to be proof of George's guilt, when of course, in reality, it proves nothing other than that the profile was moulded around the suspect.

Operation Oxborough had spent an estimated £2,000,000 and thirteen months hunting the man who killed Dando. The murder squad must have asked themselves how much longer it would take to get sufficient evidence to prove George's guilt, and what would be the cost financially, temporally and through criticism? Under the Police and Criminal Evidence Act no further applications for extensions could be made, and so Campbell knew George would either have to be released until more evidence was obtained, or charged. The investigation had been hard and they had been unable to find anyone who was more likely to have committed the murder. After all, George was the only significant suspect the police had questioned in thirteen months of investigation, and if George was not charged there would be little chance of finding someone else to charge. As the Assistant Commissioner of the Metropolitan Police Force, Brian Moore, commented after the trial:

"It was a stranger attack. It was not seen by anybody, the killer was not seen at the time, and very little forensic evidence was left behind. There could be no more difficult environment to investigate a case."[15]

---

[14] A Crown Prosecution Press Release issued on 30 July 2002
[15] *BBC News,* 2 July 2001.

And so, on 28 May 2000, the public was informed the police had made a breakthrough with their expensive and high profile investigation, when a spokesperson for the Metropolitan Police issued the following statement:

"Barry Michael George, aged 40, unemployed, of 2b Crookham Road, Fulham, south-west London, was tonight charged with the murder of Ms Jill Dando on April 26, 1999, at 29 Gowan Avenue, Fulham. He will appear at west London magistrates court tomorrow morning."

It would be almost a year later, when the trial finally began, on 4 May 2001, after several weeks of legal argument, that he was to stand before a judge and jury in Court Number One at the Old Bailey.

Chapter 5:

The evidence against George

"You have deprived Miss Dando's fiancé, family and friends of a much loved and popular personality. You are unpredictable and dangerous ..."[16]

No doubt the reader will notice how short this chapter is in comparison to the following chapter, which aims to defend George by contradicting the evidence against him. By no means is this deliberate. The length of this chapter is merely a reflection of the scant evidence against the man who has been imprisoned on a charge of murder.

First it is important to give a summary of the trial and those involved. The prosecution case started on 4 May 2001 and lasted for five weeks. The case was presented by Orlando Pownall QC, and the main prosecution witnesses were Susan Mayes (who had identified George as the man she had seen on Gowan Avenue on the morning of Dando's murder), Ramesh Paul (a member of staff from the local taxi firm Traffic Cars, who claimed to have met an agitated Barry George on the day of the murder and two days later when he allegedly falsified an alibi), a number of members of staff from Hafad (who provided evidence conflicting with George's account of his movements on the day of the murder, and his suspicious actions two days later), David Dobbins and Susan Coombe (who both provided evidence of George's 'fascination' with firearms) and Robin Keeley (the forensic scientist who compared the particle of alleged firearms discharge residue from George's pocket, with that of the particles found on Jill Dando).

The defence case lasted two weeks and finished on 22 June

---

[16] Mr Justice Gage when sentencing George to life imprisonment on 2 July 2001.

2001. The defence counsel, Michael Mansfield QC, called a number of witnesses to demonstrate the prosecution's case *'hung by the merest of threads'*. The main defence witnesses in George's defence were Susan Bicknell (who provided George with an alibi), Elaine Hutton (who helped corroborate George's alibi), Dr John Lloyd (a forensic scientist who argued the particle was unrelated to Dando's murder) and Mark Webster (who argued against the significance of the textile fibre).

After the trial judge, Mr Justice Gage, completed his summing up, which lasted for two days, the jury retired to consider their verdict. They reached their verdict only after five days, split over a weekend.

5.1: Obsessions

The Old Bailey heard from the prosecuting counsel, Orlando Pownall QC, that George has *"an exaggerated interest in well known figures"*.[17] The police found material to show George had an interest in celebrities such as Freddie Mercury. Searches of George's flat recovered business cards and other material relating to *'Bulsara Productions Inc'*, a phoney business of which George claimed to be a director. George also was found to use the name 'Barry Bulsara' (Bulsara was Freddie Mercury's real surname). An edited photograph of George with the lead singer of the rock group 'Queen' was also discovered. The title of the photograph was *'Freddie Mercury and cousin'*. It is a fact that George informed people he was Mercury's cousin, when in reality they were not related in any way.

It is true George had emulated the lives of certain well-known figures such as Thomas Palmer, as well as Freddie Mercury and at an early age, Garry Glitter. The question that needs to be answered is, however, did he have an obsession or any interest in Jill Dando?

The police and the prosecuting counsel believed George had an unhealthy interest in Dando. The police could not prove such a theory although they believed George might have harboured unhealthy feelings towards the victim. The prosecution during George's trial, however, tried to show George was obsessed with Dando and tried to convey this view to the jury. In order to

---

[17] From a speech by Orlando Pownall, on Friday 4 May 2001.

demonstrate George had a fixation with Dando, the prosecution relied upon evidence recovered during the searches of 2b Crookham Road.

Amongst George's collection of newspapers, newsletters and magazines officers had found a small number of articles referring to Dando. Those present at George's trial heard that eight articles were found in George's flat which were printed prior to the victim's death. In addition to the articles predating 26 April 1999, over forty articles were found in his collection that referred to the investigation into the murder of Dando. These included articles from the BBC's in house newsletter, *Ariel*, which George had collected every week. The prosecution believed such a high number of articles indicated an unhealthy interest in the victim.

As has been discussed, there was a presumption Dando's killer had been obsessed with the victim. They believed that as George appeared to be obsessed with the victim he could have been her killer.

The police developed a large number of previously undeveloped photographic films recovered from Crookham Road. It transpired, through study of these photographs, that George had taken pictures from his television screen of newsreaders and other television presenters. Although no photographs had been taken of Dando, despite her regular appearances on television, the police and prosecution believed George had an exaggerated interest in female television presenters and celebrities in general.

In his appeal on *Crimewatch*, which had taken place while George was the prime suspect, DCI Campbell stated his belief that the murderer had either an obsession with Dando or an obsession with women. The photographs developed from rolls of undeveloped film found in the suspect's home showed George had an exaggerated interest in women. This was because George had taken photographs of four hundred and nineteen different women. This indicated the suspect had an unhealthy interest in women.

The police also discovered evidence to suggest George engaged in following women. During the 1980's he had been interviewed for harassment, although no charges had been made against him. George's criminal record matched the profile of a man obsessed with women.

5.2: Loner

When George was being investigated Campbell was of the opinion that Dando's killer must be a social outcast, a loner. As stated in Chapter 4 the *Crimewatch* appeal had asked for people to report anyone they knew who, amongst other characteristics, was a loner. As George had few friends and does not have good social interaction skills probably due to his personality disorders, he fitted the detective's idea of a loner, which was used to further prove his guilt.

5.3: George's interest in firearms

George had, during the 1980's, used the alias Thomas Palmer. Palmer had been one of the SAS soldiers who had taken part in the operation to rescue hostages during the Iranian Embassy siege. George liked the heroic image of being in the SAS and so he began to use this alias.

Amongst the undeveloped photographs recovered from 2b Crookham Road there were two images which particularly interested the police and later the prosecution. The first photograph was taken from a distance and shows a man holding a Heckler and Koch MP5 replica machine gun and the second, previously undeveloped photograph, showed a man holding an 8 mm Bruni handgun. Experts stated the guns were both blank firers and were therefore not weapons. However, this showed the police George had an interest in firearms. The second picture has often been described as sinister. The picture shows a man standing with a gun in his hand, whilst wearing a mask.

Upon being shown these two photographs George commented they were taken at an SAS base. He did not believe he was the man shown in the pictures. The police believed it was indeed the suspect shown holding the guns and they took George's words to be a sign he was being deceitful.

The police interviewed David Dobbins regarding George's interest in firearms. The prosecution also called him as a witness in order to be questioned about the issue during the trial. Dobbins had known George during the 1980s when they lived in the same hostel. When the Dobbins family moved elsewhere, George occasionally visited them. During the trial Dobbins told the court how on one occasion in 1986 George had entered their home, dressed in a combat jacket, military belt and jeans, and produced an imitation 8 mm Bruni blank firing firearm, with which he discharged a blank round. Dobbins described the effect the incident had upon his family and himself when he said, *"It was pretty scary. It was like he was trying to frighten us."*

This witness also informed the court 'Thomas Palmer' (Dobbins only knew George by this alias) had at some point owned an imitation Heckler and Koch MP5 machine gun. When investigating the location of George's two blank firing guns, police officers discovered that Dobbins and a friend had broken into George's home during the mid 1980s and stolen the weapons. George had reported them stolen. Incidentally, a few weeks after George was convicted, David Dobbins hung himself.

The prosecution called a second witness to further discuss the defendant's interest in firearms. Susan Coombe had lived in the same hostel as George in 1985.

Whilst living at the hostel Coombe had on one occasion made a visit to George's room. During this visit George had allegedly shown the witness a gun he kept in a shoebox under his bed. This particular firearm was neither of the firearms shown in the undeveloped photographs found in George's flat. At the trial Coombe described and drew a picture of the small silver gun she had seen fourteen years before Dando's murder. From these sources of information it is believed George may have kept a third gun; possibly a blank-firing Browning. Searches at Crookham Road, and subsequent research, failed to locate it. No one who knew George from his days at Crookham Road knew of this weapon, and Dobbins did not claim to have stolen it.

George has denied he owned a third gun. This suggests either he forgot about its existence, that Coombe was lying or mistaken, or George was lying. The detectives and prosecution favoured the latter possibility, believing George was lying about his ownership of a third firearm in order to conceal the extent of his interest in firearms. The small silver gun could not have been the weapon used to kill Dando, but it was believed this was further corroborating evidence of George's 'obsession' with firearms and all things military.

In 1981 George joined the Territorial Army under the name 'Steven Majors'. During his period of service for the TA, in which he attended twenty-nine training sessions, George was able to fire weapons on a few occasions, whilst under supervision. The prosecution claimed as a result of his twenty nine training sessions at the TA, George acquired sufficient experience to be competent with firearms and live ammunition.

In addition to his service in the Territorial Army, during the summer of 1982 George made an application to join a gun club. Although his application was turned down the police and prosecution believed George had occasionally fired pistols on the premises, whilst his application was being considered. During the trial, Pownall claimed George had been *"principally involved in pistol shooting"* whilst at the club.

Handwritten lists, in George's handwriting, were recovered from 2b Crookham Road. These listed a number of different firearms including the two blank-firing guns the suspect had owned prior to them having been stolen. These lists also included grenade launchers and other such weapons George had heard of.

Further evidence of his interest in firearms was found during a search of George's flat in the form of a shoulder holster.

Officers read the firearms magazines and books recovered during searches of George's flat. In one of the magazines an advertisement was found which proved to be of interest in the investigation. The advertisement offered deactivated-reactivated guns. As the murder weapon could have been a deactivated-reactivated firearm this was, in the opinion of the prosecution, compelling evidence that George had an interest in reactivated firearms.

The prosecution compared the evidence of George's interest to the interest the killer had with firearms, according to the psychological profile provided to Oxborough investigators. Orlando Pownall claimed during the trial on Tuesday 8 May 2001:

"The gunman would have had an interest in firearms - so did the defendant. The gunman would have had an interest in altering or reactivating blank-firing guns - so did the defendant."

5.4: Witnesses and identification

Unlike the police investigation, the trial focussed upon the testimonies of nine witnesses, eight of which had attended identity parades (either live parades or video parades). These witnesses included the key witnesses who had reported sightings of a man close to or at the crime scene, immediately after the shooting. The prosecution witnesses were those who provided the best descriptions and whose descriptions were of men who had not been eliminated from the investigation. These witnesses were also those who had provided statements and (in the majority of cases) identification evidence which, in the minds of the prosecution counsel, consisted of compelling evidence that it was George who was seen on Gowan Avenue on the day of Dando's murder. The prosecution alleged that the eyewitnesses who provided evidence during the trial had provided police with descriptions which shared characteristics in the man's appearance, and more importantly that these characteristics described George.

Details from the statements provided are included in the appendix. In this chapter, when referring to a witness, the letter designating each of the sightings will be provided so the reader can refer back to what each witness told the police following the crime. During the trial, a witness named Theresa Normanton testified (the appeal judges like to call her by her middle name, Belinda, for reasons unknown to anyone other than themselves). She made her statement to the police at a later stage than the others and so her statement is not mentioned in the appendix. It will be discussed in this chapter where relevant.

George participated in one live conventional identification parade. After being viewed by witnesses by this means he stated he did not wish to participate in future identity parades (as was his legal right). Therefore, future witnesses participated in parades which showed video images of the face of George along with eight other faces. By the time of the identity parades George had grown a goatee beard and moustache.

The first sighting considered was sighting A, made by Helen Scott (the witnesses were not questioned in this order during the trial). Scott reported seeing a man on 25 April 1999 (the evening before the murder) around 20:00. During the trial Scott stated that the man was in her view for around two minutes. At the video identity parade she picked out a man who was not George, stating she was eighty to eighty five percent sure she was correct. This man was number eight in the parade whereas George was number two. The prosecution relied upon her evidence at the trial however, so it could be argued that although Scott could not identify George, she may have seen George because her description provided to the police was similar to the descriptions given by other witnesses who may have also seen George.

The next sighting to be considered was sighting B, made by Susan Mayes. This woman was the key prosecution witness whose evidence would, in the prosecution's eyes, prove George's guilt. During the video identification parade she attended she asked to see numbers two and eight again. After seeing both again she commented she was *"very sure"* that between 06:57 and 07:00 on 26 April 1999 she had seen number two (George) opposite Dando's home.

Stella de Rosnay saw a man, whose description is included in sighting C, for ten to twelve seconds at around 09:30 on the day of the murder (her daughter-in-law believed it to be 09:40). At the video identity parade she could not decide between number two and number eight commenting, *"For me for the moment it would be number two or eight ... I would say number two."* However, she conceded she was not at all sure and could not make a positive identification. The following day though Stella made the following statement:

"I watched the video twice and immediately ruled out seven of the males. When I saw number two on the screen, it suddenly brought something back to me. I recognised his face as the man I'd seen passing by my window on 26 April 1999 ..."

Charlotte de Rosnay reported sighting D. Charlotte is the daughter-in-law of Stella and was with Stella when they both saw a man at around 09:40 (according to Charlotte). The two descriptions do vary although this could be considered to be due to the varying lengths of time they had each viewed the man. The basic descriptions were, however, the same. At the video identification parade Charlotte specifically stated she did not think the man she had seen on the day of the murder was on the video parade. This is clear in reading her comments; when she was asked whether the man was present she replied, *"No I don't think so."* During the trial, however, number two (George) was described by Charlotte as being the *"predominant contender"* despite the fact she had no belief he was the man she saw when staring at an image of his face. The prosecution took her testimony as yet further evidence to suggest George was on Gowan Avenue prior to the murder.

Terry Normanton made a statement at a later stage in the investigation and so her description is not included in the appendix. Her statement showed she reported a man who appeared to be 40 years of age, 5'8 in height, of medium build with black hair which was long and slightly wavy, but not down to his shoulders. The man had no facial hair and his face was described as being *'not narrow'*. She commented he could have been Mediterranean or sun tanned. The man was wearing a black suit and no tie and he had a mobile telephone. Normanton had been six to eight feet away from the man she had seen. At the video identity parade Normanton could not make a positive identification. The reason for this (according to her) was the men in the video identity parade had facial hair whereas the man she had seen did not. During the trial she stated she was sure it was George she had seen on the day of the murder. This (according to the prosecution) was further evidence that George was on Gowan Avenue prior to the murder despite his statement he was elsewhere at the time.

Terry Griffin, the postman who reported sighting F, was called as a prosecution witness. Discussion of his evidence is not relevant here, for he provided more evidence for the defence than he did for the prosecution, and he did not see Barry George. However, the prosecution claimed that as he had seen a Mediterranean man on the day of the murder that man could have been George because Susan Mayes had described a Mediterranean man and she picked out George during the video parade.

The evidence provided by the key witnesses Richard Hughes and Geoffrey Upfill-Brown (sightings J and K respectively), who almost certainly saw Dando's killer, will be omitted from this section. The next chapter is more suitable for discussion of the evidence of these two men. However, again the prosecution used the information provided by these witnesses to assist them in their argument that George was present on Gowan Avenue and fled the crime scene immediately following the murder. They used the evidence of these two men because their statements provided descriptions which were allegedly similar in certain respects to those of other witnesses who believed it could have been George, though neither of these two witnesses identified George as the man they saw.

The final prosecution witness to discuss here is Janet Bolton. Bolton reported sighting L to the police. She had seen a man at some point between 11:35 and 11:40 on the day of the murder and therefore her information was very important because Dando had been killed just after 11:30. Bolton did not attend a parade and therefore it cannot be known whether or not it was George she saw running down Gowan Avenue. Despite this, Bolton was called as a prosecution witness to give evidence against George. Her description was said to tally with other descriptions of a man seen around this time and therefore she could have seen the killer. Because her description was similar in certain respects to the one provided by Susan Mayes it was believed George could have been the man seen by Bolton.

The prosecution claimed that as the nine eyewitnesses had provided statements which possessed similarities regarding the features of the men seen, then they had all seen the same man. They then argued that, as one witness said she was "very sure" the man she had seen was George, then it was probable the other witnesses had also seen George. For example, in her initial statement to the police Susan Mayes described a man of Mediterranean appearance. She was not alone in describing a man who appeared to be from the Mediterranean region. As Mayes identified George it was believed others who reported seeing someone who appeared to be of Mediterranean origin also probably saw George. This, according to the prosecution, provided compelling evidence that George was watching the home of Dando prior to the murder and therefore must have been the killer:

> *"We suggest that you can be sure he was there at 7am and later at 10am and was paying close attention to No 29 ... Why is he lying about his movements, if these identifications are correct and reliable? What reason did he have for being there? The crown suggests he was there hoping that Miss Dando would appear."*[18]

---

[18] Orlando Pownall speaking on Friday 4 May 2001.

5.5: George's actions on the day of the crime and his suspicious actions two days later

During the first week of the investigation, Oxborough detectives received phone calls from staff at Hafad and London Traffic Cars (as has been explained in the previous chapter). As the investigation progressed more pieces of information were entered into HOLMES regarding George's actions on the day of the murder and his suspicious actions two days later.

Staff from Hafad altogether made four telephone calls to the incident room. Those calls, when taken together, reveal that a man named Barry Bulsara of 2b Crookham Road, Fulham, visited the advice centre on the day of the murder without having made an appointment. The callers, Leslie Symes, Susan Bicknell and Elaine Hutton, could not give a precise time at which the visit was made. There was a general consensus it had been between 11:00 and 11:50. However, when police later interviewed the three members of staff and their colleagues this consensus had altered, thus removing any firm alibi George could have relied upon. They now believed George could have arrived at some point between 11:00 and 14:00. This inability to agree meant Hafad staff could not provide George with an alibi for the time of the murder.

On the day of the murder he had been agitated when he arrived at the centre. He told the members of staff to whom he spoke that he had problems with his GP, his housing department and other organisations (George used to regularly complain about services he was receiving. Many believe he did this to occupy his time when he had nothing better to do).

At some point before 13:00 George arrived at Traffic Cars in order to travel to Colon Cancer Concern so he could collect some information regarding colon cancer and other bowel disorders. A member of staff in the taxi office, Ramesh Paul, remembered the encounter he had with George. When questioned by police, and later Pownall and Mansfield, Paul recalled how agitated George had been while in the office. George had asked for a free ride because he did not have any money with him. Paul told how he laughed at George and told him he could not have a ride if he could not pay the driver.

Paul became increasingly suspicious when George, upon being told to leave, remained in the office. He commented on how the suspect had become agitated and appeared to be in a world of his own. George, allegedly, would not sit down; he kept walking up to a window in order to look up and down the street.

The prosecution alleged that as George had appeared to be agitated following the murder, at both Hafad and Traffic Cars, this suggested he could be responsible.

The police and prosecution were aware George had arrived at Traffic Cars just before 13:00 on the day of the murder. However, having studied CCTV footage of a street close to Hafad (Stevenage Road) they believed George must have visited the advice centre after 12:45 before visiting the taxi company. This was because the footage showed a man wearing a yellow top (George was certainly wearing a yellow shirt when he arrived at Hafad and Traffic Cars) walking in the direction of the advice centre at around 12:45. A witness named Julia Moorhouse provided evidence proving George had spoken to her at around 12:30 on a small street near the centre. After speaking for a few minutes George had walked along Stevenage Road. An expert in mobile telephone communications told the court that George had made a telephone call on his mobile phone, to check his remaining credit, at 12:32. The call had lasted thirty-five seconds and, according to the expert, it could not have been made whilst George was in Hafad. According to George's account of events he had been in Hafad at this time although he was never quite sure of exact times. It was believed the call was made from the Bishop's Park area, which is nearby the advice centre. When George approached Moorhouse, he had a mobile telephone in his hand.

The prosecution linked these three pieces of information together in their attempt to show that the defendant was still on his way to Hafad at 12:30. He would therefore have had sufficient time to carry out the murder before returning home to get changed and then head out towards the advice centre in an attempt to falsify an alibi, they argued.

It was the suspicious actions of George on 28 April 1999, two days after the crime, which caused staff at Hafad and Traffic Cars to report this man to Oxborough. It was mainly this that resulted in him coming into the picture. On this particular day, George entered Hafad and appeared to be very distressed. He told the members of staff he encountered that he feared people thought he had killed Dando. He wanted to know what time he had visited on the Monday of that week. He also asked what colour clothing he had been wearing on the earlier visit. He told the staff he was intending to show he was not the killer and asked whether, if needed, he could rely on them to corroborate his claim that he was not responsible. He had appeared to be abusive when staff could not remember for certain the time of his arrival. Orlando Pownall stated during the trial, George was *"threatening and intimidating in his manner. He insisted on knowing what time he had attended the centre."*

When George was at Traffic Cars he made Ramesh Paul write down the time at which George had been at the taxi company's offices on the reverse of a business card and then sign the card. Paul wrote *'1:15'* and signed it. The police later found this card during a search of George's flat. He made Paul tell him what clothing he had been wearing on the day of the murder because he wanted to prove he was not wearing the same type of clothing as the killer. During George's trial Paul recalled the words he had received from George with regards to this; George allegedly told Ramesh Paul, *"I was wearing yellow like the colour of the sun. You must remember!"* Paul was very suspicious by this behaviour, and during the trial he commented that George *"practically shoved it [his wish to know when he was at Traffic Cars] down my throat".*

While in the office at Traffic Cars, Ramesh Paul believed he heard George muttering he did not want to be blamed. Paul was not paying much attention, as he believed George was in a world of his own and was a nut case.

This is all suggestive, according to the police and prosecution, that George had, through his actions two days after the crime, sought to falsify an alibi for his whereabouts at the time of the murder. His odd behaviour was eventually taken by the police to be an indication that his visit to the two offices two days after the crime was an attempt to falsify an alibi by forging a false impression into the minds of the staff he had spoken to. During the trial Orlando Pownall asked:

"What did the defendant have to fear? Why did he feel impelled to seek verification of his movements? Were his actions merely an irrational response to a misguided belief that he might become a suspect, or were they the actions of a man who knew he was responsible and was doing his level best to create an alibi?"

Suffice it to say, despite the full story regarding this point not having been provided in court, the prosecution took the latter view. They did not believe the actions of the suspect were consistent with the actions of a man who had no involvement in any criminal activity. This view would, in the absence of all evidence, have seemed to be the most plausible. However, in the next chapter it will be shown the most plausible explanation was in fact the former view.

It would be claimed by Pownall on 4 May 2001 that George's actions were out of proportion for an innocent man:

> *"His reaction to her death was out of all proportion to what one might expect from an individual who was not an admirer and would not have even recognised her. He visited shops and sought letters of condolence. He even suggested to a local council that they should consider a memorial."*[19]

The prosecution took the view George had an exaggerated interest in the aftermath of the murder, indicated by him having taken flowers to Gowan Avenue and his collection of condolence cards which he had lost in the mess in his flat. The prosecution believed these actions were uncharacteristic of an innocent man. In the eyes of the prosecution and the police, his actions suggested he was guilty.

5.6: The particle

During one of the searches conducted at 2b Crookham Road a coat belonging to George was removed, along with other items. This particular item of clothing was a Cecil Gee coat, which George had bought many years previously in 1988.

Routinely, all of the suspect's clothing was checked for the presence of possible forensic evidence. Up until checking this coat no forensic evidence had been found on George's clothing, and so there was no physical evidence linking him to the crime. A taping of the left inside pocket of the Cecil Gee coat revealed one microscopic particle, which was believed to be firearm discharge residue. The particle consisted of three basic elements: aluminium,

---

[19] Orlando Pownall speaking on Friday 4 May 2001.

lead and barium. Forensic tests had found on the victim's hair particles of aluminium, lead, barium and antimony, which had been released from the gun when the bullet had been discharged. Although the particles found on the victim contained four elements, it was possible that the particle found in George's coat could match those because not all particles contained all four elements. One particle on Dando's coat contained just aluminium and barium. Very little residue had been found on the victim; only three or four particles were discovered, presumably because of the close proximity of the barrel to the victim's head upon discharge, which resulted in most of the residue entering the victim.

It was believed the particle found in the pocket was of the same type as those particles found on Dando. This to them was compelling evidence George had fired the shot that killed Jill Dando. As you have previously read, it was this particle which, in the absence of other evidence, eventually proved to be sufficient evidence for a charge to be made.

During the trial Mr Robin Keeley, the prosecution's expert witness, commented it was his opinion that the particle found in George's pocket could only have come from a gun.

It was this particle along with the identification provided by Susan Mayes which would prove to be the prosecution's argument. The prosecution told the jury *"this aspect of the case provides compelling evidence of his [George's] guilt"*.[20]

5.7: Other forensic evidence

A thorough examination of the victim's clothing was made in the hope that some forensic evidence had been left by her killer. In addition to the particles from the gun, a single polyester fibre was found on Dando's raincoat. The fibre was compared with items of clothing belonging to George. It was discovered the blue-grey fibre could have been of the same type as fibres from a pair of trousers removed from Crookham Road.

The forensic evidence at the disposal of the police and prosecution was limited, but in their eyes it amounted to significant evidence which contributed to the overall compelling evidence which could be used to implicate George.

---

[20] Orlando Pownall, speaking on 8 May 2001.

5.8: George's lies to the police

What is a lie? Vrij defines a lie as, *'A successful or unsuccessful deliberate attempt, without forewarning, to create in another belief which the communicator considers to be untrue.'*[21]

George did not testify in court for it was determined that due to his epilepsy he was medically incapable of being questioned in a courtroom situation. Therefore it cannot be said George lied in court. However, detectives believed, during interviews at Hammersmith Police Station, that George had made a deliberate attempt to hide the truth.

In addition to what the police and prosecution believed to be lies spoken by George regarding his presence in photographs holding firearms, Oxborough and the prosecution counsel believed George had lied when questioned about other relevant issues.

During the police interviews George denied knowing of the celebrity prior to her death, stating he did not know of her *"in the flesh in any shape or form"*. The police did not believe he could be unaware of a woman who lived within half a mile of his flat, and who had appeared on several television programmes as well as featuring in the tabloids and magazines.

George's claim seemed unlikely when it was considered he had lived within half a mile from the victim's house and the victim had appeared on several television programmes and been featured in various magazine and newspaper articles before her untimely death. Indeed the court heard George had eight articles which featured Dando in some way from before her death, and even more articles dating from after her death. Detectives also discovered that a man matching George's description, who claimed to be Freddie Mercury's cousin, had possibly mentioned *"the lady from Crimewatch"* to a woman in a jewellers shop. This story was not tested in court and so it cannot be verified. However, George's denial of knowing Dando was interpreted as a lie. George claimed that he only knew of Dando's name after her death, at a time when many people across the country were talking about the incident. Again, the police did not believe him. The prosecution would also state their scepticism regarding George's responses during police interviews, with Orlando Pownall telling the court he

---

[21] (Vrij. 2002: 176).

believed George's claims were *"patently false"*. When the video-recorded interviews were shown to the jury, undoubtedly George came across as being deceitful.

It was also believed that George was being deceitful when asked about his links with Gowan Avenue; the street on which the victim had lived. He claimed he had no links with the Avenue. However, police, through searches and other methods of investigation, discovered this was not true. A few years before Dando's death the suspect had been a registered patient at the doctors' surgery located a few doors away from 29 Gowan Avenue. Studies of the photographs which George had never developed revealed George had once taken a picture of a woman as she walked along Gowan Avenue.

One further piece of information suggested that George may have had further links with the victim's street. This was a story about an incident which had occurred during the mid 1990s, told by a woman interviewed by the police. She told how a man, who was certainly George, showed her and her child the way to a building in Fulham. As they walked, George pointed to a street which may have been Gowan Avenue (the woman did not know Fulham at all) and commented *"a special lady"* lived there. This information could be completely irrelevant to the issue of whether or not George shot Dando, because the name of the street referred to has not been determined. Even if it was Gowan Avenue then the 'special lady' could have been anyone, perhaps the woman who George had photographed. Pownall informed the jury, however, that George did know a *'special lady'* on Gowan Avenue and therefore it could be concluded, George was trying to hide his connections with Gowan Avenue and his interest in Jill Dando.

5.9: Any other evidence

The surveillance on George revealed he was growing a beard and moustache. This was taken to be an indication that the suspect was anticipating having to participate in an identity parade, and therefore he was making efforts to disguise himself. The police wondered why an innocent man should wish to disguise himself in what appeared to be anticipation of being viewed by witnesses. This information was, in the eyes of the police, very important. George was arrested when it was learnt that he was growing facial hair.

During a search of 2b Crookham Road the police found a business card for 'Bulsara Productions Inc.' with the word *'Dando'* written on the reverse side, in George's handwriting. This was not considered to be a largely significant piece of evidence but it was mentioned at the trial. In fact as its significance was considered to be so low, like many pieces of supposed evidence, the card was only just admissible. However, it was used to further demonstrate the prosecution's belief that George had an exaggerated interest in Jill Dando.

5.10: George's criminal record

Details of George's criminal record were of course not presented to the jury, as a person's past is not indicative of current guilt; people can reform. Of course, many people who commit crimes do re-offend upon release from our penal institutions. This is not the general rule however, despite what many prejudiced individuals may believe. As the media on the whole was prejudiced against George it is, in a sense, good that a person's past actions are rarely discussed during a trial. This aspect, however, did assist the police in determining George was possibly responsible for the shooting outside 29 Gowan Avenue. It was George's criminal record, along with other factors, which made George the prime suspect.

George had, prior to his contact with the police regarding the Dando murder, committed crimes of a serious nature. In 1980 George pleaded guilty in court to impersonating a police officer. He had intervened in an argument in the street and had shown a clearly fake police warrant card which he had made, although it fooled one woman who was relieved a police officer had intervened in the dispute. He received a fine for this crime. Also during 1980 George was charged with indecently assaulting two women on separate occasions on the same day. He had tried to kiss one and touch her breasts, and he put his hand up the other woman's skirt after asking her out. He was convicted of one assault and received a three month suspended sentence.

In 1982 he attacked a woman but this time, unlike the other two occasions, he did attempt to rape the woman. In January 1983 George was allegedly found hiding in some bushes outside Kensington Palace. It was claimed he had in his possession a length of rope and a knife. It was reported he was arrested but, after questioning, was released without charge. Soon afterwards however he was interviewed in connection with the attempted rape that had occurred in 1982. He was charged, pleaded guilty in court and sentenced to thirty-three months in prison.

Although this evidence is circumstantial in its nature, Orlando Pownall, of the prosecution counsel, claimed on the whole it proved George was the one responsible for ending the life of Jill Dando, when he stated on Friday 4 May 2001 in his opening speech that the police had pieced together -
"...*compelling categories of circumstantial, forensic and scientific evidence, which, when taken together, prove that he [George] was the man in Gowan Avenue who was responsible for killing Jill Dando*".

To the student without a questioning mind this indicates George was guilty as charged. However, this is only one side of the debate, and so in the next chapter the case for the defence will be presented.

Chapter 6:

Arguments to suggest George is innocent

> *'...and yet it must be confessed that circumstantial evidence can never be absolutely convincing, and that it is only the critical student of such cases who realises how often a damning chain of evidence may, by some slight change, be made to bear an entirely different interpretation'.* [22]

This chapter will argue against the evidence discussed in the previous chapter.

In the last chapter the prosecution's assertion that George was obsessed with firearms and Jill Dando was stated. It also told how the evidence presented at trial was considered to be *"compelling"* proof of George's guilt. In this chapter it will be demonstrated the evidence cannot be considered to satisfy the burden of proof and between the mid 1980's and 1999 George had undergone a tremendous transition during which his interest in firearms had been reduced and his behaviour significantly improved.

6.1: Obsessions

As you have read, George is said to have had obsessions with certain celebrities.

At this point it is necessary to fully understand the word 'obsession' and its implications. The words 'obsessed' and 'obsession' are difficult to define. The English Oxford dictionary gives the definition of the word obsession as *'state of being obsessed; persistent idea,'* and obsessed as *'thinking about someone or something all the time'*. So we can assume if someone is obsessed with something, they presumably think about the particular thing continuously or very frequently.

---

[22] (Conan Doyle. 1988: 16).

How many people can be said to have obsessions? Undoubtedly, a large proportion of the population has something which interests them so much it forms a significant part of their lives. Whether the interest is with cars, trains, sport, women, men, their job, a particular celebrity, or something completely different, many people have what could be described as an obsession; it is not an uncommon characteristic of large numbers of individuals although many would deny they have such a developed interest.

There was once a television interview where a presenter met a small group of women who were huge fans of Sir Cliff Richard. They travelled all over the world and went to all of his concerts and many other charity events where he had appeared. They owned videos, books, all of his records and CDs etc. and many other related items. Sir Cliff was their life. He dominated their lives and without him no doubt a gap would have existed within the lives of these women.

This may be sad and many would consider this interest to be an obsession. However, this interest is not a bad thing, and it is certainly not dangerous.

In the same way, George was a fan of Freddie Mercury as well as many other celebrities. He had books about Queen's lead singer, and he even had an edited picture of himself with his arms around his idol. George likes this singer, just as so many others do. George shared his interest with others, a theme to be discussed in more detail shortly.

Yes, George may well have been obsessed with Freddie Mercury, so much so he changed his name to Barry Bulsara (Bulsara being Freddie Mercury's real surname). Just because he had what could be described as a keen interest in an inspirational figure in the world of music, does this mean George could have had an obsession with Jill Dando? As has already been explained, the psychological profile of the killer which police used indicated Dando's killer would have had an obsession with her, or an obsession with women. However, as was stated in Chapter 4, this opinion only came into being when George was in the picture, and no evidence to suggest he had a fixation with the victim has been found. By the time George had emerged as a possible suspect in the Oxborough investigation, the police had formed the view that a man who was an obsessed fanatic murdered Dando, and as was described in Chapter 5 the prosecution alleged George did have such a fixation with the television presenter.

The police did find a number of articles referring to Jill Dando in George's flat. During George's trial it was stated that eight articles predated her death. However, the police have since, rather confusingly, stated George had *six* articles predating the shooting. This new figure has also been used by the Justice For Barry campaign who say George had *'approximately six'* articles referring to Dando printed prior to 26 April 1999. These articles which featured Dando dated from 1990 to 1999. The police also found over forty articles, printed after the murder, which reported the police investigation. None of these articles were cut out, highlighted, placed in a scrap-book or marked out in any way in order for them to be easier to find.

Strangely for a person said to be obsessed George did not have a copy of *The Radio Times* printed and sold the week before the shooting and which had Dando on the front cover.

George was a hoarder of newspapers and the BBC in-house newsletter *Ariel,* which he collected as he was a former employee of the BBC. Over eight hundred newspapers were found at 2b Crookham Road and so the occurrence of six or eight articles about Dando, which dated before 26 April 1999, is to be expected (particularly over a nine-year period). Dando was in the newspapers fairly frequently in the months prior to her murder. The tabloids had discussed her engagement and her changing roles at the BBC, presenting new programmes and ceasing to present programmes she had in the past. The occurrence of eight articles can hardly be said to be evidence of an obsession. If he was obsessed with her, he would have had far more articles. And he possibly would have had a copy of at least one of the three issues of *The Radio Times* where Dando had appeared on the cover, and these would have been cut out or highlighted in some way so the articles could be found more easily. His flat was a mess, with papers underneath rubbish having been there presumably for many months. The papers which did feature Dando were lost underneath the rubbish, and so it would have taken him many hours to find the articles; after all George would have had to search through over eight hundred newspapers. Talk about looking for a needle in a haystack! If he was obsessed with Dando, he would not want them to be lost. He would want them where he could access them easily. Imagine how many celebrities and people in the public eye were featured more than once in those papers. The majority of people do not read all of the articles in a newspaper or magazine. So George was probably unaware he had these articles, and even if at some point he had read them he may well have paid them little attention and simply forgotten about them. He may not even have been aware of the presence of the newspapers in his flat, for there was so much rubbish accumulated over the years it was difficult to walk around inside the flat.

Whether it was six or eight articles which referred to the victim prior to 26 April 1999, the incidence of so few references from a nine-year period is in conflict with the view of George being obsessed with Dando. In fact, it is the lack of articles that demands explanation.

Following Dando's death the media followed the investigation perhaps too keenly. Newspapers and television news programmes covered developments almost every day during the first few weeks of the Oxborough investigation. Therefore, anyone who collects newspapers and magazines and other such sources of information, as George does, will have inevitably collected many articles regarding Dando's death, and the police investigation into her death. Due to the fact that George had articles after Dando's death, he was accused of having an unusual interest in the inquiry. This point will be discussed in Chapter 6.5 where it will be shown his actions and interests were not uncharacteristic of an innocent man.

George had no photographs of Dando in his possession except those printed in the newspapers after her death. He had no photographs taken from the television. He had taken photographs of other women from the television, including newsreaders, but none were of Dando. This is highly suggestive. Remember that at an early stage of the investigation the police eliminated one man who had tried to develop photographs he had taken of Dando from a television screen, without even questioning him. Yet the fact George had photographs of other celebrities, who were not the victim, was seen to be significant.

George never seemed to develop photographs for some reason, and so all of his camera films (many hundreds of camera films) were found intact indicating that none of the negatives had been removed that could be photographs of Dando. George also had no photographs of Dando's house, yet police found undeveloped photographs of other houses in the area. Also on the theme of pictures, George had no Dando pornography. Some perverted individuals like to take the heads of celebrities and place them on the bodies of models. The pictures are then placed on websites. This form of pornography has caused much embarrassment for many celebrities and many celebrities are unaware they are featured on such sites. Despite having Internet access, George did not visit such sites. The police had made efforts to trace everyone who visited the sites featuring Dando.

George had no video recordings of any of the television programmes Dando had appeared in. There is also no evidence to suggest he had ever made attempts to meet her, or any of her friends. There is also no evidence to suggest he had ever visited her house. This is unusual for an obsessed individual if they know where the person they are obsessed with lives. George had visited Freddie Mercury's house when he became interested in the singer. He also used to talk to one of Freddie Mercury's friends.

As has already been mentioned, the state of George's flat made it incredibly difficult to find anything. It would have therefore been impossible for him to remove any evidence to suggest he had an obsession.

The discussion of George's *'obsessions'* can actually be used in his defence. A common theme with George is his love of discussing what he is interested in. George is unable to hide his interests, and would not want to. He has even approached complete strangers in the street and initiated conversation. Almost immediately on those occasions he began to discuss his interests. George would tell people he was Freddie Mercury's cousin. He had hired a limousine on the first anniversary of Mercury's death so he could go to the former home of the singer posing as Barry Bulsara the 'cousin' of Freddie Mercury and sign autographs. George gave business cards for 'Bulsara Productions Inc.' to people he met, pretending he was a director for the business. He showed people his books about Freddie, and his edited photograph of *'Freddie Mercury and cousin'*. He offered interviews to journalists to discuss the *"family connection"*. Everyone who knew George knew of his 'obsession'.

When George was interested in stunts and was posing as 'Steve Majors' he was interviewed about his abilities as a stuntman. George took great pleasure in discussing his interest in stunts and in September 1981, using the name Steve Majors, he arrived in Long Eaton Stadium in an attempt to persuade the manager to allow him to carry out a daring stunt. The stunt involved roller skating down a seventy foot high ramp, leaping forty feet into the air over four double decker buses, and landing upon a twenty foot high structure.

The event was arranged to be held on 19 September and thousands bought tickets to watch George's *'death-defying leap'*.[23] He successfully completed the jump but injured himself upon landing. He did not mind because he received attention and in doing so he could share his interest with complete strangers. His performance was shown on television and was featured in local newspapers.

On the eve of his attempt he entertained an audience at an ice skating rink in Nottingham. This gave him further opportunity to show people his interests and gain attention.

A few years later George attempted to re-enact his leap over four buses for a children's television programme so he could once again receive attention and show his interest in stunts. This time, however, he failed and injured his thigh. The programme was never broadcast.

On 26 April 1999 George spoke to a complete stranger about the helicopters flying over Fulham searching for the gunman who had shot Dando.

However, George NEVER mentioned the name Jill Dando to anyone before her death, which would be unusual for a man who was incapable of keeping his obsessions and interests to himself, if he was in fact obsessed with Dando. People like George feel a need to talk about their interests because they feature in their minds so frequently; it heightens their experiences to discuss their interests with others. At the time George was being investigated, but before it was possible for the police to determine whether George was obsessed with Dando, DCI Campbell commented on *Crimewatch* that the killer would have *"an unhealthy interest in Jill Dando and more importantly it is unlikely to have been kept a secret"*.

Psychologists believed this was a characteristic the killer would possess, but clearly George did not possess such a characteristic.

As was explained in Chapter 3, it would seem the gunman was an obsessed man. He could have been an obsessed fan who was angered by Dando's betrayal of what he believed to be love, and was possibly also angry because Dando would be appearing on television less frequently. Or he could have been an ex boyfriend

---

[23] *The Derby Evening Telegraph*, 21 September 1981.

who had been jilted yet still harboured feelings for the presenter and became furious when he learned of Dando's impending marriage. George was neither of these.

It was also claimed George had an obsession with women; Campbell of course had claimed the killer would have had an obsession with Dando or with women, his theory possibly based upon George. This was claimed because of the presence in George's flat of undeveloped films containing images of four hundred and nineteen women. However, it must be noted the majority of these photographs had been taken in the early 1990's and so it would appear George's interest in women had at least partially diminished by 1999. The fact none of the photographs were ever developed and no witnesses claiming George had stalked them in 1999 had come forward further suggests George had undergone a transition by which his behaviour greatly improved. Even if George had an obsession or unhealthy interest in women, it is not a sufficient cause to kill one specific woman who would be missed and whose murder would spur a major manhunt.

The discussion of George's 'obsessions' is only relevant in the sense that it shows his character. Much of the information presented against George is completely irrelevant to whether or not he committed a crime. For example, it has been shown George had an 'obsession' with Freddie Mercury but this has no bearing on whether he killed Dando. It was used to insinuate George had an exaggerated interest in famous people and therefore he could wish to shoot a celebrity. It is a rather bizarre logic. Evidence should only be considered to be admissible if it is sufficiently relevant to the case being discussed. If it is not sufficiently relevant to an issue in the case then it should be considered to be inadmissible.[24]

6.2: Loner

The killer was thought to have been a loner. The word 'loner' is defined as being a person *'who prefers not to associate with others'*. This word is a modern term of abuse to add insult to the damaged lives that many people have. A loner is someone who

---

[24] (Smith, J. C. 1995: 12).

spends time on his or her own, and because of this suspicion often immediately falls upon them when certain crimes are committed. Was George a loner? Does he deserve this derogatory label?

In short, the answer is no. George wished to have friends as much as anyone else did. It is for this reason he carried out a stunt in which he leaped over four buses injuring himself in the process, and for this reason he visited the home of Freddie Mercury on the first anniversary of the star's death pretending to be his cousin and signing autographs. It is for this reason that he worked as a volunteer at a centre for Japanese people. For this reason alone he sought relationships and in 1989 got married. It is also for this reason George approached strangers in the street and spoke to people. The staff in shops, advice centres, cyber cafés, the local library, launderette and so on, were accustomed to this man who often came in just for a chat. George sought friends and social interaction.

It seems, sadly, if a person is withdrawn and unfortunate enough to have a poor social life, they will frequently be accused of being a criminal. It must be recognised there is a fundamental difference between being a loner and being lonely. In any case, neither of them is an indicator of a criminal.

6.3: George's interest in firearms

Before I defend George regarding the view of his obsession with firearms, I would like to share an analogy, which is very relevant here.

When I was younger my family and I often went on camping breaks. We were members of a camping club that organised 'rallies'; events at certain locations which large numbers of members would attend. One such annual rally, which still occurs to this day, had a Western theme. Each year many people of all ages, mainly men but women often participated, would dress up in cowboy costumes and, for a weekend, play like children with their blank firing guns or cap guns. It was quite an amusing spectacle to see grown men, who had gone to great lengths to create impressive costumes and had spent small fortunes on firearms, play cowboys and Indians. Many had built their own guns; it had been difficult for them to do this, I was told. I have never seen as many sparks since viewing one man's home-made shotgun. The noise was unbearable and certain events were painful, when all of the guns were being fired simultaneously and as a result large amounts of firearm discharge residue were flying around.

The men were in their element playing like little boys in a school playground. They were often seen sneaking up on their partners, gun in hand, in an attempt to frighten. On several occasions complete strangers tried to frighten my family and me by sneaking up on us from behind. Trying to frighten people was all part of their game. It was a very odd experience but one which enables an understanding of George's childish interest in firearms.

Give a man a toy gun and he will revert to childhood. Give a gun to a man who has the level of maturity of an adolescent and he will almost certainly play with it in the same way as many young boys play. Therefore George, who is immature, can be expected to play soldier. Most boys do and many grown men do. When George dressed in combat gear he did not intend to appear sinister or evil; it was a game. George, like most children, engages in role-play. However, George did mature to the degree that by 1999 he no longer wished to play with guns.

George had used the false name Thomas (or Tom) Palmer at some point during the early to mid 1980s. Many people only knew him by this name. George tended to change his name whenever his mind became interested in something new. When George became interested in stunts he began using the name Steve Powers, when he became interested in Freddie Mercury he became Freddie's 'cousin' Barry Bulsara and when he was interested in firearms he used the name Thomas Palmer. When he no longer called himself Palmer his interests had moved to the world of music and to his admiration of Freddie Mercury. Hence he became the singer's 'cousin'.

For several reasons it is clear that by April 1999 George no longer had the same level of interest in firearms he had displayed in the mid 1980s. He still had what he termed a healthy interest in guns and I am inclined to believe him. The police found magazines relating to firearms at 2b Crookham Road. However, these were many years old, dating from the 1980s, and as George was a hoarder he kept hold of these even when he no longer read them. A man with a current 'obsession' with firearms would have magazines and specialist material that was produced recently rather than many years ago. If he were obsessed then he would want to keep up to date in the world of firearms. George did not do this.

During the mid 1980s George had been very open about his interest in guns. He had shown his replica firearms to people and had once fired a blank round at a family he had befriended. The prosecution produced two witnesses who showed George had what could be described as an obsession with firearms. However, both of the events described by these witnesses had occurred during the 1980s. The prosecution could not produce a single witness who could substantiate their claim that George had an obsession with guns in 1999. The residents of Crookham Road were not subjected to the antics George was once renowned for during the 1980s.

In 1981 George joined the Territorial Army. The appeal judges mentioned he joined the Territorial Army in 1981 and left in 1983, which is incorrect. Anyone reading these dates could be forgiven for thinking George would have had a large amount of military training. However, as you will later learn, you should treat with caution anything the appeal judges said. George joined the Territorial Army at the very end of 1981 and had left less than one year later after failing to complete his basic training; George only attended twenty-nine training sessions. The TA is an organisation whose members attend relatively short meetings once a week which are not compulsory, and whose members occasionally participate in weekend trips away. Much of the time is spent in exercising and in practicing drills and other such activities. George did fire weapons on a few occasions, while under supervision at the training sessions. These weapons were self-loading rifles and machine guns, not handguns.

There is an incorrect notion, created by Orlando Pownall, that George fired pistols while he was a probationary member at the gun club. The club's rules prevented him from firing weapons. The club's rules required applicants to gain a reference from an employer or other such person. However, as George was unemployed he knew of no one who could be a referee and assist him in the application process. George's application was promptly rejected and he soon ceased to visit the club. Haddon Pearce, the club's pistol captain at the time, has told that to his knowledge George never fired a gun while on the premises. Instead, he simply stood watching others shooting. The jury, however, were told the exact opposite. The discussion of George's involvement with these organisations by the prosecution led the jury to believe George was a man who had used firearms on many occasions when this is far from the truth.

There is no evidence at all to suggest George had any degree of competence with weapons. There is also no evidence to suggest he had fired any type of gun since 1982.

Also during the early 1980s George had made an attempt to join the regular army. Again his application was turned down. During a search of his flat police found an application form for the army. It was a fairly recent form, although it dated from before 1999. It was never sent. Why? His interests had moved on, that's why.

During the period of intense interest in firearms in the 1980s, George had bought some replica blank firing guns. The police found undeveloped photographs of him holding the guns. However, police found no guns (fake or real) in his possession. No one who knew George knew he had any guns, which would be odd if he was in possession of such firearms, as he had frequently shown them before when he did own such items.

As has been stated earlier, the police believed George had lied when he claimed the man holding replica firearms in the photographs shown to him during police interviews was not him. The police believed George was lying in order to conceal the extent of his interests with guns. Both of these photographs were taken during the 1980s and George had never seen it due to the fact he did not develop the photographic film. Seeing it for the first time, whilst at Hammersmith Police Station, he probably did not realise it was indeed him; he probably forgot the picture had been taken. He probably did not recognise himself; he was wearing a mask in the photograph taken from short range, and the other photograph is taken from a distance.

There was a definite transition in George's interests. His enthusiasm with firearms had diminished by the 1990s although it had never disappeared. It was replaced with an interest in music. George stopped calling himself Thomas Palmer, which in itself is an indicator that he no longer had such an interest in guns, and he began to call himself Barry Bulsara. He not only began to use the name Bulsara, he took on the role of Barry Bulsara, the 'cousin' of Freddie Mercury. He created business cards of his business, 'Bulsara Productions Inc.', which stated he, along with the surviving members of Queen, were directors of the company. He also claimed he was a director of the Freddie Mercury Fan Club. With thoughts of Freddie Mercury occupying his mind beyond 1999 there was no room for such an interest in firearms. George's favourite programme at present is a music show, and not any military or firearms orientated programme.

In 1999 George did still have an interest in guns and the military although this was significantly different to his earlier interest. It is inaccurate to suggest that George had, as the prosecution alleged, an obsession with such items. Even accepting George's limited interest in guns, the next point to consider is, did he have the knowledge to obtain the illegal and relatively specialist adapted weapon which was used to kill Dando?

In 5.3 Orlando Pownall was quoted as having said, *"The gunman would have had an interest in altering or reactivating blank-firing guns - so did the defendant."* The police and the prosecution believed George had such an interest in altering weapons, but it is immensely difficult to see how there is sufficient reason to accept such a hypothesis. The murder weapon was a 9 mm semi-automatic handgun which had either had its barrel shortened, had been a blank firing gun that had been adapted so it could fire live rounds, or it had been deactivated and later reactivated. Any one who watched the *Cutting Edge* documentary will know George is incapable of even the simplest tasks which require technical ability, such as repairing a puncture on his bike. Therefore, it is safe to assume George could not himself have succeeded in altering a gun in such a way. And so if George was the killer he must have bought the weapon already altered.

In addition to the adapted gun, the killer used an adapted cartridge. The bullet and cartridge used by the gunman were found outside 29 Gowan Avenue. The cartridge exhibited crimping marks described in Chapter 3. These are incredibly rare and no experts from Britain, the USA or Russia who were consulted by Oxborough detectives had ever seen such marks. They had a practical application; it is believed they may have been created in order to tighten the bullet in the cartridge in order to reduce the noise created when a shot was discharged. This seems to be the most reasonable explanation. The person who made the marks must have had highly specialist knowledge in firearms and firearm manipulation. Even if the killer did not make the crimping marks he must have been aware of them. A person does not obtain a highly specialised firearm and unusual ammunition, unless they had specifically asked for them. Therefore, the killer must have understood the alterations to the gun and bullets would have made his task more effective. George would not have had this knowledge; he had a fairly rudimentary knowledge of firearms acquired from books and magazines available to the public. The killer must have had knowledge that superseded this.

How easy would it have been to obtain such a gun? The murder weapon was a highly illegal gun, rarely seen and therefore one of only a small number. It had been altered in a manner enabling its owner to carry out a kill without causing a great deal of noise and the bullets had been altered for the same purpose. Therefore it would be an incredibly difficult task for anyone to obtain such a weapon. The person would have to have contacts in the underworld or the black market. George did not have good social skills and he did not have contacts. How then could he possibly obtain such a weapon? It is not the sort of item you can buy from a shop or that you can acquire through mail order.

George would have had no need to buy such a gun if he wished to kill. He would have bought a simple gun, which had not been altered. After all, such a basic weapon would have been sufficient for a one-off murder. Does George have the intelligence to realise an adapted gun would significantly increase the chance of successfully evading justice? All those who know him, or have met him, do not believe so. Why would he buy a specialist gun, which would presumably cost a small fortune, and then throw it away after killing Dando, when a much simpler and cheaper weapon would have been sufficient? There is no evidence to suggest George was intending to commit more than one murder and the weapon has never been found in his possession.

It has been suggested George had an interest in reactivated-deactivated firearms. The prosecution base this claim upon an advertisement present in one of the magazines found at 2b Crookham Road which offered reactivated-deactivated firearms (it did not offer altered ammunition). It must be remembered there is no proof at all that the murder weapon was a reactivated gun. It must also be remembered, George had over eight hundred newspapers and many magazines in addition to these. In these there must have been many thousands of advertisements. An advertisement of an item is not evidence of the person buying the item. Magazines and newspapers will have many articles, and typically also contain many pages of advertisements. Most people do not even bother reading these, let alone buy the product or service offered. Just because George had an advertisement for such a gun, does not mean he possessed any guns. He also had articles for private investigators but he never hired one to follow Dando, or acquire information about her or Alan Farthing. Also, the advertisement was featured in a magazine dating from 1987; twelve years before Dando was shot.

6.4: Witnesses and identification

The issue of 'witness' statements and identification is one which requires lengthy discussion. The questionable nature of this evidence was sufficient to be a ground for appeal. As you have read in a previous chapter, several people saw suspicious men in Gowan Avenue and the vicinity of Gowan Avenue from the evening before the murder up until shortly before the murder, and also they saw suspicious characters shortly after the murder up until around twenty minutes later. It must at this point be stressed, no one saw anything suspicious at the time of the murder, and no one saw the murder. Also, none of the witnesses who reported sightings to the police following the murder saw anything which seemed to them to be sufficient cause to contact the police until they heard of the incident which had resulted in Dando's death.

As has already been stated, most of these descriptions were attributed to the same man. In an earlier chapter it was shown these could not have all been the same man, and it was suggested the different people present could not have all been involved in a plot to murder the celebrity. Indeed, as you are aware, one of the men seen on the day of the murder was later discovered to be a gas man who was completely uninvolved with the shooting and therefore was eliminated, with the sighting not being discussed in court. Just because a witness saw something they thought was suspicious, it does not mean the man they saw was a criminal.

Before discussing the evidence of 'eye-witnesses' of the 'killer' who gave evidence during the trial, some general information regarding witness testimony is required.

It is well known a witness's memory becomes less reliable as time goes by; memories fade and alter over time. In the case of the witnesses who reported sightings from the day of Dando's murder none had a good reason to memorise the man's appearance in anticipation of attending an identity parade a year or more later.

Many had only seen the man for a matter of a few seconds. Therefore when it came to the identity parades it is likely the image of the man they had seen, which had been stored in their minds, will have altered in some way however slight the alteration happened to be.

Richard Hughes and Geoffrey Upfill-Brown attended a live, conventional identity parade on 26 May 2000. Terry Normanton and Terry Griffin attended video parades on 14 August 2000, sixteen months after the murder. Susan Mayes, Stella de Rosnay and Charlotte de Rosnay attended video parades on 5 October 2000, eighteen months after the shooting. Helen Scott attended a video parade on 23 January 2001, twenty one months after Dando was killed.

The delay between the first, live, identity parade and the first video parade, has been explained by the fact that it took time to compile the images. However, this is not an excuse for the length of time between the different groups of people attending parades. The video was ready in August yet four witnesses saw it at a significantly later stage. One has to wonder what effect the time lapse had upon their ability to recall a face and make a correct identification.

Witnesses can also make mistaken identifications because they can recognise a face but incorrectly recall where they had seen the face.[25] Eyewitnesses can therefore observe a crime or suspicious activity, then later see the face of an innocent person which they come to believe is the face of the perpetrator of the crime or suspicious activity they had earlier observed.

When more than a year has elapsed, it is increasingly likely a witness could incorrectly believe an innocent person they had once seen could be a criminal. George spent most of his time, during the day, walking around the streets of Fulham. Therefore it is possible that at least some of the witnesses, all of whom (with the exception of Stella de Rosnay) lived in Fulham, may have seen George at some point prior to the identification parades, but not necessarily on the day of the murder itself.

Research of identity parades where the true criminal is not present has suggested witnesses will often pick out someone rather

---

[25] (Ainsworth. 2001: 72).

than admit they cannot make a positive identification.[26] Often the suspect is picked to spare the embarrassment of a witness, even when the witness was not sure the person they had seen was on the parade.

A case which is relevant here is the Adolf Beck case. In 1895 Beck was accused of swindling women out of articles of jewellery. Twelve women made positive identifications, indicating Beck was responsible for the crimes committed. However, it was later proven that without a doubt Beck was not responsible for the crimes he had been accused and imprisoned for.[27]

As a result of mistaken identifications, which have been made on numerous occasions resulting in miscarriages of justice, the judge at a trial is now obliged to use Turnbull guidelines so jurors are warned that mistaken identifications can occur. The members of the jury should be told to examine the duration of the sighting, how close the witness was to the suspect, in what lighting conditions the sighting was made, what, if any, previous acquaintance the witness had with the person seen, what interval there was between the observation and the identification and whether or not there are discrepancies between the description provided by a witness and the actual appearance of the accused.

Mr Justice Gage correctly warned the members of the jury of the dangers of mistaken identification. They were able to decide whether or not an incorrect identification had occurred. However, the decisions made by the jurors are not necessarily correct.

One final point to make here is, a common theme in the testimonies of eyewitnesses is the overestimation of time. A study by Loftus *et al* tested the ability of witnesses to correctly estimate the length of time of an event.[28] A robbery was staged and shown to volunteers participating in the test. The duration of the robbery was thirty seconds. The witnesses were asked how long they believed it lasted. The average response was two and a half minutes. Bear this in mind when reading any statements. Unless a witness looked at their watch and timed an event, then it is unlikely the witness would be able to provide an accurate duration time of the event. Their timing can be nothing more than an estimate.

---

[26] (Cutler *et al.* 1994: 93).
[27] (Smith, J. C. 1995: 202).
[28] (Ainsworth. 2001: 36).

The evidence of the eye-witnesses who testified at George's trial will now be assessed. Although it is not in keeping with the order of witness evidence discussed in the last chapter, Susan Mayes' evidence will be examined first, as she was the key prosecution witness.

As you have read in the last chapter, Susan Mayes claimed she saw George between 06:57 and 07:00, opposite 29 Gowan Avenue. The first point to note is, even if she did see George at this time, her sighting took place four and a half hours before the crime. If George was present at that time it does not mean he had any involvement in the crime; there is no evidence to prove the man seen at this time was the gunman. The police believed the killer may have stayed around waiting for Dando but this is not known for sure. Also, George states he was never there at that time. Mayes testified she was *"very sure"* she had seen George. The question is, can we be very sure Mayes is correct? There are far too many questionable points to her testimony that raise serious doubts as to the reliability of this witness. To quote the appeal hearing judgment, *"it is probable that if there had been no positive identification of the appellant, there would never have been a prosecution"*. Therefore, if Mayes' evidence can be shown to be unreliable, then the prosecution's case is destroyed.

It should be remembered the sighting occurred on an April morning when, even later in the day, the weather was drizzly and the sky was grey and dull. Therefore lighting conditions were not at all ideal.

Originally Susan Mayes stated she saw the man she reported to the police for around one minute. As shown earlier, the ability of a witness to determine the duration of an event is inappreciably difficult. When being questioned by Michael Mansfield during the cross examination for the defence, Mayes conceded she had looked at the man three or four times for a total of five to six seconds. Let me reiterate; the key prosecution witness, the witness upon whom the case against George relied, saw the man who *could* have been the killer for only *five to six seconds*.

Mayes commented on how the man she saw looked away and wiped the windscreen of a car he was standing beside, in an attempt to conceal his face. Presumably this accounts for at least two seconds of this period of time. When the witness had drawn level with the man, he looked to the ground and so again the witness was briefly unable to see the man's face. Presumably this would account for another second at least. At the one location where Mayes could have had a good look at the man's face, she was unable to see the face properly. Every time she saw the face from a good angle, she was further away. We can assume from her *own* evidence, *not* the defence's interpretation of the evidence, that Mayes had an unobstructed and direct view of the face of the man she saw four and a half hours before the crime, for around two seconds. This would mean she had little more than a glimpse of the man who eighteen months later she could apparently recognise. Of course, it is possible the estimate of five to six seconds was an underestimate. However if, as Mayes herself claimed under oath, this was the amount of time the man was in her view then we can assume that five to six seconds is not far from the truth.

Another point which we can use to show Mayes' evidence is insufficient proof of George's involvement in the crime, is the inconsistency in her statements regarding the man she saw on the morning of the shooting. During an early stage in the police investigation Mayes reported seeing a man who, amongst other characteristics, had a *"short and smart haircut"*. However, during the trial she would claim the man she saw had long and untidy hair, which bears no resemblance to her earlier statement. During the trial she was asked about this inconsistency and in response she stated the police could have misinterpreted what she said, or she may have used those words herself. Although some police officers' statements can be unintelligible it is difficult to believe someone could be foolish enough to take down a statement completely incorrectly. How can an officer hear words to the effect of *'black hair in quite long layers with the longest bits over the collar; a heavy style'* and yet write down the words *'with a short and smart haircut'*?

A further point that should be considered when looking at the evidence presented by Mayes is the fact that the car which was unnecessarily double-parked on Gowan Avenue (the car at which the man Mayes saw stood wiping the windscreen) was never traced. Mayes believed the vehicle was a taxi and she must have had some reason to believe this was the case, suggesting that the sighting might not have been in any way related to the murder. The man seen by Mayes was almost certainly responsible for the car, and its presence should be considered suspicious; why would it be double-parked when the street had plenty of parking spaces? The car was illegally parked and a man beside it was acting suspiciously, so it is reasonable to suppose the man seen by Mayes was indeed responsible for the car. The car was certainly not at the location at 07:15, and so soon after the sighting both the man and the car had disappeared. If the man seen was responsible for the car, as it would seem, then it could not have been George, for he does not own a car and due to his epilepsy he does not drive. There is no evidence to suggest George has ever driven a car.

The final point, for the time being, which will hopefully further show that Mayes' identification evidence was incorrect, or at the very least insufficient to prove George's presence on Gowan Avenue, is the fact she was given immediate post-identification feedback. Mayes was told she was correct in her identification. She was told she had picked out the right man when of course she had only picked out the suspect and not necessarily the killer. This will have inevitably increased her confidence of being correct in identifying the man she had seen on the day of the murder. Never should anyone be informed they were correct when they may not have even identified the criminal and when it is known the witness may have to testify in court. In court a witness should not be influenced by what they have heard at an earlier stage. The jury are influenced by how confident a witness is and so as Mayes appeared more confident than she should have been on the basis of her sighting, this would have meant the jury believed she was correct when in reality she was quite possibly wrong.

Luus and Wells wrote:

'...because people intuitively use confidence to judge the likelihood of identification accuracy, we argue that there is an incentive for police and attorneys to manipulate their witness's confidence'.[29]

Did the police realise they did not have sufficient evidence without a positive identification? The appeal judges believe they would not have done. Did they therefore influence a witness who could provide the impression that George had been on Gowan Avenue on the morning of the murder? It is not suggested that the

---

[29] (Cutler and Penrod. 1995: 190).

police acted illegally, for there is no evidence to prove they did so, but they may have unintentionally influenced Susan Mayes. It was certainly a foolish and unorthodox action to inform Mayes she was correct in her identification and thereby influence her opinion regarding who she saw on the day of Dando's death. In April 2003 a trial collapsed in Sheffield when it was claimed that officers from South Yorkshire Police had persuaded the key witness in a murder investigation to pick out their suspect at a video identity parade.[30] South Yorkshire Police continue to maintain they did not influence the witness in any way, however. It is interesting that Mayes' identification was made in October 2000, shortly before Barry George was committed for trial. Committal proceedings occur to assess the evidence and decide whether a trial should commence. Without Mayes' identification at this crucial time, a time at which experts were beginning to realise the particle of alleged firearms discharge residue was not strong evidence, it is likely the case would never have gone to trial.

Unless Mayes possesses a magnificent mind, with exceptional memory, it is difficult to imagine how she could see a man's face for perhaps two seconds and yet be able to identify him eighteen months later in a video identification parade where only his face could be seen. In addition to this difficulty, all of the faces shown in the video identity parade had facial hair when the man she had seen on the day of the murder was clean-shaven. The information provided here surely raises doubts as to the integrity of the evidence provided by this witness.

The next witness to discuss is Helen Scott; did she see George? Scott saw a man *the day before* the murder, who was looking up Gowan Avenue from the bottom of the road. Number 29 (Dando's house) was therefore not in his view. The fact that the sighting occurred on the day before the murder suggests it could have no relevance to the shooting of Dando. She was unable to make a positive identification and she picked out a man who was not George during the parade. It must not, therefore, be said George was on Gowan Avenue on the evening before the murder. Despite the fact it could be completely irrelevant, her evidence was considered to be admissible despite Mansfield's legal argument that partial identification is not proof of presence. Scott specifically

---

[30] *The Star* (Sheffield), 3 April 2003.

stated in her statement that the man she saw had very thick eyebrows and so it must be assumed the man did have very thick eyebrows for she was certain about this. However, George does not have eyebrows that can be described in this way; his eyebrows are in fact very narrow. Scott's evidence falls far short of the quality of evidence the prosecution needed in order to prove George was fairly close to the crime scene on the evening before the murder.

The judge at the trial, Mr Justice Gage, when referring to Scott's evidence, told the jury she did not identify George:

"in fact she identified another person. For this reason, I direct you that it would be extremely dangerous for you to rely on the evidence of what happened at the video parade in relation to this witness. The fact is she did not identify the defendant."

One has to ask why the prosecution called her as a witness to testify against George, a man she did not identify and, in all probability, a man she did not see.

Stella de Rosnay saw a man for ten to twelve seconds through a window. At the video identity parade she could not identify George as the man she saw. She later commented she believed George was the man she saw but there is a reason for this, which will be discussed later. In her first statement she commented on how the man she saw had a pale complexion with hair of a normal length, neither long nor short. This is a very different description to that provided by Mayes who saw a man of Mediterranean appearance with either long or short hair depending upon which statement you read. It is also very different to the description of the olive skinned man with long hair many other witnesses described. Therefore, how could Stella de Rosnay have seen the same man other witnesses described? It is shown in the appendix these could not all have been the same man. If Susan Mayes did see George, then Stella de Rosnay did not.

Charlotte de Rosnay is a valuable witness in George's defence. Charlotte saw the same man at the same time as her mother-in-law Stella. Charlotte would at the trial concede she had only a glimpse of the man seen out of a window from her house. Again an important point to note is that both Charlotte and Stella de Rosnay saw a man approximately two hours before the murder.

During the identity parade this witness commented she did not believe the man she saw on the day of the murder was present, but of course something (or someone) had made her change her mind by the time of the trial. Considering Charlotte had only a glimpse of the man, she certainly provided a detailed description, even commenting he had a *"five o'clock shadow"*. This is understandable because she had been exposed to many descriptions at a very early stage, which inevitably influenced her own description which she would provide to the police. Her description was influenced by discussions with her mother-in-law, and perhaps other witnesses who all lived on the same street. It is known that Richard Hughes told Helen Doble and Saunders about the man he had seen leaving the scene of the crime. After the police had questioned Doble and Saunders, these two women went to Charlotte de Rosnay's house, where inevitably they would have discussed the sighting of which they had heard. Charlotte was therefore not an independent witness and her description was influenced by external factors. Her evidence is even more questionable when it is considered she had an affair with a detective working on the Oxborough investigation, DC Peter Bartlett, something the jury was never informed of. The affair had begun four days after Dando's murder, after Bartlett took a statement from her. News of this relationship only emerged the day after the verdict had been announced. This could explain the change which occurred in her confidence.

Although Charlotte claimed she had ended her contact with the officer by the time of George's arrest, this cannot be guaranteed. Through reading an account of Mansfield's cross examination of this witness during the trial itself, regarding whether she ever received any information about George from the police, her body language suggests she may have been still in contact with the officer when George was in custody. She was certainly being defensive but Mansfield could not ask her directly about this, because the jury was not allowed to be told about the affair.

If the two were in contact, it would explain why Charlotte became more confident by the time of the trial that it was George she had seen on Gowan Avenue on 26 April 1999. Prior to this, she had expressed her belief she had not seen the suspect.

At one point Charlotte had pressed charges against Bartlett for harassment. Bartlett was charged with this offence. This is suggestive. It was not until 18 February that she dropped the allegations. Whether or not she maintained contact with Bartlett after George's arrest, the liaison could very well have had an effect upon the trial.

In court, in the absence of a jury, Michael Mansfield commented upon the effect that this affair could have had upon Charlotte's testimony:

> "They continued a relationship when he [Bartlett] had been warned not to. It is most unfortunate that a witness of this kind, given her testimony, should have any liaison."

Charlotte described the man she had seen as having been a pale man, with pink skin, which does not bear any resemblance to the olive skinned man seen by many. One major flaw in her evidence is that in her statement made on 30 April 1999 she said that she did not see any man at 09:40 on the day of the murder yet later, whilst having an affair with Bartlett, she stated that she saw the man at 09:40. I do not suggest her change of story came about as a consequence of the affair, but a change of story certainly took place. Charlotte's evidence certainly does not prove that George was on Gowan Avenue. After all, she did not think that the man she saw was on the identity parade. Her evidence does not come even close to showing that George could have been the man that she saw, and the prosecution were wrong to state that the man could have been George because there is no evidence to substantiate such a theory.

Terry Normanton's evidence is very interesting. Normanton was included as a witness in the trial despite the fact that she was unable to make a positive identification, yet her evidence was used as further *'proof'* that George was waiting on Gowan Avenue on the morning of the murder. Anyone reading her testimony would believe that her evidence was impressive and that she had a good opportunity to view the man she saw. She testified that as she was walking he was looking in her direction and she could see him in front of her for two minutes and she had a clear view of him for one minute. At one point she was within six to eight feet of the man she later described. The first obvious point to make here is that if Normanton had a clear view of him for one minute, and she was walking in the direction that he was looking, then at some point the two must have been very far apart. As mentioned earlier in this section, people naturally overestimate time. If her information is correct then she would have had an excellent opportunity to view the man and provide a useful description to the police soon after the crime.

It is therefore unfortunate that Normanton has an autistic condition that makes her mind unable to connect events until a period of time has elapsed. It took her a *year* to realise that she had seen a man on that particular day who could have some relevance to the inquiry. Even when on two separate occasions she was asked if she saw anything relevant to the murder investigation she responded negatively. Despite this, in court under oath, Normanton stated that she had made a statement at an early stage in the investigation. One has to ask: if she could state so incorrectly or be mistaken about such a matter when she had sworn an oath, then what else could she have been mistaken about? Bear this in mind when reading Normanton's evidence.

On the 14 August 2000 Normanton attended a video identity parade. When staring at the face of George she was not sure if he was the man she had seen on the day of the murder. When asked if the man she had seen was present she responded, *"I am sure, I am not quite sure. I cannot remember a moustache."* However, she stated that number 2 (George) *might* have been the man.

Despite the fact that she could not make any identification during the parade, in court Orlando Pownall stated that she had identified George. By the time of the trial yet another transformation in the confidence of a witness had occurred. When being cross-examined by Mansfield, Normanton told how she was sure that George was the man she had seen on Gowan Avenue at 09:50 on 26 April 1999. This witness had not made a positive identification and she had only decided that George was the man when time had elapsed and when she was not looking at his face.

As further proof that Normanton had seen George, Pownall stated that the witness saw a man who did not have a goatee beard and therefore she could have seen George, *"She did not merely identify the defendant, but claimed that the man did not have a goatee beard on April 26. She was right."*[31] This does not at all prove that Normanton saw George; it simply means that she saw one of the many males who do not have a goatee.

Although she had told the police, a year after the crime, that she

---

[31] Orlando Pownall speaking on 4 May 2001.

had George in her view for around two minutes, Normanton conceded that in reality she had only seen the man for a *"shortish space of time"*. These are her words, not the defence's interpretation of her testimony.

Her autistic condition may well have made her recall characteristics of a man she had seen at any point in time, or a man she had just heard about. During the course of a year a number of comments overheard, pieces of information read in the newspaper or watched on the television and the frequent display of an E-fit of a man believed to be involved in the crime, can influence a person by making them believe that they may have seen something which in reality they did not. Normanton lived on the same street as Dando had lived and therefore she took an interest in the case. Every day, for the first few weeks following the shooting and on many occasions thereafter, Normanton received information of a man who was taller than 5'7, had long dark hair and who was clean-shaven. The media frequently referred to a man with a mobile telephone. On the day of the murder, if she had seen anyone, she may have seen a man who was completely unrelated to the crime and whose characteristics she may never be able to truly recall. As a result of external influences, in the course of the year she may have heard of a man frequently discussed in the media and by other witnesses she lived near, and so as a result she too began to believe she had seen the killer.

There are two sources of information that affect a witness' statement to the police. These are the original sighting, and any external influences which affect the memory of the sighting. Over time these two sources can come into conflict with one another, with the external influence affecting the memory. Peter B. Ainsworth from the University of Manchester believes this can dramatically affect the evidence provided by an eyewitness in their testimony:

"Over time the information from these two sources may be integrated in such a way that we are unable to tell from which source some specific detail is recalled. All we have is one 'memory'."[32]

---

[32] (Ainsworth. 2001: 56).

Indeed, Terry Normanton commented that if the man depicted in the E-fit had been on the parade she would have identified him, when there was no disputing the fact the man Sappleton described bore little resemblance to the killer, but importantly the man in the E-fit looked nothing like George. Therefore clearly Normanton's evidence has been influenced by outside factors. The above quotation applies to other witnesses too. Earlier in this section it was told that Charlotte de Rosnay had received external influences which probably affected her description by the time she came to provide information to the police. Unfortunately the jury do not appear to have considered such factors sufficiently.

Terry Griffin was one of the witnesses who provided a description of a man of Mediterranean appearance on Gowan Avenue prior to the murder. On being asked during the video identity parade if the man he saw on the day of the murder was present, Griffin said *"No"*. He did not say, *"I'm not sure,"* or *"He could be."* He positively stated the man he saw after 10:00 on the day of the murder was not on the parade and was therefore not George. This is interesting because multiple witnesses described a Mediterranean man on Gowan Avenue on the day of the murder, yet Griffin saw a Mediterranean man who was certainly not George. The prosecution themselves stated it was inconceivable for two men of similar appearance to be acting in a strange manner on that day in that area. And so if this was true and Griffin saw a Mediterranean man who was not George on the day of the murder, then it would not be possible for a second suspicious man of Mediterranean appearance to have been present. Further proof George was not the man seen by Griffin, is a few weeks after the murder a man who most certainly was George approached him. Griffin was unable to recognise him as the man he had seen on the day of the murder despite speaking to George for some time. Why the prosecution called him as a witness is difficult to comprehend.

As is demonstrated in the appendix both Richard Hughes and Geoffrey Upfill-Brown saw the man who attacked Dando leave the crime scene. Therefore these two men must be considered to be key witnesses in the investigation.

Richard Hughes reported a man described in the appendix (sighting J). The man was seen closing the gate at the front of Dando's house. Hughes originally stated that he only saw the side of the gunman's face even though, as has been stated, he later admitted that he saw three-quarters of the killer's face and that he would be able to recognise the man.

Hughes attended a conventional identity parade and was therefore able to see the height and build of the men in the line-up from both the front view and the profile view. Despite these views he could not make a positive identification, which is suggestive as Hughes is a witness whose identification would be valuable. He saw the killer whereas Mayes may not have seen the killer. A sighting of a man four and a half hours before a shooting is insignificant compared to an identification of a man seen immediately following a shooting. Nevertheless at the parade Hughes could not pick out the man he had seen on the day of the shooting. Instead he believed one of the foils was, to use Charlotte de Rosnay's phraseology, the *"predominant contender"* although no identification was made. This shows there is no evidence to suggest the man seen by Hughes was George.

Geoffrey Upfill-Brown, who reported sighting K, is another witness whose identification evidence could be considered to be extremely valuable. It is even more valuable when it is considered he *"was expecting to have to remember it [the man's description] because of the way the man was behaving. I watched him very carefully and made every mental note I could."* As the appeal judges themselves noted, Upfill-Brown could be expected to appreciate the importance of remembering what he had observed. It is therefore important to note he did not recognise George at the identity parade, which again highlights the point there is absolutely no evidence to suggest it was George who fled the murder scene immediately following the murder of Dando.

Janet Bolton did not attend an identity parade (the reason for this is unclear and contradicted in the appeal judgment) and so it really was improper she should have been called to provide evidence against George when she did not even identify him as the man she saw. Her evidence was very poor, with her description being vague (see sighting L recorded in the appendix). Her statement was made on the day of the E-fit being released (30 April 1999) and so it could be the case that the E-fit influenced her description. She stated the man she had seen looked very much like the man shown in the E-fit. Bolton described a white male with dark hair who was wearing a suit, which is severely lacking in detail. She could give no estimation at all of the age of the man, which makes one wonder why she was called to be a witness. Bolton was one hundred yards away from the man and she was anxious that a traffic warden might catch her on a yellow line, so she was not in the correct frame of mind to remember a man's appearance. Indeed she believed the man could be a traffic warden, causing her to hurriedly leave the area barely looking at the man.

On 28 May 1999 she made a further statement in which she commented the man she saw shortly after the murder might have been wearing a red tie although she could never be certain of this. None of the other witnesses remembered such a tie, including Richard Hughes and Geoffrey Upfill-Brown. It must also be considered, Bolton saw the man running on the opposite side of the road to which the other sightings on Gowan Avenue had taken place.

As she did not attend a parade, there is no evidence to suggest she saw George. Her evidence was insufficient to warrant her attending a parade, and so it is insufficient to warrant consideration.

As was explained in the last chapter, the prosecution alleged the witnesses provided evidence that had continuity in the characteristics described. As George matched these characteristics, in the view of the prosecution this was seen to be proof that George was spotted on several occasions on Gowan Avenue prior to the murder and following the murder, and therefore this was considered proof George was the murderer. Is it true there was continuity in the descriptions of witnesses? This is a point already touched upon in this section. The answer, simply, is no. Although most witnesses provided estimates of height and age that were similar, there are many aspects of appearance which do not correspond with one another. At some point between 09:30 and 09:40 a man wearing a navy blue or grey suit, a blue shirt and a tie, was seen running down Gowan Avenue. However, at 09:50 Terry Normanton apparently saw a man walking down Gowan Avenue who was wearing a black suit, white shirt and no tie. Realistically these were two different men. And even if they were not, they could not be George, for ten to twenty minutes is insufficient time for him to travel to his flat and get changed before returning to Gowan Avenue, particularly when the de Rosnays saw the man running in the opposite direction to George's flat.

None of Hughes, Upfill-Brown, Charlotte de Rosnay nor Stella de Rosnay described a man of Mediterranean appearance. However,

Susan Mayes, Terry Griffin and others described a man who appeared to be of Mediterranean origin, with some describing the man as having olive skin. The difference between olive skin and white, pale skin is clear to anyone. The de Rosnays described a man with hair which was neither short nor long, whereas other witnesses described a man with long hair. Therefore it is clear there was no continuity in the descriptions provided by witnesses.

The jury was overwhelmed by the prosecution's claims that the men seen by witnesses had common features and therefore must be the same man, despite the fact only one person could make a positive identification. The prosecution alleged George had the appearance of the man described by witnesses and they stated (erroneously) that people who knew George would describe him in the same way as witnesses had described the man they saw. The jury was not informed that family and friends of George did not believe he had such an appearance. It is said he has a Mediterranean appearance and Susan Mayes saw a man who could be described as Mediterranean, and she allegedly saw George. Can George be described as a man of Mediterranean appearance? It would seem not and Robert Henderson does not believe so.[33] However, the opinion of two people is only favourable to the opinion of a single individual. For this reason a survey was conducted in order to seek the views of others.

The survey was conducted via the Internet to allow a large number of people over a large area to participate. A website was built on which three photographs of George were uploaded; two of a bearded George and one of him clean-shaven. There were no indications of who was shown in the photographs and it was asked that if anyone should happen to recognise George then they should not participate in the survey.

A simple message was written on the site, which asked for participants to e-mail me with a description of the man they could see in the pictures. No description was offered, and no leading questions were asked, so it could be determined if anyone would look at the photographs and state that he appeared to be of Mediterranean origin.

When the initial responses were received each of the participants were e-mailed with one simple question; does the

---

[33] (Henderson. 2001: 4).

person shown in the photographs appear to be of Mediterranean origin?

The number of responses was disappointing; only thirty-five people provided me with descriptions, and of these only thirty provided me with an answer to the second part of the survey. However, thirty-five is higher than nine and therefore the survey results are of value when determining how closely George matches the descriptions provided by the nine eye-witnesses who gave evidence at the trial.

In addition to the thirty-five, several contacted me to say they knew that George was the man in the pictures. Others did not understand the question and provided me with such information as *'one looks like a passport photograph'*.

The responses were generally very good. Here is an example of the quality of the responses:

'A rather square face dark brown hair, brown eyes. Low flat ears, slightly round nose. Thick neck. Thin top lip. Prominent, but slightly thin eyebrows. It is hard to tell from the colour pictures.'

Note that numerous witnesses described the man seen in the Gowan Avenue area as having had a round shaped face.

With regards to the preliminary descriptions, no one described George as Mediterranean in appearance despite the fact the participants had been asked to describe George in a way in which anyone who had not seen the pictures would be able to produce a visual image of him in their minds. One person commented he could have originated from the Mediterranean, but this participant offered alternate locations such as the Middle East. He was not at all sure. It did not help that in the photographs showing a frontal view of George's face, George had a goatee beard and moustache, giving him more of a foreign appearance. Once the survey had been completed, consultations with some of the participants indicated it was George's facial hair which made him look less English. However, on 26 April 1999, George was clean-shaven.

Multiple participants commented that George looked white and pale. Some had commented on how he appeared to be English. This was before they had been asked if George appeared to have originated from the Mediterranean.

On the whole the respondents did not believe that race is an important factor when describing the appearance of George. Of the thirty-five only one had suggested a possible Mediterranean origin. This is suggestive when compared to the four of the nine who had believed the man they saw on the day of the murder was of Mediterranean appearance.

When asked if George looked Mediterranean, of the thirty who responded seventeen maintained he definitely does not look like he is from that region of the world. The following two responses are worthy of inclusion:

'My first reaction is that he doesn't seem like he is from Italy or Spain or Mediterranean descent. I am a Flight Attendant in the U.S. And have received training for almost 24 years on observing people for example - Hi-Jackers, to be able to describe for Law Enforcement officials. I don't know if this will be of use to you - I am by the way 1/2 Italian and 1/2 Irish.'

And,

'No, I would not think or say he was Mediterranean. It would never even enter my head to think so.'

Of the rest, eleven believed it was possible George appeared to be from the Mediterranean, although many told me they would not have considered this had they not been asked directly. A typical response is shown here:

'It's possible, but it wouldn't jump to the front of my mind. Actually, I would think Eastern European.'

One person did not know what a person originating from the Mediterranean looks like.

Only one person believed the suspect looked as though he was of Mediterranean appearance. To reiterate, only one out of the thirty who had completed the survey believed this. As this person had not suggested it in their initial description it would appear the participant did not think George looked strikingly Mediterranean. It would seem, through the results, that George does not look noticeably Mediterranean, especially when clean-shaven, whereas witnesses described the man they saw as Mediterranean in appearance. Therefore, the man seen on Gowan Avenue must have had very noticeable Mediterranean features whereas this survey indicates George does not have such features. It is interesting to compare the characteristics provided by witnesses who allegedly saw George on the day of Dando's murder with the characteristics of George's appearance as described by participants of the survey. One of the most striking characteristics of George's face is the distinctive shape of his nose. One of the participants of the survey described his nose in the following way:

'Nose is odd. End/tip is like a slightly squished small playdo ball, which is then flattened as the nose continues to the forehead. Odd.'

This description of George's nose was not unique. Seventeen of those who responded to the survey commented on the strange shape of George's nose. It is therefore interesting to note that not a single witness described a man seen on Gowan Avenue prior to and following the murder, as having a strange-shaped nose, despite some of them providing detailed descriptions.

George does not look like the man described by witnesses who may have seen the killer. The man seen by the witnesses was not the man who is currently serving a life sentence in Whitemoor prison.

Consider for a few moments: on 27 April 1999 Susan Mayes described the man she saw at between 06:57 and 07:00 on the day of the murder, as having a *"short and smart haircut"*. But by the day on which she gave evidence in court, her description had altered to a man with long layers of collar length hair with some bits over the collar, which is clearly a very different description. Stella De Rosnay could not be sure at the identity parade and she was unable to make a positive identification of the man she saw prior to the murder. However, the day after the identity parade all of a sudden she commented *"When I saw number 2 [George] on the screen ... I recognised his face as that of the man I'd seen passing by my window on 26 April 1999."* Charlotte de Rosnay, when asked if the man she saw on 26 April 1999 was on the video identity parade replied, *"No I don't think so."* Yet following the identity parade she had a remarkable restoration of memory and became confident the man she had seen on the day of the murder was number 2, George.

It is important to note, as many have noted and as was discussed at the trial that these three women shared a lift home from the police station following the parade, and by this point in time Susan Mayes had received confirmation she had been 'correct' in her identification. It would seem to be an unlikely coincidence therefore, that following this car journey all three women became remarkably more confident that the man they had seen, who in fact was almost certainly two separate people, happened to be number 2 in the parade. A definite change occurred and there can be little doubt that this was as a result of the three women swapping notes so to speak regarding their experiences.

Of course, the jury was allowed to consider the effect of the journey home. However, the jury may have read too much into Mayes' confidence when in fact she was only really confident because she had been told she had picked out the correct person. She had only identified the suspect, which is not to say she had identified the killer.

Even if Mayes was correct in picking out George, and therefore she was correct in her belief it was George she had seen opposite 29 Gowan Avenue on the morning of 26 April 1999, it does not mean George was involved. Also, her identification was the only positive identification. More importantly seven of the eight witnesses who attended identity parades failed to make a positive identification, including the key witnesses who reported sightings of a man at and close to the murder scene immediately after the murder.

The prosecution related the majority of the witness statements to George in a way which implied all of the witnesses saw George when clearly they did not. In all probability most of the witnesses did not even see the killer. Robert Henderson says that the identification 'evidence' is *"laughably inadequate"*.[34] It is not difficult to agree with him.

6.5: George's actions on the day of the crime and his suspicious actions two days later

The possibility/probability that George could not have been at the murder scene at the time of the murder will now be discussed. Remember Dando was shot at around 11:30 on the morning of 26 April 1999.

---

[34] (Henderson. 2001: 4).

During his summing up the judge, Mr Justice Gage, directed the jury that if it could be determined George had an alibi at any point between 11:00 and 12:00 then he could not have been responsible for murdering Dando. This is because of the distances involved; after the murder George would have to have returned to his flat via Fulham Palace Road and Fulham Road in order to get changed. It can be argued compellingly that George had an alibi during this period of time. Unfortunately, however, when considering the evidence during his appeal the judges got the time at which George had arrived at one location, Traffic Cars, wrong. For this reason when reviewing the case they decided George could not have had an alibi. However, as hopefully you will now see, this is not at all true.

It is known on 26 April 1999, George certainly visited both Hafad on Greswell Street, which is just over half a mile from the scene of the crime, and the London Traffic Cars office, which is on Fulham Palace Road. To remind you, George believed he had been at Hafad from around 11:00 until shortly before 13:00, but probably after 12:30. He was, he thought, at Hafad at the time Dando was murdered shortly after 11:30.

As has been stated the staff at Hafad believed the time of George's visit to the disability centre had been between 11:00 and 14:00. It is known from Ramesh Paul and the business card George asked him to sign that George left Traffic Cars at 13:15. During the trial Paul stated his belief that George *"was there quite a long time ... fifteen minutes. I wouldn't say that it was less than fifteen minutes."* Therefore George arrived at the taxi office at 13:00 at the latest and not at 13:15 as the appeal judges incorrectly believed. Paul told the court George could have arrived as early as 12:55. After leaving Traffic Cars in a taxi George was driven to Colon Cancer Concern, which was a few miles away from Fulham. He stayed at the cancer centre for a short period of time before making his way home.

It is a fact his movements from around 13:00 (possibly 12:55 or even slightly earlier) until later on, certainly after 14:00, are accounted for. He could not have been at Hafad during this period of time.

However, this still leaves us with the question of when George visited Hafad. Could it have been between 11:00 and 12:00, or between 12:00 and 13:00? If it was between 11:00 and 12:00, then George could not have killed Dando. The police could never determine when George visited the centre because of the conflicting staff accounts, and so it could not be determined whether or not George had an alibi. However, there is a chance George does have an alibi and he could not have been at Gowan Avenue when the murder was committed.

The members of staff at Hafad were individually able to provide more precise times as to when George was present at the advice centre. During his visit on the day of the murder George was passed around different members of staff because he had not made an appointment yet he required help. Eventually he was passed on to a member of staff who did speak with him, Susan Bicknell. Bicknell gave evidence in court regarding the visit. She stated, as she had stated in her police statements, that George was with her at 11:50. Bicknell contacted the police a few weeks after the murder. However, she had made a note of the time a week after the shooting in order to inform the police in case it had any bearing on the investigation. She had good reason to remember this time and she has never wavered. It was Bicknell's first day of working at Hafad on the day Dando was killed, with George being her first client, and so she would not have been confused over times. She was not wearing a watch on that day but she looked at the clock, which according to her was never more than five minutes wrong during the whole time she worked at Hafad.

Bicknell stated she could have been speaking with George for around twenty minutes. Of course it is possible this is an overestimation but we can assume even if it is fifteen minutes is not far wrong. George had been very agitated because he needed help with problems mainly relating to health (he believed he had back problems but his doctor refused to believe him). He had gone into considerable detail about his problems, showing letters, which he had in a carrier bag, from doctors and psychologists. Bicknell was *"very concerned"* which suggests she spent some time with him. George continued to discuss his problems even when he was told they could not help him on that day. An appointment was made for the following day. A symptom of Asperger's syndrome is that sufferers can talk for lengthy periods of time irrespective of whether or not people are listening or interested in what is being said. Also, Susan Bicknell has a tendency to talk for lengthy periods of time before getting to the point. George had also continued talking to the other members of staff for periods of time before he had been passed on. George was sat in the waiting area in between speaking to different members of staff. He was also probably at the centre for a period of time before he began to be dealt with. This suggests George was at the centre for a considerable amount of time. Having read a lot about George's character, and having spoken to his friends and relatives, it is also probable that after having been dealt with he remained in the centre for some time, picking up leaflets and reading information (he collected medical information after all). Of course, there is no evidence of this but it is a point worth considering and which has not been sufficiently considered in the past.

If Bicknell was correct with her view that she was speaking to George at 11:50 then George could not have murdered Dando. Dando was shot just after 11:30. If George was the gunman, it would mean he ran down Gowan Avenue, along Fulham Palace Road, up Fulham Road and onto Crookham Road and to his flat. He would have had to change his clothes (the gunman was wearing a dark wax/Barbour style jacket that went down to his knees and dark baggy trousers, but George was wearing a yellow top and jeans when he went to Hafad and Traffic Cars). It would have been necessary to wash his hand (which would have had blood upon it) and anywhere else that was covered in blood, then pick up his carrier bag containing the letters and run to Hafad. All that in the space of less than twenty minutes. This is not at all possible.

Is there any corroborating evidence to support the view that George was at Hafad between 11:00 and 12:00? Elaine Hutton also worked at Hafad. She was working next to Bicknell while George was being spoken to. Hutton phoned the police two weeks after the murder. In her phone call she told Oxborough detectives 'Barry Bulsara' visited the advice centre at 11:50. This of course supports Bicknell's claim and therefore would suggest George was completely innocent. However, a year after the crime, when Hafad staff were interviewed for the first time by the police, Hutton altered her story slightly with her view now being George visited Hafad *"around midday"*.

Lesley Symes spoke briefly to George on the day of Dando's death. On the 28 April 1999 Symes became the first member of staff at Hafad to phone the police. During her telephone call she claimed George had visited the centre at around 11:00. If this was the correct time then again George could definitely not have committed the murder. However, once again a year after the crime the time provided by a member of staff had changed to after lunch. Another member of staff also now stated the visit was made at around 12:30 with a colleague stating it could have been as late as 14:00.

Which timings can be considered to be the truth? Susan Bicknell stuck to 11:50 rigidly which is suggestive. It must be remembered Bicknell was the woman who spoke with George and so she has the greatest reason to remember at what time the defendant was present at Greswell Street. Hutton stated it was around noon which means it could very well have been 11:50 as she had stated originally (original statements are often the most accurate). Symes had altered her time a year after. Her original timing could not have been far wrong for she had informed the police of the time so soon after the event and after just having been asked by George which time it was he had been there. A year had elapsed before the alteration occurred and memories can alter over time. None of the other people who provided times to the police a year after Dando's death had provided times to the police earlier on. This is odd as they would have been aware their colleagues had provided information. They would have known the times Bicknell, Hutton and Symes had provided to the police and so if their times were different to those the other three women had stated, then surely they would have phoned the police. This point makes me very sceptical regarding the information provided by those who stated George had visited Hafad as late as 14:00. By the time these individuals provided information, a reward for £250,000 had been offered for information leading to an arrest. It has in the past been suggested these later times may have been introduced so long afterwards in the hope they could acquire some wealth. It must be noted that Rosario Torres, who believed George made his visit between 12:30 and 13:00, also strongly believed it was not Bicknell who dealt with George. There is no disputing it was Susan Bicknell who spoke with George. Therefore if Torres was wrong about this, is it not possible she could have been wrong about the time of George's visit?

Going by the early accounts, there is a consensus that George arrived at Hafad between 11:00 and 11:50. Even later on the statements suggest George was at the advice centre at 11:50. It is more reasonable to rely only upon the earlier evidence, and if this is done then George certainly has an alibi. The following will further show George was at Hafad between 11:00 and 12:00.

The prosecution allege George arrived at Hafad at some point between 12:47 and 12:50, before going to Traffic Cars. They base this opinion upon a CCTV image, which is very blurred and was only just deemed admissible as evidence. This CCTV footage showed a man in yellow heading along Stevenage Road towards Hafad. The prosecution believed it could not have been a coincidence that two men in the area could both have been wearing a yellow top. The man (if it was a man) could have been wearing a yellow raincoat or a yellow jumper; it was impossible to tell. George was known to be wearing a yellow shirt when he visited Hafad. To anyone with common sense, if this person in the CCTV footage was George, then he certainly was not on his way to Hafad. For starters, the person in the footage was not carrying a bag but George had taken a bag of letters with him to Hafad. Secondly, he was not wearing or carrying a jacket. However, both Susan Bicknell and Leslie Symes remember that when George arrived at Hafad he was wearing a yellow shirt underneath a jacket. And finally, George arrived at Traffic Cars around 12:55. Therefore, how could he possibly have arrived at Hafad just before 12:50, waited to speak to someone and eventually be dealt with by Susan Bicknell for fifteen to twenty minutes and then walk the five-minute or more journey to Traffic Cars within only five to ten minutes? It is evidently impossible; to suggest the person in the CCTV footage was George is to show the ridiculous reasoning of the prosecution.

The evidence provided in court by Julia Moorhouse allegedly further corroborates the prosecution's argument that George visited the advice centre after noon and therefore could have committed the murder. Moorhouse's evidence was discussed in 5.5. At around 12:30 on the day of the murder, George approached Moorhouse in the vicinity of Hafad. The prosecution, therefore, believe that after talking to this woman George made his way to the disability advice centre. However, Moorhouse could not recall seeing George holding a carrier bag of letters. She also could not recall seeing George with a jacket; he was not wearing a jacket; as Moorhouse was able to determine, he was wearing a long sleeved yellow shirt of some sort, and she cannot remember him carrying such an item of clothing. This is not to say conclusively that George was not in possession of a bag and jacket while engaging in conversation with the witness. However, as Moorhouse was able to provide police and the court with a very good recollection of the meeting, such as George's cleft lip and a detailed description of what was said during the conversation, surely you would expect her to have remembered a bag if George had been carrying one. Of course, it was a year after the crime before Moorhouse was first interviewed although she had reported the event to the police early into the investigation. However, George could not have been carrying a bag and jacket when talking to this particular woman.

It is important to establish whether George met Moorhouse before, or after, visiting Hafad. George was agitated about his fears regarding his health when he visited Hafad on the day of the murder. Indeed he made a scene about it and he only calmed down after the staff had put a lot of effort into trying to pacify him. When the first member of staff met him, George was already highly agitated. He believed he had been treated badly by doctors who did not believe he had illnesses he claimed to have. If George had spoken to Moorhouse before visiting Hafad then he would have referred to his problems, particularly if he had the bag with him, which he must have done if he visited Hafad immediately after talking to this witness as the prosecution alleged he had done. If he did not have the bag and jacket with him when speaking to Julia Moorhouse (as seems most likely) then this would mean that after visiting Hafad he returned home and then went out again for a walk. George would not have thrown away the jacket and the bag of letters for they were important to him. His health concerns were of the utmost importance. The view George could have gone for a walk after visiting Hafad is very likely as George spent most of his time walking around the streets of Fulham, particularly around the Bishops Park area, which is where the conversation with Moorhouse took place. George was certainly calm when he was speaking to Moorhouse. He was able to talk about his interests in a way which for him is normal. As he was not agitated about his health problems then he must have spoken to this particular witness after the staff at Hafad had calmed him down. It was only after leaving Hafad that George was calm because an appointment had been made for him to have his problems dealt with. If George had spoken to Moorhouse after visiting Hafad, then he was definitely not responsible for the murder of Jill Dando.

Another point to consider here is, the conversation between the two took place on Doneraile Street, which is just off Fulham Palace Road. It is very possible George was heading towards Traffic Cars, which is on Fulham Palace Road, when he saw a woman he wanted to approach; Julia Moorhouse. The over-flying helicopters gave him the opportunity to attempt to impress her and so he took a diversion; he decided he would talk to the woman he liked the look of and then go to Traffic Cars. He spoke to this witness for five minutes before walking to Traffic Cars, possibly taking a circuitous route that meant he was caught by CCTV cameras.

George arrived at Traffic Cars around 12:55 but no later than 13:00. It is, as shown earlier, unrealistic to believe George could have visited Hafad between speaking to Moorhouse and visiting the taxi firm. The evidence provided by Ramesh Paul (the member of staff at Traffic Cars) can be used to further prove the visit to Hafad occurred earlier than the prosecution believe. Paul provided a detailed and on the whole accurate account of his meeting with George on the day of the murder, when George attempted to get a free taxi ride to a location two miles away in order to collect some information about bowel cancer. He was worried that he had bowel cancer, and he had gone to a hospital about this in March 1999. Paul commented that George was agitated when he visited Traffic Cars but this was because Paul refused to give him a free ride and also because Paul told George to *"fuck off"* and continued to be hostile to him for the whole time he was there. George had not been agitated before this; he was just being his usual self, appearing to be in *"a world of his own"* as Paul would later tell the court. George believed he could get a free ride because people with disabilities such as his could obtain a card entitling them to free rides from taxi companies. This is partly why he had visited Hafad earlier that day. When he was refused the free ride to the cancer centre he desperately needed to visit, he became concerned and worried.

Importantly, Paul never commented that George had a carrier bag or jacket with him. If George did not have the bag or jacket with him when he arrived at Traffic Cars then this is further proof he had visited Hafad before noon, and therefore it is further proof George could not have killed Dando. He must have returned home to take the jacket and bag back so he did not have to carry them with him; the weather had, by this time, improved and so there was no need for him to carry the jacket with him.

It is rather unfortunate the police did not contact Colon Cancer

Concern, which is where George travelled to in the taxi. The police never asked staff at this centre whether George was wearing a jacket or carrying a bag. If the member of staff who spoke with George reads this book then I would welcome contact.

George's account that he entered Hafad around 11:00, and stayed for nearly two hours, was wrong but then George never really knew at what time he had been present at the centre. After two years could you possibly expect an innocent person to know precise details about their movements? The important issue is that when studying the timings in this case it seems absurd that George could only have arrived at Hafad after 12:45. The prosecution's argument in this regard cannot be proved. It could only be proved that George's recollection was wrong which, most probably, the jury took to be an indication that George was lying when in reality he could simply have been mistaken. There was no proof George was not at Hafad between 11:00 and 12:00 and yet there is good evidence to suggest he was there at some point between these times, which if correct, shows George is certainly innocent.

As you read in the last chapter, George visited Hafad and Traffic Cars on 28 April 1999. It was this suspicious action which caused Hafad staff and Ramesh Paul to contact the Oxborough investigation incident room. The police, prosecution and appeal judges believed that the second visit to each of these places two days after the murder was George's way of attempting to falsify an alibi by forging a false impression in the minds of staff. Contrary to popular belief this is, as will now be demonstrated, completely untrue.

When being questioned by police about why he went to Hafad and Traffic Cars on 28 April 1999 George responded, *"I went back there basically to account for my movements so if a situation did come up, I could address it to my solicitor."* In court the jury watched all of the police interviews, which had been videoed. They were therefore aware this was George's explanation as to his movements.

Of course the jury may not have believed the defendant when he claimed the reason why he went to Hafad and Traffic Cars two days after the crime was to gain information in case the police questioned him. They presumably wondered why an innocent man would be so worried that he could be questioned in relation to a crime he had no involvement in. However, the jury was not aware of George's past criminal activities and therefore they were unaware George had been questioned in relation to the murder of Rachel Nickell as a result of his past criminal behaviour. Rachel Nickell had been savagely raped and murdered on Wimbledon Common, south-west London, in 1992. Upon his release from prison in 1984, George's relatives, in particular his stepfather, had told him to behave himself because whenever a serious crime took place he would be a suspect. When he was questioned in connection with Nickell's murder, George realised his relatives were right and since that point in time he became fearful of being questioned for other crimes he had not committed. When George heard that Dando had been murdered near to where he lived he expected the police to come and question him once again. After all, he had been interviewed in connection with the Nickell murder even though he was completely innocent (in November 2004 detectives discovered that DNA linked a murderer named Robert Napper to Nickell's death). Therefore in anticipation of more questioning he visited Hafad and Traffic Cars so he could prove to the police and his solicitor he was not responsible. Unfortunately his actions had the opposite effect.

Few members of the public are familiar with the routine 'informal' police interviews, which take place as part of a murder inquiry. The amount of questions that are asked, and the probing nature of those questions, would make many people, especially people who suffer from paranoia, very worried. George wished to be prepared for a visit by the police.

The jurors were also unaware that George has been diagnosed as suffering from paranoia and therefore he frequently believes he is going to be accused of crimes he has no involvement in. George wrongly believed people were accusing him of the crime and they were commenting on how he looked like the E-fit (he probably meant the description issued by police). This explains his mutterings about how he did not want to be blamed. Such worry is not indicative of guilt, it is more indicative of a paranoid disorder; a disorder that George certainly has. At present he is paranoid in prison, convinced people are plotting to kill him. If the members of the jury had known about his paranoia and the interview regarding the murder on Wimbledon Common then perhaps they would have been more willing to believe George's words shown above which they heard in the videoed police interviews. They would certainly have realised George's behaviour two days after the murder was not as irrational as Orlando Pownall led them to believe.

There are no references to George having made any suggestion to any members of staff he spoke to that he was present at any particular time. Pownall himself remarked, George *"insisted on knowing what time he had arrived at the centre"*.[35] His actions therefore, were clearly those of a man seeking information rather than those of a man wishing to influence what people may tell the police.

George has been accused of acting out of proportion for an innocent man. His actions following the death of Dando apparently were uncharacteristic of someone who had no involvement in the crime. It is true he suggested to the local council that a memorial should be constructed, collected condolence cards and took flowers to Gowan Avenue. However, is this out of character for a man who had no involvement in Dando's death?

George's actions were not necessarily out of proportion for an ordinary member of society mourning her death. Many people react in such a way following the death of someone of national significance, even if they were unaware of their name (something which will be discussed later in this chapter). This is evident from the number of flowers laid. Flowers were not commonly laid at the scenes where people had died; it was something which really began when flowers were laid following the death of Princess Diana. Many people travelled half way across the country to lay flowers when Holly Wells and Jessica Chapman were murdered. An indication of whether George's actions were out of proportion or not would be to look at how he reacted to the deaths of other celebrities.

Like many people in this nation, he was upset when Princess Diana died. George certainly went onto the streets of London on the day of the funeral, holding a large placard with the words *'Queen of Hearts'* written upon it. It is well documented and indisputable that he was terribly upset on hearing of the death of his idol Freddie Mercury. George went out of his way to hire a limousine to travel to the house of the late Queen singer on the first anniversary of Mercury's death. He also became an acquaintance with a friend of Freddie Mercury's. Of course, he never had anything to do with the

---

[35] Orlando Pownall speaking on Friday 4 May 2001.

deaths of these individuals; however he responded in the same way to the deaths of these as he did to Dando's death.

As Dando lived so close to his home and as he had recently regained his faith, George felt it would be morally correct to mourn her passing. Actually, his mourning would provide him with something to talk about so he could approach women and make conversation. He could tell them how Dando lived nearby, because he had found out following her death they lived within half a mile of each other. He could make up stories about seeing a man nearby on the day of the murder who could have been the murderer (of course, these stories were later proven to be false but they gave him a topic of discussion). He could also attempt to impress women by saying he had met Dando when with his 'cousin' Freddie Mercury. Again, this was untrue, as neither George nor Freddie Mercury had ever met Dando. However, it gave him the excuse to play on his fantasy that he was related to Queen's lead singer. It also provided him with something to occupy his time; an alternative to complaining about services he was receiving. He exploited Dando's death to make conversation but that does not necessarily mean he was in any way involved in the dreadful crime. *'Would the highly efficient killer who apparently staked out Jill Dando's Fulham house, coldly executing her before calmly leaving the scene, leaving no clues to identify him, then go around the streets talking like a prat about the murder?'*, George's campaign has asked.

And so, it is my belief that George acted no differently on hearing the news of Dando's death than he would have done had anyone else been killed close to where he lived. He took advantage of Dando's death to attempt to have social relations but that is all. It must be noted the jury was not informed of one important point which can further show George's actions did not indicate guilt. This point is, George has been diagnosed as suffering from Histrionic Personality Disorder; a disorder whose sufferers draw attention to themselves and react to events in a dramatic way.

His actions regarding her passing are indicative of someone wanting to take an interest in order to talk to people about a topic which was in everyone's mind. His actions were not out of proportion for an innocent man.

6.6: The particle

Jurors love forensic evidence. It makes their job so much easier if a criminal leaves a fingerprint at the scene of a crime or the prosecution are able to rely on DNA evidence, or some other form of forensic evidence which links the criminal to the scene of the crime. Unfortunately for the members of the jury, who had been sworn in to listen to the evidence in the case of Barry George, they were presented with only one piece of forensic evidence worth considering, and even that piece's relevance to the crime is highly debatable. I am of course referring to the particle of supposed firearm residue found in the inside pocket of a Cecil Gee jacket belonging to George.

As has already been described, a taping from inside the left inside pocket of a jacket belonging to George revealed a particle, which the prosecution wishfully interpreted as evidence of George's direct involvement in the incident which ended the life of Dando. The particle is microscopic at 11.5 microns in size, which is approximately 0.0125 millimetres. Compositional analysis showed the particle was made up of three elements; barium, aluminium and lead. The particle had the same composition as the particles found at the crime scene on the victim. It must be noted here that just because the particles matched, it does not mean they came from the same source. They were comparable in so much as they had the same chemical composition.

At this point in this argument it is important to discuss the coat in which the particle was found. George's Cecil Gee coat was dark blue in colour and was not particularly long. When combining the descriptions of the clothing worn by the killer, provided by Richard Hughes and Geoffrey Upfill-Brown, it is clear the gunman's jacket was dark, probably black, and it was a three-quarter length wax or Barbour style jacket which went down to the man's knees.

If George was the killer, he could have put the gun into the pocket of the Cecil Gee jacket when returning home after the shooting. This could explain why the particle came to be in a jacket which did not resemble the one worn by the killer. However, the particle could have found its way into the pocket a substantial amount of time before Dando was killed.

George bought the Cecil Gee coat in December 1988 a few months before his wedding. As George had a stronger interest in guns during the 1980s than he did in 1999, he may at some point have had a blank firing gun in the pocket. He never denied having had a gun in 1989 but he always has denied owning a gun after this year, which is almost certainly correct. Firearm discharge residue does not wash out completely when a piece of clothing is washed even many times. There is no way of dating FDR and so the particle may have been in the pocket for as many as ten years before the murder, depending upon how frequently George had his jacket washed.

There is absolutely no way whatsoever in which it can be said with any certainty that the particle found in George's jacket pocket came to be there due to the fact a discharged gun which had been used to murder Dando had been placed into that pocket. In fact, it is possible the particle could have come from a firework, as some fireworks have the same composition as the particle. As George had an interest in guns and firearms, presumably he had an interest in gunpowder. Who is to say, George had not picked up a firework at some point? With the large numbers of fireworks being found on the streets it would not be impossible. Also, the particle could have been left in the pocket as a result of a blank-firing gun having been placed in the pocket. The particle consisted of three basic elements, which could be from a number of different guns if a gun was the source of the residue.

As has been explained, the expert witnesses consulted by the prosecution and who appeared at the trial commented that the possibility that the particle came from a firework or blank-firing gun was small. However, this possibility could not be ruled out. Indeed, the defence expert Dr John Lloyd, who has thirty years experience as a forensic scientist, said it was possible for the particle to be from a firework. He believed the particle was too small to be significant, as you would expect more particles to be present if the jacket held any relevance to the crime. He stated that to rely upon such questionable evidence was *"incredible"*, mainly due to the size of the particle that played a huge part in the prosecution's case. Dr Lloyd told the court:

"It has been suggested that a single particle could be a relic of something which occurred a year before. It is quite a unique suggestion. The claims that it is so related are based on scientifically unsupported assumptions. The evidence is dependent on flawed police procedures. It is my view that this evidence is not reliable as evidence of the defendant's involvement in the shooting

... There is no particular reason why this particle can be so related to the shooting of Miss Dando."

The prosecution's expert witness, Mr Keeley, himself openly stated when being questioned by Pownall and not Mansfield, *"The most you can say is that it could have come from that ammunition [the ammunition used to kill Miss Dando] ..."*

Clearly the issue of whether the particle relates to the crime is important. There are serious doubts as to the relevance of the evidence in the trial. If this highly questionable evidence was not available, then the Crown Prosecution Service would have found there was no case to answer. And yet, the particle could be from a firework. It makes a mockery of the justice system when such questionable evidence is presented at a trial.

In the USA firearms discharge residue is known as gunshot residue (GSR). In that country many agencies have stopped testing for GSR because they are aware there are too many misleading and erroneous results to make the test reliable.[36] They have told how such particles can find their way onto a suspect in a number of ways, even when the suspect has not fired a gun.

And now the issue of contamination must be examined; the *"flawed police procedures"* Dr Lloyd was referring to.

Before the jacket, along with other items of the suspect's clothing, was taken to a laboratory for forensic examination, Gallagher decided it might be a good idea to take it to be photographed. He did this so witnesses could be asked if they remembered the man they had seen on the day of the shooting wearing the coat; even though the key witnesses described a wax or Barbour style jacket.

Removing the Cecil Gee jacket from the packaging it had been sealed in to ensure its integrity as evidence should any forensic evidence be discovered, Gallagher took it to the Scenes of Crime Branch's photographic studio on Amelia Street.

It must be noted that ammunition which had been recovered in a raid had been photographed in this studio at some point in the months preceding the arrival of George's Cecil Gee jacket. This studio had also, one year prior to George's jacket having been photographed there, contained Dando's clothing as well as the bullet

---

[36] (Houde. 1999: 168).

and cartridge used in the murder. Is it not possible therefore that particles could have been deposited when evidence from Gowan Avenue and the other ammunition were taken to the studio? Keeley did not believe this was likely although he admitted it was possible. It is known the studio is not cleaned in any specialised way; it is just dusted and cleaned using an ordinary household vacuum cleaner, in the same fashion as any other office is cleaned. This is rather foolish when forensic evidence is often taken to the premises, and therefore minute particles may remain within the rooms for significant periods of time.

At the laboratory, where it was searched for the presence of forensic evidence, the jacket was placed on a work surface in many positions and so both the inside and outside came into contact with one another. The pocket was then pulled inside out and placed on another part of the jacket. Therefore if, during the time in which the jacket was put down at the photographic studio, any part of the jacket had picked up a minute particle, then the inside pocket could very well have come into contact with the particle. It could very easily have become stuck to the jacket and when the jacket was put into different positions the particle could have moved to the part of the jacket on which the pocket was placed.

The photographs taken at Amelia Street were not even shown to witnesses and so the purpose of the photographs was not fulfilled. The taking of photographs of the jacket may have caused contamination needlessly; it may have been a flawed and pointless procedure that has resulted in the imprisonment of a man.

The jury was unsure about the possibility of contamination. During their deliberations this issue evidently played on their minds as they considered it. During the deliberations they asked Mr Justice Gage if they could again see the jacket in which the particle had been found. It was after this second viewing that the members of the jury on the whole became satisfied that contamination had not occurred, even when no experts could rule out such a possibility. No doubt the fact the particle was found in an inside pocket reduced the possibility of contamination in the minds of some of the jurors. As the particle had been found in an inside pocket it must have seemed unlikely it could have found its way into the pocket from a work surface it came into contact with.

However, the photographs taken of the jacket do have a purpose here: the jacket was displayed in a way in which it would be worn, with a white shirt and red tie underneath. Therefore, the inside of the jacket will have been exposed to the air for some time. Also the shirt may have picked up a particle as it was placed onto a surface. When the jacket rubbed against the shirt a particle could have entered the pocket.

Unfortunately the defence did not cover sufficiently the possibility that contamination could have occurred during the police search of George's flat. Mansfield dedicated large amounts of time to what, in his eyes, was the main way in which contamination could have occurred; at the photographic studio. There is only so much time to be spent arguing the possibility of contamination without turning the proceedings into a farce. Inevitably other possible causes of contamination could not be discussed as fully as one would like. Mansfield probably believed the jury would have realised contamination could well have occurred, for the prosecution witness agreed with this, and therefore it was dangerous to consider the particle to be evidence linking the defendant to the crime. Mansfield correctly showed that the officers who made the search which recovered the jacket in which the particle was later found were not wearing forensic search suits. The search team, who were drafted in from police stations all over London, were wearing 'search blues' instead of the disposable forensic suits used during searches where it is believed forensic evidence may be present. Search blues are blue shirts and blue trousers. All but one of the police officers was wearing rubber gloves instead of forensic gloves. Most had cleaned their shoes but none, including the adviser, were wearing the overshoes required during forensic searches.

Due to the fact the clothing worn by all members of the search team was not disposable, anyone who had come into contact with firearms or ammunition in the past would have forensic evidence on their clothing. No tests were carried out to see if the articles of clothing had any particles on them. If this was the case then contamination could quite easily have occurred as a result of a police officer bringing particles into the flat themselves. Also no members of the search team remember having been asked if they had been involved in searches where firearms or ammunition had been recovered.

A police constable who handled the Cecil Gee coat, and opened the inside pockets of the coat, P.C. Cain, had on an earlier search handled firearms ammunition. He was wearing the same clothing as he had worn when he found the ammunition. Therefore, if at any point he had touched his clothing with his gloves, before handling the jacket, the particle could have been transferred onto his gloves and then onto the pocket.

It was rather foolish on the part of those conducting the search to have worn ordinary search clothes, as they were fully aware of George being a suspect in a murder investigation and they were looking for evidence to prove this, which of course would consist of forensic evidence.

It is conventional procedure to take samples of the police vehicle, in which the items recovered in a police search are placed, prior to the search. This is in order to determine whether forensic evidence was present prior to a suspect's belongings having been placed within it, which if present could contaminate the items belonging to the suspect and result in it incorrectly appearing that a suspect possessed, for example, firearms. However, the van in which George's belongings were placed when they were removed from 2b Crookham Road was not sampled. The jury was not sufficiently informed about this point.

The jury did not hear any information relating to one very important point that could indicate contamination was not just a possibility but a probability. Unfortunately the information did not emerge until after the trial, and although it was supposed to have been discussed during the appeal hearing at the Court of Appeal, the appeal judgment makes no reference to this. Had it been presented to the jury then they may have believed contamination probably did occur and therefore they may have believed the particle did not constitute evidence.

This point is that numerous witnesses, including a church minister, the Reverend John Hale, have told how on 17 April 2000, the day on which the Cecil Gee jacket was removed, they saw four armed police officers enter George's flat.

DCI Campbell and his team have denied a presence of armed officers in the suspect's flat. However, the suggestion that guns were taken inside the flat just prior to the jacket having been found, is compelling. A risk assessment, which is always conducted by the Metropolitan Police when they plan a search, will certainly have shown there was a potential threat which required armed officers to be present. After all, George was a suspect in an investigation of a crime that had involved a firearm. The police had also been informed George allegedly owned guns (see 4.1 where the calls made to the incident room early in the investigation were discussed).

Scotland Yard was contacted regarding this point. As a result of their secrecy, they were simply told I was a writer conducting research and could they answer this question:

'If it is known that a suspect may own firearms would police, when wishing to conduct a search of the suspect's home, carry firearms with them? If so, is this a common practice?'

The response received was interesting. The email office wrote,

Dear Sir,
Thank you for yur [sic] email ... not for us to give away our secrets but probably yes
EMail Office
New Scotland Yard

If firearms were taken into the flat then this could account for the presence of the particle. As has already been stated, when he found the jacket PC Cain opened the pockets. If there was a gun nearby at the time then FDR from the weapon could have found its way into the pocket. The weapon would have been discharged at some point prior to the visit to Crookham Road and therefore FDR would have been on it.

When considering just one possible explanation as to how contamination could have occurred, the possibility that the evidence could have been damaged is unlikely although possible. However, when multiple plausible explanations are considered, such as in this case, the possibility becomes significantly higher. There can be no disputing the police procedures were dangerously flawed, and so there can be no guarantee the alleged firearm discharge residue, if it was even FDR, has any bearing whatsoever upon the case. It cannot prove George shot Dando dead.

During the trial Mr Justice Gage told the members of the jury that because of its weak nature, the particle could not be considered evidence in its own right; it could only be used to corroborate other evidence, he believed.

6.7: Other forensic evidence

As was stated in 5.7 a single fibre was found on the victim's raincoat. This was approximately 0.5 mm in size. It was unfortunate for the prosecution to argue that two pieces of minute evidence linked George to the shooting.

It was claimed the fibre could have originated from the trousers found in George's flat. It could equally have originated from any pair of trousers which were made of the same material. George is not the only man who owns trousers like those found in his flat. Who is to say the killer was not wearing a pair of trousers which happen to be of the same type as those owned by George? There was no evidence to suggest the fibre did certainly originate from a pair of trousers. It may be prudent to refer to the case of Derek Christian at this point. Christian was convicted of murdering an elderly woman named Margaret Wilson though he has good reason to maintain he is innocent. The prosecution against him relied heavily upon the evidence of textile fibres. However, it was shown that multiple garments could be produced from fibres which are *'microscopically indistinguishable'* from one another. For example, it was shown that a rugby football shirt had fibres matching those from a sweatshirt.

It must be remembered Dando had visited a shopping centre just half an hour before she was killed. It is possible the fibre may have found its way onto her raincoat as she brushed against someone. No doubt people will argue the fibre was transferred due to lengthy contact. This is not necessarily the case, and it must be remembered the killer only made physical contact for a few seconds. Similarly the fibre could have originated from a paramedic or one of the other individuals who attempted to offer first aid.

Dando's coat had also been in contact with the interior of her car just moments before the shooting. Did the car seat have fibres placed there as a result of someone having sat in the car who happened to be wearing clothing composed of such fibres, which became transferred when the raincoat came into contact with the interior of the car? We shall never know if this was the case because the police did not feel that it was necessary to carry out forensic analysis of the BMW. It was not deemed relevant at the time.

Due to the fact that the fibre was so minute, at only half a millimetre in length, only three of the four necessary tests were carried out. Dye was not extracted from the tiny piece of material. Therefore, it could not be determined the fibre matched those fibres from George's trousers. As Dr Zakaria Erzinçlioglu correctly writes, two fibres may appear to be identical, but unless the dye is removed from the fibre then it cannot be determined they are the same colour, let alone they are from the same source.[37] As the dye from the fibre found on Dando's raincoat was not extracted, and therefore was not fully compared to fibres from the trousers belonging to George, there is no way in which it can be said they are identical.

Mark Webster, a forensic scientist, commented on how the single fibre could be completely unrelated to the shooting, *"A single grey polyester fibre is not in my view significant evidence. It is not something you should rely on."* The appeal judges even commented, *"This was not more than a weak support for any connection to the 'raincoat' fibre ..."*

It is impossible to state whether the fibre has any relevance to the crime. It is simply too common to constitute as evidence linking George to the murder. The prosecution, however, claimed this contributed to the 'compelling' case against George.

One significant finding of forensic tests, the only significant evidence in this case regarding forensic science, was the absence of firearms residue in George's flat. Despite a very extensive forensic search of George's belongings and his flat, the police failed to find any particles other than the one found in the Cecil Gee coat which was discussed in 5.6 and 6.6. It would seem, therefore, that if whatever had caused the particle to be deposited in the pocket had ever been in the flat, it had constantly stayed in the pocket. The killer was not wearing a Cecil Gee jacket however. Therefore, to be the killer it would probably be the case that he would have had to switch the gun from the pocket of the coat he was wearing at the time of the murder into the Cecil Gee jacket whilst still outside the flat. Only in that way could he bring the gun into his home without depositing particles.

This lack of forensic evidence inside of the flat could indicate there had never been any firearms, which fired live ammunition, in the home of George. As George had moved into 2b Crookham Road during the mid 1980's and no particles were found in the flat

---

[37] (Erzinçlioglu. 2000: 218).

despite him rarely cleaning, this is further corroborating evidence that George was not obsessed with firearms during the 1990's and particularly not at the time of the murder. It also increases the likelihood that the particle came to be in the pocket of the Cecil Gee coat as a result of contamination.

6.8: George's lies to the police

Anyone who has a child will know children will lie to protect themselves. Children will lie to try and prove they did not do something they have been accused of *even if* they did not do anything wrong in the first place. In such cases a child will lie by distorting facts and hiding certain facts in order to convince the adult they did not do anything wrong. In the eyes of psychologists George is not mentally retarded, because his IQ is slightly above the threshold of seventy. However, there is no disputing the fact he is emotionally, psychologically and behaviourally immature. George also has a poor memory, which means he could be construed as lying about past events when in reality he genuinely has no recollection of them. Of course, he would recall committing a murder and covering his tracks, if responsible for the crime. Remember this when reading of George's alleged lies; he may have lied, if he did lie, in order to protect himself even if he was not responsible for the crime committed. The issue of whether or not George lied to the police is obviously an important one.

The Police and Criminal Evidence Act 1984 states that people who are mentally disordered can often provide information that is unreliable, misleading or self-incriminating. It should be remembered the police were fully aware that George was mentally disordered. However, when George provided unreliable and misleading information during the police interviews, those who questioned him did not bear the words of PACE in mind. Instead they took what is perfectly ordinary behaviour for someone with disorders such as those which George possesses to be a sign he was lying.

George suffers from epilepsy. Most people are aware sufferers experience seizures or fits, which are very visible. However, most people are not aware that epileptics can also suffer from 'absent seizures'. When a person experiences an absent seizure they temporarily lose awareness of what is happening. George is known to have these seizures frequently, particularly when he is stressed. When in an interview situation sufferers will lose track of what is being discussed and will often become confused. For this reason those who do not understand the illness will believe the person being interviewed is lying, or being misleading.

The *Cutting Edge* documentary included a comment by Professor Gisli Gudjonsson, who said:

"[George's] brain is highly abnormal. His functioning is highly abnormal. When you're dealing with somebody who has the kind of deficits that Mr George has then obviously it makes them vulnerable to the legal process. It makes them vulnerable because they may be misinterpreted."[38]

It was discussed in the last chapter that George apparently lied about his links with Gowan Avenue. George claimed he was unaware of the fact he had once been a patient at a doctor's surgery on Gowan Avenue. It is undoubtedly difficult for many to understand how a man cannot realise he went to a surgery. As it is hard to comprehend such a concept, many will believe that when he said he had no links with Gowan Avenue, he was lying. It should be noted, George was only briefly a patient at the surgery. However, some may still have difficulty in believing he did not realise the connection he had had with Gowan Avenue. The police took his lack of awareness to be a sign of deceit, which they interpreted as indicating he was hiding the truth in order to get away with the crime. Having once been a friend to someone who bears many striking similarities to George, an alternate explanation can be offered through the use of an analogy.

A few years ago I was walking through Chesterfield with two friends of mine. We were walking to another friend's house. Our route took us past a primary school which one of the friends, who I shall refer to as Mike, and myself, attended for many years. It had been four or five years previous to this event that we had both been pupils at the school, but during our time in secondary school we had to visit the primary school once or twice a year. Both Mike and myself had visited the primary school just months earlier. Clearly then, we had spent a large proportion of our lives at that school.

---

[38] *Cutting Edge*, 2002.

As we walked, Mike pointed to one of the buildings (it was the cafeteria in which he had eaten his lunch every school day) and exclaimed, *"That's a small school!"* He was surprised when I pointed out to him it was the school we had both attended for at least six years. Indeed it was difficult to convince him of the fact. This analogy shows certain people can be completely unaware they have had links with a place in the past, even if they are taken to the place itself. Perhaps George was simply unaware he had connections with Gowan Avenue in the past.

George told the police he did not know of Dando before her death but the police did not believe this (see 5.5). However, there is substantiating evidence of his claim. George had once been trying to impress a woman in a jewellery shop by talking about the people he had apparently met with his 'cousin' Freddie Mercury. Along with Princess Diana, George had apparently met the lady from *Crimewatch*. He did not know, or at least he did not appear to know, Dando's name. This indicates his claim that he did not know Dando before her death was right insofar as he did not know her by name. It also further suggests that the claim of George being obsessed with Dando, is false.

Inevitably some people at this point will ask how a man who lived within half a mile of a woman who appeared on many television programmes could not know her name. Firstly, it should be pointed out hardly anyone in the Gowan Avenue area of London knew Dando was a local resident. Indeed, some people who lived on Gowan Avenue itself were unaware she was a neighbour. Of course, George walked the streets a lot but even he did not have reason to know because Dando rarely went to her own home, and she was often abroad. Even so, is it realistic that George could not know the name of someone who was described as a *'household name'* by so many people? To prove this is highly possible I will recount my own experience of hearing the terrible news of Dando's murder on 26 April 1999.

On that particular Monday, I was at school. When I heard Dando had been killed I was in an afternoon lesson preparing for an exam. As the lesson progressed two other students entered the classroom and informed my teacher that someone had just been on the Internet and they had read Dando had been killed. I clearly remember the reactions of many of the people in the room. My own first reaction was: *"That's terrible, but who is Jill Dando?"* I did not have any idea of who she was, although when the students said she read the news two faces came to mind; the face of Dando herself, and the face of a Channel 5 news reporter. I was not sure who Jill Dando was. A friend I was sitting with did not have any idea whatsoever who Dando was. I could not explain because I did not know. My teacher also did not know who Dando was and others in the room either could not be sure or did not know. The students who came in informed us but even after this there were those of us who did not know.

At the end of the school day I walked up to where my mother collected my brothers and me from school. My grandma was with her. I told them both that Dando had been killed. I remember neither my mother nor grandmother knew who Dando was. I explained, and eventually my mother worked it out, but my grandma did not know to whom I was referring.

Therefore, clearly Dando was not the household name people believed her to be. I had frequently watched *Crimewatch* but I was not aware of her name. Even the vicar who was asked to conduct Dando and Farthing's marriage, was completely oblivious to Dando's fame when he was first spoken to. It is therefore not unreasonable to believe that George may have been unaware of who she was. If so then this would be further evidence he was at no point obsessed with her. After Dando's death everyone knew her name. It was hard not to with all the media coverage. The Dando murder shook the nation in a way similar to Princess Diana's death, albeit on a smaller scale.

6.9: Any other evidence

As was stated in 5.9, George started growing a beard and moustache while he was under surveillance. As was also discussed in 5.9, this was interpreted as an attempt on George's part to disguise himself. Why would a man wish to disguise himself a year after committing a murder? If he was responsible for the terrible crime then he would have disguised himself soon after the murder because it is known he was worried people would identify him as the man described by witnesses. Even if he was attempting to disguise himself then this could mean he was trying to prevent an incorrect identification. It is known George feared people believed he looked like the man depicted in the E-fit; the man police still wanted to question. He feared if he had to go on a parade he would be incorrectly picked out so he started to grow a beard to ensure he looked less like the man in the E-fit, a man who was definitely not George.

George, like many people, changed his appearance at times. When the police had noticed he was growing a beard and moustache, George had just celebrated his fortieth birthday (George's birthday is 15 April). Perhaps he felt it was a time to mark the milestone in his life with a change of image. It is a fact that George marks changes in his life with a change in his appearance. George still had the beard and moustache after the trial, many months after the identity parades had taken place. Therefore, if the reason for growing the hair was for disguise there was no longer any need for such facial hair but he retained both the beard and moustache.

There are two reasonable explanations that can be offered to explain the presence of the word *'Dando'* on the reverse of the business card found in George's flat. Firstly, George may have written down the name as a reminder of how to spell it so he could write out the letter of condolence he sent, or a reminder he had to take flowers to Dando's house. Many may believe this to be impossible, as Dando is only a five-letter word and simple to spell. However, Lomax is also a five-letter word and is almost equally easy to spell. Often people will write *'Lomas'* or *'Lomac'*. People have even believed it is spelt *'Lowmacques'*. Therefore, it is not impossible that a man with learning difficulties could not be one hundred percent sure of how to spell an uncommon name.

Secondly, the name Dando may not have referred to Jill Dando. This is probably the true reason why Dando's surname happened to be written on the reverse of the business card. It is known, through evidence recovered during searches of his flat, George had at some point been interested in a gymnast known as Suzanne Dando. He had made a note of her name. Could the writing upon the business card also be a reference to this woman? George is in the habit of writing out lists and names repetitively. There is also a musician known as Evan Dando who plays with 'The Lemonheads'. Evan Dando and The Lemonheads are signed on the EMI record label. Queen, George's favourite rock group, was also signed on EMI. Could George have used the Internet to search for EMI for information about a group he was very interested in, found that Evan Dando was also signed to the label and decided to go to buy music by this performer who happened to have the same surname as the victim? In order to remember the name of the musician he may have written it on the back of one of his music business cards before going to a music shop. Even if it did refer to the victim it certainly does not prove George was involved in the crime.

The prosecution used these pieces of information in their attempt to prove George was responsible for killing Dando. In reality, like so much of the 'evidence' used in the prosecution's case, they could have been completely unrelated to the victim and therefore completely irrelevant.

6.10: George's criminal record

Yes, George did impersonate a police officer. He wished to join the police force, and so when his application was turned down he began to play the policeman so he could emulate the life of his father. He was also allegedly arrested for being in possession of a knife outside the home of Prince Charles and Princess Diana, even though no records of this arrest exist and the claim results from one police officer having contacted the press. Following George's trial certain newspapers, including national broadsheet papers, picked up on this point and made false claims stating George attempted to murder Diana. These newspapers have created a large amount of confusion regarding this incident. However, if the event took place then George was certainly released without charge. It is difficult to accept that the sequence of events was as described in newspapers. If George had been in possession of a knife and was waiting outside the home of the heir to the throne, and it was viewed he was even a slight threat, then he would have been detained for a longer period of time than the few hours he was. The police were allegedly satisfied he posed no threat, and they must have had sufficient reason for this.

In the early 1980s George had indecently assaulted one woman and attempted to rape a second woman. His actions are inexcusable. However, as detestable as this makes him appear to be, attempted rape and murder do not equate to one another.

After George's release from prison in 1985 he is not known to have committed a single criminal offence. That is not to say he was a law-abiding citizen between 1983 and 1999, but it certainly suggests an improvement in his behaviour, as prior to 1983 he had been caught so easily after having carried out crimes.

Another point regarding his past criminal actions, which can be used in his defence, has already been discussed in 6.5. George was interviewed following Rachel Nickell's murder, which could explain why he was nervous and so went to Hafad and Traffic Cars on 28 April 1999.

George had always chosen secluded areas when attempting rape or similar crimes; it was his trademark so to speak, so if he killed Dando why did he do so outdoors when she was about to unlock her front door? It would be wiser to wait until she entered her home. If the killer had been around for some hours, he would have known no one was in the house. Of course, rape presumably was not the motive but even so it was foolish to kill outdoors in the daytime when there is a more suitable alternative.

6.11: Any other arguments in George's defence

Michael Mansfield shared with the court his view that the killer was a Serbian assassin. He commented, *"For Miss Dando to have been murdered by such precision shooting with a single muffled shot, it has to be the work of a professional assassin."* In order to add weight to his theory, he relied upon the evidence of Major Peter Mead. According to Major Peter Mead, a ballistics expert, the shooting of Dando was near perfect. During the trial he claimed, *"It is difficult to imagine how it could be bettered."* The jury, however, obviously believed George was capable of near perfection in carrying out a professional-style killing. They must have been persuaded by the prosecution's argument that George was a firearms obsessive who had experience in using guns. This is, of course, untrue and in reality there is not a shred of evidence, contrary to the prosecution's view, to suggest George had any degree of competence with firearms.

It is difficult to imagine how George, a man with little dexterity and an inability to think in complex ways, could have carried out such a near perfect execution.

George is not an intelligent man. He can read but he cannot always understand what he reads. He may appear to be intelligent when he uses words such as *"ascertain"*, but he has an IQ that is significantly below average. In addition to this, his ability to plan, organise and execute tasks was tested prior to the trial. George was found to be in the bottom one percent of the population with respect to this. Therefore how could he possibly plan and execute a murder in daylight, which needed a high degree of intelligence, and succeed in evading justice for approximately one year? George is not clever enough to kill in the way in which Dando was murdered.

Professor Gudjonsson has commented on George's ability to perform the crime he has been convicted of:

> *"All I can say is that when you're talking about a person who is disorganised, has significant brain damage, and finds it difficult to organise and plan his activities, you have to ask yourself how this person could have performed an efficient act of executional killing."*[39]

George is right-handed. As shown in Chapter 3 it is very likely that the killer was left-handed. Michael Mansfield strongly believes Dando's murderer was left handed and there can be no doubt the killer used his left hand to inflict the fatal wound. George has very unsteady hands according to his ex wife and those who know him. Apparently he has difficulty putting coins in a wallet. Therefore, it is hard to believe he would use his weaker left hand to carry out a task that required high manual dexterity to succeed in escaping justice.

If George was the gunman could he have acted normal, normal for him, after just carrying out a vicious shooting? The majority of those who have met him and spoken with him seriously doubt he could have done. His fellow prisoners doubt he could be capable of such a crime, as do the prison officers at the prisons he has served in. If the prosecution claims were correct then George would have gone to Hafad and Traffic Cars following the murder. At Hafad George had been able to do something he frequently did, complain. Could he have blanked out, or appeared to have blanked out, the fact that he had just murdered a woman and replaced the thought of Dando lying on the ground bleeding to death with his own concerns regarding his health and his housing association? Could he also have approached a woman he liked if he had killed someone less than an hour earlier? Surely if he had just murdered someone he would have been too agitated to consider chatting-up a woman. It must be remembered that George is the sort of person who is very emotional.

---

[39] *Cutting Edge*, 2002.

He has constantly maintained his innocence and has never slipped into a trap by which he could provide an incriminating statement. A man like George almost certainly would do so if he was guilty; you need intelligence to lie. After his first appeal hearing, George made the following statement:

> "I did not murder Jill Dando and I believe that one day the truth will come out. I only hope and pray that this happens in my lifetime. I have spent over two years in prison for a crime I simply did not commit. I have struggled hard during this prosecution against me to keep my faith in the British criminal justice system. Today, that faith and belief has been destroyed."

It is most unusual for a man of George's intelligence and psychological disorders to constantly maintain his innocence. Especially so when being interviewed by the detective (Snowden) who is allegedly amongst the best interviewers in the Met, and who is more able than DCI Campbell himself at extracting confessions, or indications of guilt, from the guilty.

Gallagher (an author who has written about stalking) believes that stalkers who kill celebrities like to associate their name with that of the victim.[40] He believes they gain some pleasure and/or relief from discussing how, and often why, they killed their victims. The same is true of obsessed fans in general. Chapman, upon being caught, readily confessed to the murder of John Lennon.

Dr Susan Young, who has studied George, does not believe he is capable of committing a crime and evading justice for a year.[41] She also does not believe he could maintain his innocence:

> "If Mr George committed this crime I think he would have found it very hard to keep quiet about it. He's the type of person who would be saying 'I killed Jill Dando, I killed Jill Dando, I killed Jill Dando.' He'd be telling you about it over and over again. He's so rigid in his thinking that he becomes focussed on certain topics. Particularly during a ten week trial when this is the whole topic of conversation. If he did it he'd find it extremely difficult not to ... own up."[42]

---

[40] (Gallagher. 2002: 128).
[41] *Cutting Edge*, 2002.
[42] *Cutting Edge*, 2002.

If George were the killer then why would he have turned left from Dando's house and then travelled down Gowan Avenue? 29 Gowan Avenue is between two-thirds and three-quarters of the way along the avenue from the bottom. Therefore the killer had more than twice as far to travel on foot when heading left than if he had turned right, before he could leave Gowan Avenue. Also, there is a slight curvature on a section of the avenue and as a result of this anyone who is near the junction of Gowan Avenue and Fulham Palace Road is unable to see number 29. A murderer would wish to seek shelter soon after a kill, so he was not on view to any more witnesses.

To get to his flat from 29 Gowan Avenue, if he were the killer, George would have had to go down Gowan Avenue, run along Fulham Palace Road and up Fulham Road until he reached Crookham Road. This is a lengthy route that would leave him exposed to public view for a long period of time over a large distance. Fulham Palace Road is a very busy road. It would also mean that any police cars in the area who may have been alerted could possibly see him on his way to his flat. It is important to note no witnesses reported seeing anyone acting suspiciously along Fulham Road, which happens to be a busy road with many businesses on it, or Crookham Road. If George murdered Dando he must have taken this route back to his flat.

If George was the killer then it would have been sensible to turn right. By turning right he would have left Gowan Avenue far more quickly, move along Munster Road or one of the other streets in the locality (perhaps Rostrevor Road), until he reached Crookham Road and the safety of his flat. This was a shorter route, at almost half the distance than the alternative, and also this route would have meant he encountered fewer people and therefore there would have been fewer witnesses. Fulham Palace Road and Fulham Road have many pedestrians and vehicles passing through. However, the smaller streets in the opposite direction are less busy with little traffic and very few pedestrians.

George is not very fit and so one has to ask why he would take a longer, incredibly risky, route back to his flat if he had just killed a woman. One possible reason why the killer turned left will be discussed in Chapter 10.

Chapter 7:

Further discussion of the evidence

'There is nothing more deceptive than an obvious fact.'[43]

The evidence presented to the court during the trial was contentious. The difficult task the jury faced is reflected in their inability to reach a unanimous verdict, and the thirty-two hours taken to reach a majority verdict. The members of the jury cannot be criticised, they did what was expected of them and were deprived from hearing evidence that was of great importance.

Both the identification issue and the issue of the particle are highly debatable and it is on these pieces of 'evidence' that the prosecution depended. The only supposed evidence which could be 'proven' in court was that provided by Susan Mayes when she said she saw George four and a half hours before the crime. Without this evidence George would almost certainly be a free man today. This is the nature of the prosecution's supposedly compelling evidence.

Why, despite Dr Lloyd's testimony, did the jury believe the particle was from a firearm? Of course, the jury was given the choice of whether they should believe this was firearm discharge residue or whether it could be from another source. The relevance of the forensic 'evidence' is a very controversial issue. The jury was correctly warned that they should consider the evidence for themselves. Despite this, ten of the jury members decided it did suggest George was guilty. The appeal judges stated, *"In our judgement, the jury could safely be left to assess the risk of contamination."* However, the question is, could the jury safely be left to assess the risk of contamination, a concept unfamiliar to them? It is highly unlikely they would fully understand the problems of forensic evidence.

The vast majority of members of the public are not educated in

---

[43] Sherlock Holmes speaking in *The Boscombe Valley Mystery*.

forensic science. It has long been a belief that fingerprints are an infallible means of identifying the perpetrators of criminal activity. Recently there has been speculation that it is possible that two people can indeed have the same fingerprint. Also, over the years people have been convicted of crimes based upon the incorrect identification of prints.

This issue has been highlighted by one case in particular, where the fingerprints found at the scene of a murder were wrongly identified as the prints of a police officer, Detective Constable McKie. This resulted in a review of the reliability of fingerprint evidence. Michael Mansfield, who has represented people who claim their prints were wrongly identified, commented in response to the above case:

"We were constantly being told that to question fingerprints was like questioning two and two and so we didn't. They thought that it was a science. We now discover it is no more exacting than comparing two shades of blue."

Although the identification of fingerprints is not an issue here, this shows forensic science does have weaknesses. If errors can be made in the identification and comparison of fingerprints, is it not possible that errors could have been made in the identification and comparison of a particle which is only *believed* to be firearm discharge residue? Especially when the study of such particles is a relatively new branch of forensic science compared to the use of fingerprints.

Living generations have grown up believing that science equals the truth, and if science indicates a person is guilty then they must be guilty. The assumption science is infallible is a dangerous one. Indeed, science is little more than a means of attempting to gain the solution through experimentation. It falls short of the truth in many cases.

The jury in a trial is composed of twelve, or in the case of Barry George eleven, ordinary people. The concept of the jury system is that a jury is made up of randomly chosen people – who by their nature will have varying degrees of knowledge, experience, education and ability. There is no level of qualification required in order to be asked to do jury service and a vociferously opinionated juror with limited scientific knowledge could decide the accused's fate. It is my contention that, members of the jury should be selected from the members of the population who are able to keep an open mind even when confronted with evidence described as *"compelling"*, when in fact such a description is nothing short of ludicrous.

Some form of assessment should be made of all potential jurors. In some states of the USA jury commissioners are appointed on an annual basis to choose those eligible members of society who are suitable for carrying out the duty.[44] Questionnaires are sent out to ascertain the level of schooling of people who may be selected for jury service. In California multiple-choice tests have been conducted to determine how suitable possible jurors are for the role. The tests aim to determine the degree of suitability through assessing the individual's level of literacy, knowledge of basic legal terminology and procedure, intelligence, memory and perception.[45] A similar system of selection should be adopted in this country. There should certainly be tests which determine the level of scientific knowledge possessed by a potential member of a jury if a case demands knowledge of scientific issues and concepts such as the possibility of contamination.

This is, of course, debatably in conflict with the concept of obtaining a representative cross-section of the population. However, is it not in the interests of justice to have a jury consisting of twelve individuals who are all capable of performing the duty they are expected to perform? If the justice system will not allow for juries to be selected upon their ability to listen and understand both sides of an argument, then in cases where the evidence is as questionable as in the case of Barry George, a jury should not be sworn in at all.

There is a school of thought in this country that in cases such as this one the defendant should have the option of whether he or she would like to be tried by jury or tried by a judge alone. This option should be provided, as a jury is inexperienced in legal matters and often cannot comprehend scientific matters and the limits of circumstantial evidence. In the case of Barry George an experienced judge would have been able to see the circumstantial evidence against him was insufficient to prove guilt. A panel of experienced judges could be used if it is thought that trial by a single judge alone is not a fair system.

---

[44] (Cornish. 1968: 33).
[45] (Cornish. 1968: 34).

Rosalind Wright, director of the Serious Fraud Office, much of whose career has been involved with public prosecution of a wide variety of offences, commented on the George case when discussing her view that trial by a judge alone should be an option available to a defendant:

> *"One trial where a defendant would profitably have elected for trial by judge alone was the Jill Dando case. I think that if the defendant had elected for trial by judge alone, he would have been acquitted. I think the evidence was very weak."*[46]

It cannot be stressed enough the evidence against George was scant and unsatisfactory. To convict a man on such tenuous, circumstantial evidence is to make a mockery of the British justice system. It is saddening to think a man's liberty has been taken away because the evidence as a whole suggested guilt.

And so the inevitable question is why did the jury believe George was guilty when presented with such flimsy evidence? Well, members of the jury, as has already been stated, are ordinary members of society. They are supposed to be representative of the population. How can twelve individuals be a fair representation of around sixty million people? If another jury had been selected, who is to say that they would have taken a completely different view of the evidence and presented a *'Not Guilty'* verdict?

It is a popular view, the celebrity status of Dando affected the chances of true justice being achieved. Henderson believes the celebrity status which Dando held was responsible for this miscarriage of justice. It is for this reason he calls his article *Barry George and the Celebrity Effect: A Miscarriage of Justice in the Making*. Mr Justice Gage had informed the jury they should put personal feelings out of the way but this was appreciably difficult, if not impossible, for all eleven of the members of the jury who decided the fate of George to do. There can be no doubt this was a contributory factor.

The prosecution, presumably the jury, and the judges who decided George's appeal should be dismissed, believed the evidence as a whole was enough to prove George's involvement in the crime. This is not enough to decide the fate of a man. Never should a case

---

[46] *The Guardian*, 16 October 2001.

be decided upon the evidence as a whole when it consists entirely of circumstantial evidence.

For a moment let us relate the evidence as a whole to a picture created through the artistic technique of pointillism. Of course in pointillism the picture as a whole is more important than the individual dots of which the picture is composed. However, in order for the picture as a whole to be correct, the individual dots themselves have to be correct. The same is true of evidence.

If the jury had known the FULL story, including the questioning of George in relation to the murder of Rachel Nickell, and the fact George had photographs of four hundred and nineteen women, none of whom were Dando, and they had kept an open mind when confronted with the prosecution's rhetoric, then the outcome of the trial could have been very different. The jury may have been wrongly influenced into believing George was a monster if such information was included, but on the other hand they could have gained important information which suggested George could not have killed Dando.

The majority of this case is based upon assumptions and possibilities when it should be based upon fact. Why should the prosecution doubt the times given by people like Susan Bicknell and Ramesh Paul, when Paul's time was logged immediately and Bicknell was adamant she was correct, but then not doubt the times given by others who could not even be certain it was George they had seen? Clearly the prosecution believed or dismissed the timings of the witnesses to serve their purposes. It seems the justice system listens only to what it wants to hear, and ignores anything which contradicts its view. This is not justice.

It is important for us to not only read of the arguments which occurred during the original trial, but also the comments made during the two appeal hearings which decided the jury had delivered a correct verdict. If the evidence against George was insufficient to prove guilt then surely the Court of Appeal would have realised this, would it not? And if the Court of Appeal did not realise then surely the Law Lords at the House of Lords, the highest appeal judges in the country, would have realised would they not? It was hoped this would be the case but the alarming truth is, the appeal judges did not study the trial details correctly. This lack of attention to detail is clear when reading the Court of Appeal's judgment, which are available on the Internet. Insufficient care has been made, which has resulted in numerous factual errors, the odd contradictory statement, as well as points that do not make sense.

At one point in the judgment, the judges state Dando was murdered on 26 September 1999 when of course it was 26 April 1999. As they have correctly written the date elsewhere, this can be explained as a simple error although an error still it is. However, other indicators of the appeal judges' inability to accurately record dates can be found in the judgment. This is rather worrying when you consider these are supposedly amongst the great legal minds of the country. They claim George was charged on 29 May 2000 when of course he was really charged on 28 May 2000. They state that the E-fit compiled by Sappleton was released on 30 May 1999, when in reality it was released on 30 April 1999.

It was also said the jury was capable of evaluating the effect the affair between Charlotte de Rosnay and the police officer involved in the murder had. However, the jury was not informed of such a liaison. The affair had been discussed in court before a jury had been sworn in, and was not revealed to the public until the trial had been completed.

The judges are not very good with names either, as they call Terry Normanton *'Belinda'* Normanton.

They make the contradiction that was discussed in Chapter 6.4 regarding the reason why Janet Bolton did not attend an identity parade.

Finally, they display blatant disregard for facts when discussing the alibi issue and in particular the evidence provided by Traffic Cars' worker Ramesh Paul. The appeal judges claimed George entered the offices of London Traffic Cars at 13:15. This time estimate was based upon the evidence provided during the original trial, which consisted of the blurred CCTV footage discussed in Chapter 5 which suggested George must have visited Hafad just before going to the taxi office. The time provided by Paul is the only concrete evidence which was provided to the police or to the court regarding the timing of George's actions on that day. To dispute such a time by saying George entered the offices at 13:15, when it was a proven fact it was at this time he left the office, is to show how inaccurate the reasoning of the appeal judges is. In this case, making a mistake of at least fifteen minutes is a major problem, which hardly inspires confidence in the justice system.

It is most unfortunate that the assessment of the safety of

George's conviction was made by a group of judges who heard the information presented at the trial and misinterpreted it, creating many inaccuracies in their arguments that the guilty verdict was correct. Quite frankly, the appeal judges did not know what they were talking about. If they had taken the time to absorb the evidence itself, which they clearly did not do correctly, as opposed to focussing upon the argument of the prosecution, which was based upon questionable evidence, then perhaps the outcome of the appeal would have been different. The judges stated they had *"no doubt"* that the conviction was valid, but how can they have no doubt about something they did not fully understand?

The judgment from George's appeal hearing at the Court of Appeal, despite their errors, raise a very important point. Once the trial had ended a member of the jury tried to contact George's solicitor; she made many phone calls to voice her concerns. It would seem the juror wished to either change her mind regarding her decision as to whether or not George was guilty, or she wished to highlight something that had occurred during deliberations. It is known that she was very upset that George had been found guilty. She had claimed a *"terrible wrong"* and *"a mistreatment of justice"* had occurred.

The trial was lengthy as were the deliberations. The members of the jury were not allowed to return home and Gage sent them to a hotel over the weekend prior to their verdict being reached. When the members filed into the court, they looked tired, frustrated and inconvenienced, partly because they had not seen their families for some time. Many of the reports of the trial discuss the frustration exhibited on the faces of those who had to decide whether or not George was guilty. Did the large amount of time they had already given to deliberations after a long trial make them more agreeable on the verdict? Did they therefore make a rash decision to agree regarding George's fate so they could return to their families and their own lives? It is a view worthy of serious consideration.

Also regarding the jury is the belief that deliberations had occurred outside of court hours. It is most improper that such discussions should take place. It is improper because jurors may discuss the case with those who are not involved in the trial.

Michael Mansfield told the judges at the Court of Appeal that this *"potential irregularity"* would have been fatal to the safety of George's conviction. However, the appeal judges dismissed this argument, stating such views were speculative. Whatever the cause of this woman's unhappiness, it is clear some error had occurred.

George's attempt to launch another appeal at the House of Lords, in December 2002, was rejected with no reason having been given.

Essentially the whole prosecution amounted to Susan Mayes' testimony that she saw George at between 06:57 and 07:00 near the crime scene, and the supposed firearm residue. The alleged falsification of an alibi assisted the prosecution in their argument. This is hardly the most convincing of cases in British criminal history but the defendant was found guilty. In fact, many people who believe George was probably guilty say he should not have been convicted on such questionable evidence, which was entirely circumstantial.

Chapter 8:

A false confession?

"...I thought if I can't have her no one else can. I went looking for her in the area and waited for her to come home."[47]

In early December 2004 a man approached a national newspaper, claiming that he had information about Barry George that would be a massive news story. Journalists listened to what he had to say and, *'in the interests of public safety'*, printed an exclusive in which it claimed Barry George had, for the first time, finally confessed to murdering Jill Dando on 26 April 1999.

George is reported to have said:

"I sent her [Dando] flowers and got hold of her phone number and I was stalking her. I saw her on TV a couple of days before her death and something in my head told me that I wasn't going to get the chance to take her out on a date. So I thought if I can't have her no one else can. I went looking for her in the area and waited for her to come home."

Furthermore it was claimed that George was planning to have Dando's *Crimewatch UK* co-presenter, Nick Ross, gunned down in an identical manner to Dando's death because it was his opinion that Ross and Dando had been *'having it off.'* George is alleged to have said that because Ross and Dando were having a relationship, George could not take Dando out on a date. George apparently said he has a man from London on the outside, who has agreed to kill for him.

The individual who reported the alleged confession was a man who had just been released from Whitemoor Prison having served a

---

[47] Words spoken by Barry George, according to a national newspaper.

twelve-year sentence for sex crimes. He maintains that George provided the confession in a jail cell. He had no evidence at all to support his claim and, instead of approaching the police, he went straight to a tabloid newspaper to sell his story. It was only after giving his account that the police were informed, by the newspaper concerned. It is easy to question this man's motives; a recently released sex offender is unlikely to gain a good job and it would be foolish to believe the man was not paid for his story. I have been offered money for stories about George, as have his relatives. For someone who has only just been released, and has only a few pounds from the prison service, it can be very tempting to provide a story to the media if one happens to have been in prison with a notorious convicted murderer. This is not necessarily what happened, but it would be foolish to accept this man's word as fact because he had motive to lie and not a shred of evidence to support his claim, a claim contradicted by all of the evidence in this case, as will be shown.

During Michael Stone's recent unsuccessful appeal against his murder conviction, Stone's barrister told the Court of Appeal that, *"such confessions [cell confessions] are easily concocted and difficult to disprove."* This is very true and it is not the first time that Barry George has been alleged to confess to the murder.

In 2002 a tape recording of a conversation between Barry George and an armed robber was smuggled out of Whitemoor Prison and was passed on to a national newspaper. In the recording George was heard to say, in response to the question *"Why did the police arrest you in the first place, do you think?"*, *"Why? Because I, I was the person who committed the murder"*, before immediately saying he had an alibi and asking his cell mates how he could possibly have been involved when witnesses showed he could not have been responsible.

The confession was allegedly recorded accidentally. The man who owned the tape recorder plays the piano and he was recording himself playing, he claims, when George entered his cell and he simply left the tape running and was lucky in that he happened to capture the confession during the four minute conversation. There are problems with this explanation for the recording because there are sections where the tape cuts out part of the conversation, at points in the conversation where it is clear George is arguing his innocence. This is strange if the recording was merely accidental and the tape was continually running because sections of the conversation would not be cut out if the tape was constantly running throughout.

The Metropolitan Police studied the tape, as did the prosecution in his case, and neither were convinced of its authenticity. Critics of the tape have suggested that the tape had been edited, with one *'I'* and a short pause having been put in to replace words such as *'they thought.'* The newspaper involved has since spoken of its desire to repair the damage they have caused to George's campaign. They even informed me that they wished to launch a campaign for George's freedom, but only if I provided them with a vast amount of exclusive information about George. I declined their offer but this did not stop them attempting to gain information from George himself, falsely claiming I had suggested the idea to them

As such it is clear that cell confessions are indeed easy to concoct and many members of the public would find it difficult to accept a convicted murderer's claim, that a confession never took place, could be genuine. It is also clear to me that many journalists play games in an attempt to gain exclusive information. Often they will tell a person that they need more and more information otherwise a story cannot be featured in their paper. This is an incentive for anyone to exaggerate stories because some journalists say that otherwise they will not get paid.

In the recent confession, Barry George is alleged to have said that he decided to kill Jill Dando only two days before her murder, after seeing her on the television. Dando was not on television two days before her murder. She was on the night before her murder, and several days before her death, but not two days before. I find it difficult to believe anyone could plan Dando's murder in only two days, or even two weeks, let alone someone with Barry George's limited abilities. Everyone involved in the case is in agreement that the murder took considerable planning. It was a shooting described as "near perfect" at trial and it appears to have been executed with almost military precision.

If indeed Barry George did stalk Jill Dando, for which there is no evidence of him having done so, then surely he would know that she very rarely went to Gowan Avenue. He would have known that Dando no longer lived on Gowan Avenue and visited the house on an infrequent basis. No one could realistically have been able to anticipate Dando would be on Gowan Avenue that day. As such

George would have been foolish to wait around the former home of the presenter on the off chance she would return. When she did visit Gowan Avenue, Dando was usually accompanied by Farthing and so it would have been foolish to kill her at this location. If he had stalked the presenter he would have found more suitable locations to kill Dando, such as outside the home she shared with Alan Farthing, which is where she was almost every day, as George must have known if he followed her movements. Whoever killed Dando specifically wanted her to be shot outside her former home because there were so many other, easier, ways and more suitable locations to murder her.

When studying the evidence there is nothing to show that the gunman loitered around 29 Gowan Avenue. Various sightings were reported but these were certainly not of the same man. The only two definite sightings of the killer were made after the shooting. George could not have predicted his alleged victim's movements, in such a way to be able to arrive at exactly the same time as she did in only two days. During the two days concerned much of George's time had been taken up by visiting his mother, visiting the local shops and having his electrics sorted. During the early hours of 26 April (the day Dando was shot dead) George had called an emergency electrician because he was having problems with the electrics in his flat. Would he want to be kept at home, with an electrician, if he needed to wait around, looking for Jill Dando so that he could kill her on that day? Surely he would not want crucial time being taken up.

Also, if George stalked Dando and had any form of exaggerated interest in her, as one would expect if he stalked her and sent her flowers, then he would have been aware that Dando was engaged to marry Alan Farthing. The couple had announced their engagement on 31 January 1999. Therefore Barry would have known that if Dando was in a sexual relationship with anyone it would have been Farthing and not Nick Ross, therefore he would surely have a grievance against Farthing. The prosecution at his trial maintained that George was obsessed with Dando and collected newspaper articles about her, even though only eight articles were present in his flat amongst over eight hundred newspapers. Consequently George must have known Dando was planning to marry if he was obsessed. Even if he was not aware of the relationship between Farthing and Dando at the time of the murder, he must have been by the time of his trial because Farthing gave evidence discussing how they had discussed the wedding on the morning of the shooting. Why would George wait until late 2004 to decide to have Nick Ross killed when, according to this confession, he knew Ross and Dando were *'having it off'* in 1999 and was angry with Ross for preventing him from being able to take Dando out? Why wait until five years after killing Dando before getting revenge on Ross if indeed this confession is true?

The 'confession' cited above states that George killed when he realised he would not be able to take Dando out after seeing her on television two days before her murder. It is inconceivable to believe that a man even of George's intelligence could only realise that he could not take Dando out only two days before her death if he had known for nearly three months that she was intending to marry another man. What could possibly make Barry George think he had no chance of taking Jill Dando out on a date two days before her death that he did not already know?

The 'confession' may appear to be damning but I know one man certainly has confessed to this murder, and a second man who sent me what I interpret to be a veiled confession although he has the tendency to attract attention to himself, and Barry George is neither of these individuals.

A man I cannot name for legal reasons made one of the confessions in April 2004. In December the previous year he had written to the Justice for Barry campaign stating:

'Nobody seems to know what happened to the gun that was used on Jill Dando, do they? I believe I know the answer, but the police don't seem the slightest bit interested, probably because the person who supplied it is the daughter of a retired police officer. You might like to give me a ring ...'

The man had served time on remand for stalking a woman (he denies this, claiming that stalking is a *'phenomenon invented by the media'*) and making threats to slit her throat *'in broad daylight'* before being acquitted, although he has since informed me that *'if this whore had succeeded in destroying my life I would indeed have slit her worthless throat.'* He has also written a poem about the Jill Dando murder and a second poem saying how killing gives him pleasure.

It was suggested, by the Justice for Barry campaign, that the man should speak to a solicitor, which he did in April 2004. Whilst at a London solicitor's he spoke with two senior detectives from the Metropolitan Police, one of which is believed to have been Detective Superintendent Hamish Campbell. During the conversation he claimed he had been supplied with the murder weapon and had been asked to perform the execution of Jill Dando. Apparently he has a terminal illness and wanted to clear his conscience before he died, but the detectives refused to take him seriously, claiming his account of events was inconsistent with the facts. The detectives dismissed him as being mentally ill; he was an attention seeker, they believed.

The man continues to claim he was the person who murdered Dando whilst Barry George continues to deny having done so. George maintains he has never confessed because he has nothing to confess to.

The alleged confession by Barry George is incredibly questionable for the simple reason that it is inconsistent with the facts involved in the case. It seems to have been created by someone who did not know that Dando was engaged and who did not realise just how much planning was needed to perform the crime. Arguing against this confession does not prove that George did not kill Jill Dando but this 'confession' does not prove that George is a murderer. Even those who believe George killed Dando remain unconvinced by this allegation, particularly the part relating to planning Nick Ross's murder because George simply does not have any motive to kill Ross. Since his conviction George has become fully aware that Dando and Ross were only colleagues. They were not even friends. George became fully aware of this during his trial. This allegation seems to have been yet another example of a confession that is not correct. As one would expect, the police did interview George in prison about the claims, but investigations seem to have drawn to a close with no evidence having been discovered to suggest that there was any truth in the allegations. Nick Ross also does not seem too concerned by the allegations. Quite simply it does not appear to have been taken seriously by anyone other than the newspaper who paid for the story.

George denies having made any form of confession and denies having known the ex-convict who made the allegation. Although the informant was not named in the media, George knew who made the allegation because the police questioned George in relation to the alleged confession. I have spoken to a prisoner who served with George in Whitemoor Prison and he has informed me that George is unlikely to discuss his case with anyone and he does not trust other inmates at all, or confide in them. George's family have repeatedly warned him that he should not speak to other prisoners about his case because of the previous false confession and the knowledge that the press are eager to print anything about him, providing an excellent means for any fellow prisoners to earn some money. Due to his paranoia George is unlikely to discuss anything relating to Jill Dando's murder with anyone. He rarely discusses his case with family and friends. The inmate I spoke to also informed me that George can be manipulated into saying almost anything if he is asked a question in a certain way and his words can easily be twisted out of context. This is the reason why, after all, George never testified at trial.

There was one interesting point that arose from the story in the newspaper: the ex-convict stated that George was incredibly untidy, his cell was littered with newspapers, he could not take care of himself and that he needed supervision when carrying out even the simplest of tasks. This is very consistent with those who knew George before his conviction and those who have served with him in prison. George carries out tailoring work at Whitemoor Prison and if he cannot perform fairly simple tasks, such as cutting materials, then how could he possibly perform a cold, calculated murder, destroy all of the evidence and evade capture for over a year?

Chapter 9:

Reason to doubt?

"Looking at the evidence, as a whole, we have no doubt as to the correctness of the conviction."[48]

When the House of Lords rejected Barry George's legal challenge against his conviction in December 2002, his only remaining chance of having his conviction quashed on legal grounds pertaining to evidence presented at trial, was exhausted. George's only realistic hope of now walking free is if the Court of Appeal overturns his conviction upon considering new evidence rather than arguing against the legality of prosecution's evidence used at trial, as had his previous Court of Appeal hearing.

The Court of Appeal is not a court of review and so it cannot study evidence that was put before a jury, unless the jury got their verdict *'manifestly wrong.'* In July 2002 the Court ruled that there was no evidence to suggest the jury at George's trial had made a huge error and that they were entitled to reach the guilty verdict, based on the evidence presented to them. A conviction cannot be overturned simply because there is a lack of evidence pointing to guilt, because the jury had been told they could only find George guilty if they believed, beyond reasonable doubt, that he was Dando's killer. For some reason, of course, they did believe he was guilty beyond reasonable doubt. As far as appeal judges are concerned it is irrelevant whether the jury were right. The Court is not interested in guilt or innocence, because it is often incredibly difficult to actually prove someone's innocence. Instead it is concerned about whether a conviction is *'safe'* or *'unsafe'*.

What is an unsafe conviction? In the case of *R. v CCRC ex parte Pearson (2000)* it was said that a conviction will be considered unsafe if, *'on consideration of all the facts and circumstances*

---

[48] The Court of Appeal judges dismissing George's appeal in July 2002

before it, the Court entertains real doubts whether the appellant was guilty of the offence of which he has been convicted.'

In order for George's conviction to be quashed, fresh, compelling evidence, which undermines the prosecution's argument and introduces a *'lurking doubt'* is required. The Court can only examine fresh evidence if it is capable of belief, if it could lead to a successful appeal, if it would have been admissible at trial (if it had been available at the time of the trial) and if there is sufficient reason to explain why the evidence was not presented at trial. A conviction will be quashed if the three appeal judges are in agreement that the new evidence, if it had been presented to the jury at trial, might have resulted in them reaching a different verdict.

Barry George has consented to me including some of the new evidence that is being studied by the Criminal Cases Review Commission, the organisation which studies cases of suspected miscarriages of justice and decides whether there are sufficient grounds for a case to be referred to the Court of Appeal. Judge for yourself whether or not it introduces real doubts as to the correctness of the verdict.

As stated in previous chapters, blurred CCTV footage of Stevenage Road, close to Hafad, allegedly showed a figure of a man, in a yellow top of some sort, walking towards the disability advice centre at 12:44. The prosecution used this to form part of their argument that George had visited Hafad after 12:45, leaving his whereabouts at the time of the murder unaccounted for. New evidence seems to indicate that the time of the CCTV footage might have been wrong, by one hour. Instead of the footage having captured a person in yellow at 12:44, the Criminal Cases Review Commission are being asked to study evidence showing the time was in fact 11:44. Apparently an *'irregularity'* occurred on the Saturday before Dando's murder, whilst Fulham Football Club were playing at home. The CCTV camera which recorded the image of the figure in yellow, was positioned at the football stadium. If it was George walking along Stevenage Road, and the time was 11:44, then he is certainly not Dando's killer because he could not have killed Dando at 11:30, or slightly after, and travelled a number of miles to get changed and washed. It would be physically impossible in the time available. In my opinion it is unlikely the figure in yellow was that of Barry George heading towards Hafad because George was wearing a maroon jacket over a yellow shirt when he entered the centre. The CCTV footage was such a tiny issue at trial that showing the time was wrong will not call into question the safety of the conviction. It was not the only evidence which allegedly destroyed George's alibi. Julia Moorhouse had placed George near Hafad at around 12:30, as had the mobile telephone call George made at 12:32. Some members of staff argued George had arrived at Hafad after 12:30. Without undermining all of these individual pieces of evidence, in a highly compelling manner, the argument George arrived at the centre after 12:45 cannot be disproved. Destroying one component of an argument does not destroy the argument. Without proof that the figure was George and that the time was 11:44 this evidence will not cast any doubt upon the safety of the conviction

In Chapter 6 it was mentioned that, since George's conviction, four witnesses had provided statements in which it was said armed officers had been present in Barry George's flat on the day that the Cecil Gee jacket, in which the controversial particle of alleged Firearms Discharge Residue was later found, was taken away for examination. This does, if the witnesses were correct, introduce yet another reason to doubt the integrity of the particle, as was discussed in Chapter 6. When taking into account all of the innocent explanations that have been put forward for the particle having found its way into the inside pocket of George's Cecil Gee jacket, it can no longer be said that the particle was compelling forensic proof of George's guilt. The presence of armed officers, if armed officers were present, which the police deny, does play a role in undermining one of the prosecution's arguments at trial. However, at trial Mr Justice Gage ruled that the particle was not allowed to be considered evidence in its own right and therefore even if it was completely undermined the prosecution still had other evidence to use against George. The case against him relied more upon eyewitness testimony rather than forensic science and therefore undermining the forensic evidence does not undermine the prosecution. The issue of contamination had been fully explored at trial, perhaps in too much detail, and yet the jury presumably believed it had not taken place. Therefore introducing another way in which contamination might have taken place, whilst of interest, would not necessarily have resulted in the jury reaching a different verdict.

The CCRC are being asked to study new evidence relating to discussions between the key prosecution witness Susan Mayes, Charlotte de Rosnay and Stella de Rosnay, who shared a lift home following the identity parade where Mayes identified George. It is clear to me that following the drive home both of the de Rosnays became remarkably confident that they had seen Barry George when previously nether had been sure and Charlotte did not at all believe she had seen George. However, this issue was discussed at the Court of Appeal in July 2002 where the judges ruled that:

"The jury was able to assess the effect that the conversation with Susan Mayes must have had upon them and they could make full allowance for it and the other shortcomings in their evidence."

The Court of Appeal respects the decision of a jury unless they make some massive error. It makes the assumption that juries are capable of determining whether a witness is lying and that they can determine how reliable a witness is by listening to a witness's testimony. Therefore it is difficult to understand why the Court should reconsider its position on this issue, even if it is shown that the three women had discussed their experience on the parade at length. Dismissing the argument in 2002, the judges said, *"Before either witness had spoken to Susan Mayes each had independently and without prompting indicated an interest in or preference for No. 2 [Barry George]."* This is not actually true; Charlotte de Rosnay had said, *"No I don't think so"* when asked if the man she had seen was on the video. Nonetheless, the key eyewitness in George's case was Susan Mayes and any conversation that had taken place between Mayes and the other two witnesses would not have affected her evidence because she had already positively identified Barry George as the man she had seen four and a half hours before Dando's murder. This is not fresh evidence; the jury at George's trial were fully aware of it and so it is unlikely that it can be examined yet again by the Court of Appeal, unless concrete evidence proving Susan Mayes had, without realising the adverse effect of any conversation upon George's right to a fair trial, told the other two women that she had been *"correct"* in her identification and that she had identified the second man in the line up (George), is brought to light.

New evidence suggests that members of the jury at George's trial had a conversation with journalists in the lobby of the hotel they stayed at whilst deliberating. As most journalists had been portraying George in a negative light before the trial it is argued that any conversation could have had an impact upon the jury's verdict. However, Mr Justice Gage had told the members of the jury to disregard anything they had heard or read and so, even if journalists did discuss views about George's guilt, they had been warned that they should not believe what they heard. Whilst it could have had an affect upon the verdict they reached, is this new evidence strong enough to question the safety of the conviction? Could the alleged discussions with journalists result in the members of the jury getting their verdict manifestly wrong? The Court of Appeal did, in July 2002, consider allegations that *'unauthorised conversations'* had taken place with the jurors before the opening speeches were made. They dismissed the claims, commenting that they did not feel it was necessary or helpful to consider them further.

Whilst the police did consider the possibility that Richard Hughes' wife, who lived at 31 Gowan Avenue, could have been the intended victim of the shooting on 26 April 1999 they did not investigate the possibility that the gunman could have made a case of mistaken identity by accidentally killing Jill Dando when in reality he intended to murder one of her relatives. On the day of her cousin's murder, Judith Dando returned to Britain from France, where she had been living for a number of years. The cousins had spoken to one another a week or so before the tragic day, when Jill Dando had suggested that Judith could stay overnight at 29 Gowan Avenue, after arriving by ferry at Dover, rather than face the tiresome journey of driving to Bristol. Judith had a spare set of keys to the house, and she knew the code for the burglar alarm, and therefore there was no problem with her using the house. Judith Dando said that she might very well stay at Gowan Avenue, but in the end she decided to drive straight home instead. Whilst very few knew that Dando was to visit 29 Gowan Avenue, how many could have known that her cousin Judith might have visited? Judith Dando had been a captain in the British Army and, of course, Britain was at war with Serbia in April 1999.

Although Judith was still at Calais at 11:30 it has been suggested, but does not seem to have been investigated by the police, that the intended victim of the fatal shooting outside 29 Gowan Avenue could have been Judith *not* Jill Dando. Why would someone want to kill Judith Dando? There seems less reason why they would want to harm her, than the television presenter, but it is something that should at least be considered because some have claimed that the police were on a wild goose chase hunting those who wanted Jill Dando to be killed, when really they should have been looking for those who had a grudge against her cousin, a woman who was never in the media spotlight and who, because she had lived overseas, could not possibly have been known of by the likes of Barry George. The CCRC have been asked to consider this possibility whilst reviewing George's case.

During the police investigation a man, who shall be referred to as Mr V, was interviewed. He emerged as a suspect because a member of the public telephoned the *Daily Mirror* newspaper and informed journalists that he was Dando's killer. In total he has been questioned three times in connection with the murder, the most recent bout of questioning having taken place in the winter of 2004. Mr V has been convicted of offences relating to firearms and apparently knew where Jill Dando lived. He also owned a Land Rover in 1999, although there is no evidence to prove Dando's killer drove such a vehicle. The Criminal Cases Review Commission is currently investigating Mr V, a fact I mentioned in the previous edition of this book.

The police remain adamant that Mr V was not connected with killing Dando; he was working at a school in south London, they claim. Although I do not believe he was involved in the shooting, since he read *The Case of Barry George* he has been sending me large numbers of abusive e-mails, attracting attention to himself and making comments that try to imply that he was Dando's killer. He has informed me that some of my theories relating to Jill Dando's killer are indeed facts and maintains there is a connection between M95 and the shooting (*'I need to know who knows the link between J.D. and M95', 'How does M95 stand you in?'*). 'Mr V' knows what M95 is and claims that anyone with *'half a brain'* should know what it means.

One of his messages from August 2004 shows his intimidating nature:

'Unsure of the ground MR L. and so you should be, don't try to piss with the big dogs, so now we are both in the dark, I am giving you for your sake a chance to contact me you know how, you have my number, by 9.00pm tonight 23 8 2004, as you say its up to you, this is in your interest, even text me to say not on, awaiting or is J.D. too hot for you'

Another e-mail he sent states:

'I am sure you are concerned about my interests, if so you would not have commented like you have done in your work, for all to read, a bad move I think. DON'T YOU.'

Mr V is not considered by most to be a serious suspect. It is highly unlikely that Mr V was involved in Dando's murder, although he has a strange habit of drawing attention to himself. He has made contact with a number of people involved in the case to warn them not to discuss him whilst simultaneously trying to suggest he knows something about the crime and to tell them that the situation is becoming increasingly serious. Late last year a man claiming to be Mr V made threatening telephone calls to one of George's relatives although he denies he was responsible for the calls. He is, nonetheless, being investigated and his intimidating e-mails to myself are being studied because some do appear to be veiled confessions, although they might be the meaningless writings of an attention seeker.

Even if the CCRC decides it is possible he could have been Dando's killer, it will probably not help George at all. In 2004 Sion Jenkins was released from prison, on bail, after the Court of Appeal ordered a retrial. Although the Court had found his conviction unsafe it had dismissed the ground for appeal relating to another suspect who, Jenkins' legal team had argued, was Billy Jo Jenkins' real killer. The claims that the schizophrenic tramp arrested near the scene of the crime was responsible for the murder were, it was ruled, speculative and there was no evidence to substantiate it. It is unlikely that there is any credible evidence linking Mr V to Dando's murder.

Does this new evidence introduce real doubts as to the safety of Barry George's conviction? In my mind the answer, sadly, is no. Due to the high-profile nature of this case, with George being considered one of the most evil killers in a British prison – probably due to the status of his victim rather than his alleged crime because more violent murders occur on a regular basis but the alleged culprits are very rarely viewed with such notoriety – the Court of Appeal will need to take extra care if it believes George should be released. The evidence calling for his release would need to be very strong for the appeal judges to say that they believe there is enough doubt to free him, because there is still immense public hatred towards the prisoner and there is not likely to be a judge in the land (let alone three) who would want to take responsibility for allowing a man perceived to be highly dangerous to leave prison unless they could be sure the release would be worth the public criticism that would inevitably follow. This is probably the main reason why the Court did not quash George's conviction in July 2002. To release a hate figure would result in people questioning the effectiveness of the Court of Appeal regardless of whether George is innocent or not, and therefore strong evidence is needed, far stronger than that outlined above in my opinion.

If George is innocent, as I believe he is, then the only evidence that will lead to his conviction being quashed is that which undermines the key prosecution eyewitness, Susan Mayes; evidence proving Barry George's alibi; or evidence revealing the true identity of the killer.

In July 2002 the three judges at the Court of Appeal said that without Susan Mayes' positive identification of Barry George four and a half hours before Jill Dando's murder, it is *'probable'* that there would not have been a prosecution against George; he would not have stood trial without Susan Mayes' evidence. To undermine Mayes' evidence, therefore, in a compelling manner, could call into question the safety of the conviction. Susan Mayes was the key to George's conviction because she alone placed him at the scene of the crime. If it is shown, convincingly, that she was mistaken, then the key prosecution argument, that George was loitering outside Dando's home four and a half hours before her murder, and therefore he must have killed her, is fundamentally flawed. The problem is that even if she was mistaken, Mayes presumably genuinely believed that she saw George, even if the police affected her confidence by telling her she had picked out the right man, and she positively identified him, even though it is open to debate whether she was correct or not. Whilst it would not be impossible for Mayes to realise she might have made an error, it would be difficult to show that she did make a mistake. The jury listened to her evidence and accepted it, even though it is, in my opinion, totally shocking that they condemned a man to life imprisonment on the basis of a sighting lasting only six seconds. There are, however, other ways that the conviction could be undermined.

Finding the true culprit for the crime would ultimately prove George's innocence because it was a lone gunman who perpetrated this crime. However, finding the identity of Jill Dando's murderer would be a monumentally difficult task. If the police were unable to discover the identity, when spending £2 million and more than one year on their investigation, then there is not much hope of George's supporters uncovering the name of the gunman let alone sufficient evidence to prove his guilt.

I believe George's best hope of gaining his freedom is finding new evidence to substantiate his alibi. To remind you, Susan Bicknell claimed George had been with her, at Hafad, at 11:50 and George maintained he had been at the advice centre for some time before speaking with Bicknell. All that would be required to allow his release from prison would be a witness or some material evidence showing his whereabouts between 11:00 and 12:00 on the morning of 26 April 1999 because it was common ground at trial that if his movements could be innocently explained for any time during this hour, then he had to be innocent because of the distances involved, as was discussed in Chapter 6. After six years have elapsed it is not very likely that a new witness could come forward and be considered to be credible because of the passage of time, though the possibility does still remain. In April and May 2000, when George was being investigated, the police concentrated on speaking to members of staff at Hafad. They did not speak to any of the clients who had been present on 26 April 1999 even though, due to George having caused a scene because he was agitated and needed his problems resolving, somebody might have recalled his presence and be able to provide a rough estimate as to the time of his presence.

The fact appointments were needed at Hafad was one reason why George became a suspect, because he drew attention to himself for not having booked an appointment, but the appointment book could play a role in showing at what time he was present at the advice centre, if it still exists. Before he left Hafad, George had an appointment written in the book for the following day. If it could be determined when then appointments in that book were made then it could help show what time George's appointment was made. For example, if a Mr Smith booked an appointment before Barry George, at say 10:30, and a Mrs Jones booked an appointment after George, at 12:00, this would mean George was present at the centre at some point between 10:30 and 12:00. Disability advice centres, like doctor's surgeries, receive most appointment bookings by telephone and so itemised phone records would show when people booked an appointment, if this information was made available. The only problem is determining the order in which appointments were written, but this might one day be possible.

I am of the opinion that the small section of footage shown at George's trial, which showed a figure in yellow walking in the direction of Hafad at 12:44, who could possibly have been George but who in reality could have been anyone, was a red herring. However, as the CCTV camera was in a position that captured anyone walking along Stevenage Road towards the disability centre, there is a real chance that George was caught on camera as he walked to, and possibly when he left, Hafad on 26 April 1999. At the time of George's trial, in 2001, nothing could be done to enhance the quality of the footage, which was too poor to enable identification of anyone in the footage. However, technological advances are taking place on a regular basis, as evidenced by the recent breakthrough in the hunt for Damilola Taylor's killers. At the time of Damilola's murder in November 2000, and the trial of four youths who were acquitted in 2002, the CCTV footage showing a number of youths, suspected of being his killers, was too poor to allow identification. In January 2005 enhancements of the imagery, in addition to other evidence, enabled detectives to charge a man and two youths with murder.

Enhancement of the footage from 26 April 1999 could allow the identification of the figure in yellow and anyone else who happened to be caught on camera. According to Susan Bicknell, George was with her at Hafad at 11:50. If the footage could be enhanced sufficiently, and the section of the footage prior to 11:50 was examined closely, then it is very likely that if Bicknell was correct, George would be visible on the footage, if he walked along Stevenage Road. At George's trial Orlando Pownall QC claimed there were only two men on the footage heading in the direction of

Hafad. One was at 10:30 and the other at 12:44. The 12:44 figure, Pownall said, was probably George because he had been wearing a yellow shirt, even though he entered Hafad he had been wearing a jacket over the shirt. Perhaps the prosecution had concentrated too much on the 12:44 figure without considering the possibility that George might have been captured on camera at 10:30. Enhancement of the footage could also show an approximate time George left the centre, if he walked along Stevenage Road. Therefore the CCTV footage could either confirm or destroy George's alibi. It has the potential to prove his innocence, or substantiate the claim he is guilty. In the interests of justice it is imperative that this footage be enhanced.

There are several high-profile cases of miscarriages of justice where it has taken decades for the evidence required to introduce real doubts to be obtained, such as the case of Robert Brown who spent twenty five years in prison for a murder he did not commit and that of George Kelly who was hanged in 1950 only for it to be realised more than a half a century later that a corrupt police officer had suppressed a confession made by the real killer. It is my belief that somewhere there is a witness or a piece of material evidence that holds the key to George's freedom. It is just a matter of finding the evidence before it is too late.

Chapter 10:

The man who murdered Jill Dando

'The human mind is not yet like a road map where the contours have been plotted and printed in detail.' [49]

If (the word "if" is used in want of another word) George is innocent, then it leaves us with the question of who did carry out the crime on 26 April 1999 at 29 Gowan Avenue? It is not the purpose of this book to try and discover the identity of the true killer. However, some time should be spent in determining the characteristics that the killer possessed. After all, is it not true to say the best way to prove a person's innocence is to find the person who really is guilty?

By the time George was convicted of murdering Jill Dando, in July 2001, there were still hundreds of names of people in HOLMES who had not been spoken to or who had not been fully investigated yet, for one reason or another, were considered to be suspects. Detectives involved in the investigation have always maintained that the case against Barry George was compelling, despite the poor nature of the evidence. There was no one more likely to have carried out this cool, calculated, cold-blooded murder, they argue, than the almost always agitated Barry George. As in most murder investigations the police reached this conclusion without visiting all of the suspects. Could there be a more compelling suspect for this *"near perfect"* act of execution than the disorganised man with learning difficulties and significant brain damage that is Barry George?

It has been mentioned in an earlier chapter of this book that the police officers investigating the murder of Jill Dando used the services of a psychological profiler in order to gain an insight into the personality of the person responsible for the crime.

---

[49] (Britton. 2001: 120).

Psychological profiling, which is also known as offender profiling, is not an exact science and so psychologists who use this method of criminal detection inevitably make mistakes. Psychological profiling is in its infancy – indeed, this technique was only introduced in this country in 1983. The police placed too much of an emphasis upon the opinion that the gunman who ended Dando's life was a loner who had an obsession with firearms and the victim. It is interesting that the police can base much of their reasoning upon the opinion of a psychologist, when the human mind is a complex machine which makes every person's thoughts, motivations and actions, completely unique.

Having assessed the evidence, it is likely that the killer may well have been a loner who had an obsession with firearms and Dando. It is possible to learn more about his personality from the evidence which was left at 29 Gowan Avenue, and from the information provided by those people the prosecution call witnesses.

It is hoped that you, the reader, will be able to follow the arguments regarding the characteristics of the personality of the true criminal responsible for Dando's death. These aspects of the murderer will be shown to be dissimilar to the characteristics of the man who is currently serving the sentence for the crime.

We can use the statements of two of the people who made sightings of a man on and around Gowan Avenue around the time of the murder. We can use these statements to ascertain what the gunman may have looked like. As has been shown, only a few of the statements provided by 'witnesses' relate to the incident that took place at 29 Gowan Avenue. The two statements which are most likely to relate to the killer and have any bearing upon this case were the statements provided by Dando's neighbours, Richard Hughes (sighting J) and Geoffrey Upfill-Brown (sighting K). Both of these witnesses spoke to the police soon after the murder and neither conversed with other witnesses who could have affected their descriptions.

Richard Hughes reported seeing a man who was *"white in colour, with thick set broad shoulders, thick black hair, pushed back, collar length, mid to late 30s, he was not wearing any glasses."*[50] An earlier statement told how the man was wearing a darkish wax/Barbour style jacket and he looked like the comedian Bob Mills, who has a passing resemblance to Barry George but then so many people do. The

---

[50] From Hughes' statement, made on 29 April 1999.

convicted murderer David Bieber, jailed for life in December 2004 for shooting Leeds policeman Ian Broadhurst, strongly resembles both Barry George and Bob Mills. The fact Bieber manufactured ammunition, owned a 9mm handgun and had extensive knowledge of firearms, in addition to his alleged involvement in the shooting of someone outside their home in the USA, has led some people to speculate that Bieber was responsible for causing Dando's death, but there is no evidence to substantiate this far-fetched claim.

The gunman appeared to be respectable, Hughes thought, whereas no one who has ever met George could claim he looks respectable. Hughes later stated that the man was taller than 5'7. Geoffrey Upfill-Brown stated that the man was white, between 30 and 40 years old, around 5'10 and of medium build, with a mop of black hair which may have been a wig. The man had a sallow complexion and was clean-shaven. He was wearing very dark, baggy clothing. Therefore, we have a reasonably good account of some of the characteristics of the gunman's appearance: he was between 5'7, but could have been as tall as 6'0, he was aged in his late thirties and possibly of medium build, but he could have been slimly built (the clothing worn made build difficult to ascertain). As the murderer may have been wearing a wig, although only Upfill-Brown suggested this was possibly the case, the man's hair colour could not be determined with certainty. This description could be applied to many people, indicating that the evidence provided by eyewitnesses was relatively poor..

If the assailant wore a wig then we can infer three things. Firstly, the gunman's hair was no longer than the length of the wig (this is not particularly helpful). Secondly, the murderer's hair was of a different style and possibly a different colour to the thick black wig. Finally, the killer wished to disguise himself to prevent recognition, either at the crime scene at the time of the murder or at some later stage.

As discussed in Chapter 3, it is believed the perpetrator of the crime in question was left-handed or ambidextrous. If this were the case, this factor would eliminate around ninety percent of the population, as typically eight to twelve percent of people are left-handed. Therefore four to six percent of the population are left handed males. Even fewer are ambidextrous. Taking this into account along with age, height, build and other aspects of appearance, the proportion of the population that matches the physical characteristics of Dando's murderer is greatly reduced although we are still left with a large number of people who could have been responsible. Let us now consider other pieces of information that can be used to further reduce the number of people who could possibly have been responsible for the crime.

There can be no disputing the fact the killer escaped on foot down Gowan Avenue. However, it is doubtful that a man who had gone to such lengths to execute a well planned and organised murder would risk the possibility of arrest by running down Fulham Palace Road. This road is far busier with pedestrians and vehicles than the alternative routes the gunman could have used to make his escape. Yet he turned left. Therefore there can be little disputing the view that Dando's killer either lived near Fulham Palace Road or had a vehicle located near there. There is no evidence to suggest the murderer travelled far on foot. It was merely an assumption that he did so. Even a man who is unintelligent would not risk jeopardising his liberty by exposing himself to the public for more time than was absolutely necessary. It would be foolish for a man who had committed such a daring crime, a man who had gone to great lengths to avoid being seen whilst carrying out the execution, to run the risk of being seen leaving the crime scene covered in blood.

Of course, if the gunman used a getaway car he would not have risked leaving it near the crime scene as he could be linked to it and possibly identified as a result. The vehicle would have been nearby at a location where it was out of sight from 29 Gowan Avenue but not so far away that he could not reach it quickly; when carrying out a crime time is an important issue. The vehicle could have been located on a side street somewhere, probably near Bishops Park. As is shown in the appendix, vehicles whose movements appeared to be suspicious, and which were never traced, left the Fulham Palace Road area at around this time. It must be remembered George did not drive.

The criminal acted swiftly whilst carrying out the kill, leaving only three clues; the bullet, the cartridge and, (possibly) the fibre on Dando's raincoat. He had insufficient time to recover the first two clues, and the third was microscopic. As only these clues were left it suggests he had planned the operation to a high level because potentially a large amount of evidence could have been left at the crime scene when it is considered that the gunman was as close as he possibly could be to his victim. To commit a violent murder in daylight, whilst there are potentially large numbers of people in the area, requires careful planning and organisation, or sheer luck. It is more likely the crime was planned like a military operation, rather than it having been performed by someone with good fortune on his side, and therefore a degree of intelligence must have been possessed.

It is probable the killer had a criminal record. The police believed the murderer would have a history of sexual offences although little emphasis was placed on this until George's conviction for attempted rape had been discovered. Although it is possible the killer may have had a history of sexual offences, it is not certainly the case. People who have a history of sexual offences kill as a means of gaining sexual pleasure. However, this was not a sexual attack and there are no indications, other than that the victim was female, that the gunman was spurred by any sexual motive.

In reality, the murderer will almost certainly have had a history of violent behaviour, even if he had not been in trouble with the police. Someone who sees death for the first time, particularly a vicious and bloody death, cannot leave the scene without feeling some emotion. According to Richard Hughes who witnessed the killer leaving the scene of the crime, the killer was able to walk *"very calmly away"* after carrying out a vicious murder. He also had the courage, if courage is the right word, to kill a woman in broad daylight when anyone could happen to walk past. Therefore the killer probably had a history of violent crime and/or an ability to remove all human emotion before ending the life of someone without panicking. He must have been able to temporarily block out human emotion.

Dando's killer must have prevented access *'and passage to remorse'*, to quote from *Macbeth*. This could only be achieved through experience or utter contempt for the victim. George had neither experience of nor contempt for Dando.

The gunman hated his victim for one reason or another, and he could not contain his anger. He seemingly wished to humiliate Dando and end her life in an act of revenge.

The gunman had an impressive knowledge of firearms; a knowledge which was far superior to that of the average gun fanatic. He must have understood a hard contact kill would result in a reduced noise level when the bullet was fired. The gunman must also have been aware of the benefits of using an adapted weapon. He had to have been aware of the purpose of the marks on the cartridge; he would have made them himself or specifically bought a cartridge with the marks already on it. Even if he did not do the alterations himself he needed to know the workings of the black market. This was a sophisticated weapon; it was certainly not readily available to your average criminal. It would seem the killer did not buy the gun from any criminal network in Britain, therefore he must have carried out the alterations himself or bought the gun from overseas.

The murderer must have had contacts in the criminal world; few would have any idea of how to obtain an illegal firearm such as was used to execute Dando. This man had knowledge which could not be legally obtained through books in a library or through magazines such as those found in George's flat. This sort of information cannot even be easily found on the Internet and George's experience and knowledge of the Internet was fairly rudimentary.

The final point, and perhaps the most important, is one that has already been touched upon: it is likely the victim knew her killer. Three sub-points can be used to add weight to this theory. Firstly no fingerprints of people unknown to Dando were found on Dando's gate, despite the fact that the gunman was not seen to be wearing gloves as he closed the gate after himself. Secondly the victim screamed in a way which showed she was surprised, not scared. Finally the killer knew Dando would be at 29 Gowan Avenue on that particular day. Dando very rarely went to her own home, and so the killer must have known her routine. It is too much to assume the killer happened to be lucky on the day he intended to do 'the kill'. This was not an opportunist kill; a person does not stand in a respectable avenue in Fulham carrying a gun in his pocket unless he expects to use it. The gunman knew, or expected, that Dando was to be there on that day. George had no reason to know such a thing because even Dando's agent did not know she was going there on that day until shortly before she arrived.

If the last point is correct then all of this information, if also correct, can be used to help determine who the real killer was.

The man responsible for the crime that ended the life of one of our nation's celebrities possessed the qualities described above. The gunman did not have the low IQ and an inability to plan and organise that Barry George does.

Chapter 11:

Conclusions

Tempus omnia revelat
(Time reveals all)

At the time of writing this book Barry George has spent almost five years in prison (including the year he spent on remand awaiting trial) for a crime he has always maintained he did not commit. Although he has launched two unsuccessful appeals it is hoped significant fresh evidence can be acquired to enable the Criminal Cases Review Commission (CCRC) to once again refer his case to the Court of Appeal. In February 2004 the CCRC began reviewing George's case based upon the fresh evidence discussed in Chapter 9 and it is expected that George will probably know whether a referral will be made, by the summer of 2005. Nonetheless six years after Dando's murder the police maintain that they got the right man.

Almost four years on from his conviction, George still struggles to understand the situation he is in and does not seem to realise the difficulties that lie ahead for him. It is impossible to underestimate the struggle that he faces but he seems to believe that any new evidence, no matter how insignificant it might be, will lead to his release. He cannot comprehend why the authorities have recently released people they claim are involved in terrorist activities, and who allegedly pose a danger to Britain, when there is allegedly strong evidence substantiating their claims, yet they are allowing him to remain in prison, for a crime he says he did not commit, when there was only weak circumstantial evidence pointing to his guilt. George, like several other prisoners I have known who claim their innocence, believes that his release could occur at any time, and has his hopes raised easily, but he is often frustrated by the appeals process, which is always very slow. It can take two years before the CCRC completes its review of a case, even when there is compelling evidence suggesting a miscarriage of justice could have taken place, and then a further eighteen months to two years before the Court of Appeal examines the evidence.

However, is George innocent? How likely is it that he could be the victim of a miscarriage of justice? The British justice system has been portrayed as being one of the fairest in the world. This may be true but British prisons have been home to an excessive number of victims of miscarriages of justice. Between 31 March 1997 and 30 June 2003 the Court of Appeal quashed 97 convictions referred by the CCRC, deeming them unsafe. If the bureaucracy surrounding applications was reduced, and more resources were made available, then there can be little doubt that more appeal hearings would be heard, and a larger number of innocent prisoners released.

On many occasions individuals have launched multiple appeals before it has been realised they were not responsible for the offences they were convicted for. Appeal judges expect overwhelming evidence that a conviction is unsafe before they consider quashing a conviction. Often such evidence is unavailable and so the hearing fails. The appeals process is lengthy and meets with many obstacles, and so just because Barry George's conviction has been upheld it does not mean the ten members of the jury who found him guilty were correct.

According to Michael Mansfield QC in his book published in 1994 (seven years before he represented George), *'Miscarriages of justice can and do happen to anyone, at any time, for any offence!'* Mansfield added that the National Association of Probation Officers have recorded that the number of people wrongly convicted could total five hundred or more.[51] Miscarriages of justice are rare, but they are by no means as uncommon as we are led to believe.

Mansfield also wrote that excuses are always given if a miscarriage of justice is recognised. The police and prosecution counsels do not usually accept they failed. Excuses such as the public mood at the time and the pressure which the police were under in order to capture the criminal(s) responsible are among those frequently given.[52] In the case of Barry George both of these factors occurred and so it is easy to understand the possibility that an injustice has occurred here as a consequence.

It must be remembered that following Dando's death the public

---

[51] (Mansfield. 1994: 274).
[52] (Mansfield. 1994: ix).

was shocked on a scale that is not often experienced in this country. As a result of this the murder squad, led by Detective Chief Inspector Campbell, was under immense pressure to get 'their man' as described in earlier chapters. When they finally found George did they therefore read too much into the incredibly flimsy evidence? An action which was later echoed at the Old Bailey, the Court of Appeal and the House of Lords.

Is it possible to state beyond reasonable doubt that George did carry out the brutal murder of Jill Dando, or could he be one of the hundreds of innocent people serving at 'Her Majesty's Pleasure'? Taking into account all of the information discussed in the previous chapters, is it possible to state, beyond reasonable doubt, that George is guilty? Many of those who followed the trial were incredibly surprised George was not acquitted, believing the evidence was not convincing enough to send a man to a lifetime of imprisonment. George was convicted on evidence of the flimsiest nature and so it is unsurprising he has a growing number of supporters.

When concentrating on arguments to demonstrate a person was wrongly convicted of a crime, it is easy to forget the victim of the crime. It is truly hoped one day the family and friends of Jill Dando will see true justice, but I wish through writing this to show that at present the wrong person is being held to account for the terrible murder. It would appear there were two victims as a result of the shooting in Fulham on 26 April 1999; one has sadly passed away, but one remains in this world but with his life effectively ended due to a miscarriage of justice.

If this country still exercised capital punishment, then George would by now have been executed for the murder of Dando. Imagine for one moment if you will that you are the judge presiding over the trial of Barry George for the murder of Jill Dando. Imagine also that capital punishment is still in use. You have heard all of the evidence; in fact you have heard more information than the court heard at George's trial. The jury have returned a guilty verdict. You know if you accept the verdict of guilty, then George will be hung by the neck until he is dead. You also know you have the right to reject the decision made by the jury and order a retrial. Do you order that George should be killed when so much doubt exists? Or do you consider the fact he could be innocent, and try to seek the truth?

Come back to reality now. George has been convicted of murder and sentenced to life imprisonment. He has had the conviction upheld at the Court of Appeal and more recently the House of Lords has refused his attempt to appeal. Is it right he should spend his whole life in prison for a crime he may have not committed? Of course it is not. To spend his whole life in prison for a crime he did not commit is no different to being hung for the crime. His life is effectively at an end.

There is, however, one consolation for George. The consolation is that the death penalty has been abolished in Britain. Whilst George is alive he is able to undertake the enormous struggle to achieve justice.

This matter should be cleared up once and for all with an independent review of the evidence and the police investigation. It would be most unfortunate for George to spend his remaining years in prison and after his death for it to be recognised he was innocent, or at least he was probably innocent and therefore should not have spent his life in prison. If the truth has not been revealed by the time of his death and his family's deaths, then history will teach that Barry George killed Jill Dando. This issue needs to be resolved in George's lifetime so he can experience freedom once again.

Let us see justice for both of the victims.

Appendix

Discussions of the information provided by witnesses in the early stages of Operation Oxborough

As was discussed in Chapter 3 a large number of sightings were reported to the police during the course of Operation Oxborough. Not all sightings discussed here refer to the killer. The police were able to eliminate some of the sightings of men once believed to have been acting in a suspicious manner. However, it is important to mention them in order to demonstrate there were multiple individuals in the Gowan Avenue area of Fulham, who were considered to have been acting in a suspicious manner. It is likely some of those sightings that have not been eliminated, including those reported by witnesses who testified at George's trial, were not at all relevant to the murder of Jill Dando. There could be a perfectly reasonable explanation as to why, for example, a man could wish to jog down Gowan Avenue at 09:40; perhaps he was on his way to work. It must be remembered there are a large number of shops and businesses in the area as well as a doctor's surgery just a few doors down from the victim's home.

The following information derives from police statements and not trial evidence, because some of the witnesses who testified at George's trial provided information very different to what they had originally informed the police. It is these statements the police relied upon during the investigation.

When reading these sightings it should be remembered, the murder took place just after 11:30 on the morning of 26 April 1999 outside number 29 Gowan Avenue.

SIGHTING A:

Date and time of the sighting: 20:00 on 25 April (the evening before the crime).

Location of the man seen: On the junction of Gowan Avenue and Fulham Palace Road.

Estimated age of the suspect: Between 35 and 40.

Estimated height of the suspect: 5'10.

Hair colour and style: Thick, black, well-groomed hair that was straight and brushed forward. It was thicker on top and shorter on the sides. The hair was collar length.

Build: Medium.

Shape of face: Wide and round, not chubby.

Facial hair: No.

Complexion: White, but a hint of Mediterranean.

Eye colour: Dark.

Clothing: A three-quarter length coat.

Any other comments: The man had dark eyebrows that were very thick.

SIGHTING B:

Date and time of the sighting: Between 06:57 and 07:00 on 26 April.

Location of the man seen: Probably opposite 29 Gowan Avenue.

Estimated age of the suspect: Late 30's.

Estimated height of the suspect: Around 5'9.

Hair colour and style: Dark. A short and smart haircut.

Build: Stocky and slightly overweight.

Facial hair: No.

Complexion: Mediterranean, olive skin.

Clothing: A black suit, a white open neck shirt.

Any other comments: He was standing next to the vehicle described in vehicle sighting 1. He seemed to be responsible for it.

SIGHTING C:
Date and time of the sighting: 09:30 on 26 April.
Location of the man seen: The witness was looking out of a window at 55 Gowan Avenue. The suspect was running down the avenue and crossed the road as he did so.
Estimated age of the suspect: Between 35 and 40.
Estimated height of the suspect: Between 5'10 and 6 foot.
Hair colour and style: Dark brown, not short or long; a normal cut.
Build: Heavy.
Shape of face: Strong and round.
Facial hair: No
Complexion: High coloured pinkish, English in appearance. When asked by the police she did not believe he looked Mediterranean.
Clothing: A medium grey suit. She was not sure of the colour of the shirt the man was wearing. He was wearing a tie.
Any other comments: The man was smart, like an estate agent.

SIGHTING D:
Date and time of the sighting: 09:40 on 26 April.
Location of the man seen: The witness was looking out of a window at 55 Gowan Avenue. The suspect was running down the avenue and crossed the road as he did so.
Estimated age of the suspect: Between 33 and 37
Estimated height of the suspect: Between 5'10 and 6 foot.
Hair colour and style: Dark brown, wavy, lots of movement.
Build: Stocky, not overweight.
Shape of face: Square.
Facial hair: No. The man had a five o'clock shadow.
Complexion: Pale, white.
Clothing: A navy blue suit, a lighter blue shirt, possibly a tie, dark shoes.
Any other comments: The man looked smart, like an estate agent.

SIGHTING E:
Date and time of the sighting: Between 10:05 and 10:10 on 26 April.
Location of the man seen: On the corner of Munster Road.
Hair colour and style: Dark.
Facial hair: No
Clothing: A dark suit. The man was wearing a hat which he removed and put in his pocket.
Any other comments: He appeared to be looking for somewhere; he was looking in many directions.

SIGHTING F:
Date and time of the sighting: Around 10:05 on 26 April.
Location of the man seen: Opposite number 17. The witness, a postman, was at Dando's home at the time.
Estimated age of the suspect: 37 to 38.
Estimated height of the suspect: 5'10 to 5'11.
Hair colour and style: Black, straight, collar length.
Build: Medium.
Facial hair: No.
Complexion: Mediterranean, tanned, slightly brown.
Clothing: A dark top. It may have been a jacket.

SIGHTING G:
Date and time of the sighting: Between 10:30 and 10:40 on 26 April.
Location of the man seen: Almost opposite number 29.
Estimated age of the suspect: 30 to 35.
Hair colour and style: Blonde or light brown, brushed back.
Build: Stocky.
Facial hair: No
Clothing: A grey suit. Smart in appearance, like an estate agent.
Any other comments: He was speaking into a mobile phone and looked agitated.

SIGHTING H:
Date and time of the sighting: Around 11:15 on 26 April.
Location of the man seen: Outside 33 Gowan Avenue or one of the neighbouring houses.
Hair colour and style: Dark.
Facial hair: No
Clothing: A dark suit, maybe blue.
Any other comments: He appeared to be smart, like an estate agent.

SIGHTING I:
Date and time of the sighting: 11:29 on 26 April
Location of the man seen: On the corner of Gowan Avenue and Munster Road
Hair colour and style: Dark
Facial hair: No
Clothing: A dark blue suit which may have been pinstriped.
Any other comments: He was wearing glasses, which appeared to be too big for him. He also appeared to be agitated.

SIGHTING J:
Date and time of the sighting: Soon after 11:30 on 26 April
Location of the man seen: At Dando's gate. The man was said to be closing the gate behind him. The man then turned left and headed down Gowan Avenue.
Estimated age of the suspect: Mid to late 30's
Estimated height of the suspect: Taller than 5'7
Hair colour and style: Thick black hair, which was pushed back and collar length
Build: Thick set with thick set shoulders
Shape of face: Full and 'jowly'
Facial hair: No
Complexion: White
Clothing: A darkish wax/Barbour style jacket
Any other comments: He appeared to be holding something up to his right shoulder. It looked like a mobile phone. He looked very respectable and so the witness believed he must have been a friend of Dando. On first glance he looked like Dando's fiancé but it was not Alan Farthing.

SIGHTING K:
Date and time of the sighting: Just after 11:30 on 26 April

Location of the man seen: The suspect was heading down Gowan Avenue from Dando's home.

Estimated age of the suspect: Between 30 and 40.

Estimated height of the suspect: Around 5'10.

Hair colour and style: A mop of thick, black, straight hair, which was collar length. It left the impression with the witness that it may have been a wig.

Build: Medium build, but the clothing worn made this difficult to ascertain.

Shape of face: Round.

Facial hair: No

Complexion: A sallow complexion.

Clothing: Very dark, perhaps black. The clothing was baggy.

Any other comments: The suspect ran then, when he realised he was being watched, he slowed down to a brisk walk. He occasionally looked back towards number 29.

SIGHTING L:
Date and time of the sighting: At some point between 11:30 and 11:35 on 26 April.

Location of the man seen: The witness was at the bottom of Gowan Avenue (the Fulham Palace Road end). The man was one hundred yards up the avenue, at the junction of Gowan Avenue and Sidbury Street; the opposite side of Gowan Avenue to that which sightings J and K had occurred. The man was walking quickly towards Fulham Palace Road.

Estimated height of the suspect: The man was simply described as tall; the distance made it difficult to determine height.

Hair colour and style: Dark, not long.

Facial hair: No

Complexion: White

Clothing: Dark clothing. He was possibly wearing a suit, which was undone. Under this he was wearing a lighter shirt and possibly a red tie.

Any other comments: The man looked like the E-fit released by the police. The E-fit produced by the police was based upon sighting Q.

SIGHTING M:
Date and time of the sighting: 11:35 on 26 April.
Location of the man seen: The suspect quickly ran across Fulham Palace Road, almost getting knocked down by a car as he did so.
Estimated height of the suspect: Between 5'10 and 5'11.
Hair colour and style: Short, dark hair.
Facial hair: No
Clothing: A dark suit.

SIGHTING N:
Date and time of the sighting: 11:38 on 26 April.
Location of the man seen: The man was seen to quickly run across Fulham Palace Road.
Estimated height of the suspect: Between 5'8 and 5'10.
Hair colour and style: Dark.
Build: Medium.
Facial hair: No.
Clothing: The man was wearing a sleeveless body warmer over a suit.

SIGHTING O:
Date and time of the sighting: Around 11:40 on 26 April.
Location of the man seen: The man was in a local park (Bishops Park) and was seen to be climbing over railings.
Facial hair: No.
Clothing: A blue windcheater.

SIGHTING P:
Date and time of the sighting: Around 11:40 on 26 April.
Location of the man seen: The man was in Bishops Park leaning over railings.
Hair colour and style: Dark.
Facial hair: No.
Clothing: A dark coat, which went down to his thighs.
Any other comments: He was speaking into a mobile phone and appeared to speak more quietly as the witness approached.

SIGHTING Q:
Date and time of the sighting: Around 11:45.
Location of the man seen: The man emerged from Bishops Park and waited at a bus stop on Fulham Palace Road. As he waited he was standing close to the man who reported the sighting.
Estimated age of the suspect: Late 30's.
Estimated height of the suspect: Between 5'9 and 5'10.
Hair colour and style: Thick, dark hair but much shorter than the hair of the man seen in sightings J and K.
Build: Medium.
Shape of face: Round.
Facial hair: No
Complexion: He was dark and had a slightly foreign appearance.
Eye colour: Large, dark eyes.
Clothing: A dark suit and white shirt.
Any other comments: He had marks upon the bridge of his nose, which are consistent with him having worn a pair of ill-fitting spectacles. He was sweating a lot and as a result has been named 'Sweating Man' by police. He also seemed to be very agitated. An E-fit was based upon this sighting.

SIGHTING OF VEHICLE 1:
Date and time of the sighting: Around 06:57 on 26 April.
Location of the vehicle: Approximately opposite number 29.
Description of the vehicle: Maroon.
Description of the movements of the vehicle: It was stationary. However, it was unnecessarily double-parked. By 07:15 the car had left.
Any other comments: The vehicle appeared, in the witness' opinion, to be a taxi. The man described in sighting B was believed to be responsible for the vehicle. He was standing next to it and was seen to be wiping the windscreen with his arm.

SIGHTING OF VEHICLE 2:
Date and time of the sighting: 10:08 on 26 April.
Location of the vehicle: On Gowan Avenue facing towards Fulham Palace Road. It was illegally parked.
Description of the vehicle: A dark blue Range Rover.
Description of any occupants: There was a man sat in the driver's seat.
Description of the movements of the vehicle: It was stationary.
Any other comments: The occupant tapped on the windscreen and motioned for the witness, a traffic warden who had started entering the car's details into her parking ticket producing machine, to go away.

SIGHTING OF VEHICLE 3:
Date and time of the sighting: 10:10 on 26 April.
Location of the vehicle: It was first seen on Munster Road.
Description of the vehicle: Dark blue Range Rover.
Description of the movements of the vehicle: It drove along Munster Road, along Doneraile Street and into Stevenage Road, parking near Fulham F.C.'s stadium. It was driving very closely to the witness' vehicle, as if to hurry her along.
Any other comments: The witness, who reported this sighting, also reported sighting E.

SIGHTING OF VEHICLE 4:
Date and time of the sighting: 11:00 on 26 April.
Location of the vehicle: It was somewhere in the Gowan Avenue/Munster Road area.
Description of the vehicle: A dark blue Range Rover
Description of the movements of the vehicle: It was stationary

SIGHTING OF VEHICLE 5:
Date and time of the sighting: Between 11:45 and 11:50 on 26 April.
Location of the vehicle: It emerged from Doneraille Street. The witness was standing at the junction of Gowan Avenue and Fulham Palace Road.
Description of the vehicle: Dark blue Range Rover.
Description of any occupants: There were two occupants, one of whom was Mediterranean in appearance.
Description of the movements of the vehicle: It travelled very fast through a red light. It was travelling so fast it leaned over slightly as it moved.

SIGHTING OF VEHICLE 6:
Date and time of the sighting: 11:52 on 26 April.
Location of the vehicle: Putney Bridge.
Description of the vehicle: Blue Range Rover.
Description of any occupants: The driver had dark hair.
Description of the movements of the vehicle: It was heading south over Putney Bridge.
Any other comments: This vehicle was captured on CCTV, which is how it came to be provided to the police.

It must be noted, certain characteristics could have been described incorrectly, or there could have been a fault in the memory of the witness. However, most, if not all, of these sightings were reported within the first fortnight of the investigation; most had been reported on the day of the crime itself. If a witness clearly describes a man wearing, for example, a blue suit jacket and he or she is certain of the colour, yet minutes later another witness saw a man wearing a black suit, who again is certain of the colour. It must be noted, the two descriptions do not correspond to the same man, and so two different men were seen.

Sightings C and D were of the same man. The witnesses, who reported these two sightings, were together at the time and were both looking out of the same window. These two sightings occurred at the same time although one witness believed it occurred at 09:30 whereas the other believed it was ten minutes later. Sightings J and K can also be linked together. This is because the witness who reported sighting J, Richard Hughes, could see the witness who reported sighting K, Geoffrey Upfill-Brown, also looking at the same man. It was these two witnesses, of course, who are the only two people to have certainly seen the gunman leaving Dando's garden immediately after the murder. The alternative hypothesis would be that Hughes saw a man who immediately following the shooting approached Dando's dead body and was able to simply walk away very calmly, which is not very conceivable.

It would seem it is probable that sightings A and F are linked. This would appear to be the case because both witnesses reported seeing a man of Mediterranean appearance who had black, collar length hair and clothing of the same description. Both witnesses had reported the sightings, to the police, early on in the investigation while the man's appearance was clear in their minds. One must, however, exercise some caution because, due to the relatively vague nature of the descriptions, the sightings could have been of two different men. The evidence does strongly suggest both witnesses saw the same man, a man who may have had nothing to do with the crime.

It is also possible for sightings L and Q to be linked together to show that another 'suspicious' man was in the area on that morning. The witness who reported sighting L, Janet Bolton, told friends, the man in the E-fit, the man described in sighting Q, was the man she had seen shortly after the crime. The descriptions are similar; for example with regards to clothing. Bolton has always maintained she saw Sweating Man on Gowan Avenue, and therefore it is, at the very least, possible both sightings were of the same man and therefore Sweating Man had run from Gowan Avenue, through Bishops Park and onto Fulham Palace Road.

Sightings A and F were of a man who was Mediterranean in appearance having an olive complexion. For the time being this individual shall be referred to as Spiros.

Sightings C and D were of a man who was pale, white and English in appearance. Neither of the witnesses believed he looked Mediterranean and therefore these sightings were of a man who was not Spiros. It must be stressed here, as it is a fundamentally important point in this case, this man was not of olive complexion and had no Mediterranean features. For the time being this man shall be referred to as Robert.

Sightings J and K relate to the same man; the gunman. It would appear this man could not have been Spiros or Robert. This deduction is based upon the differences in clothing. Unlike the prosecution I do not adhere to the view that the killer kept returning home to get changed, thus potentially missing the opportunity to carry out the act of murder. To repeatedly change clothing is a time consuming process; a process for which there is no time for when carrying out a kill. It would be almost unprecedented for a murderer to keep altering his appearance whilst waiting for a victim to arrive. For now I shall refer to this man as Daniel.

This leaves us with many sightings unaccounted for. Can it be said these all represented different men and therefore several suspicious men were in the vicinity of Gowan Avenue? Or are some more of the sightings related to the three men described above?

It is possible that the witness who reported sighting B, Susan Mayes, also saw Spiros. This is because Mayes reported seeing a man of Mediterranean appearance, with olive skin and of a similar age and height to that of the man reported in sightings A and F. The description of this man's hair varies from the description of Spiros. In court the witness told she had seen a man who had untidy, black collar length hair despite what she said in her original statement. It is possible, sighting B was of Spiros. However, it is also possible that a second man of Mediterranean appearance was on Gowan Avenue.

One of the occupants of the Range Rover observed in vehicle sighting 5 appeared to be of Mediterranean origin. It is therefore possible, Spiros was driven somewhere soon after the murder. If we were to follow the logic of Orlando Pownall, who represented the Crown during George's trial, we would have to accept the man in the Range Rover was Spiros, as was the man seen by Susan Mayes (sighting B). This is because allegedly it is inconceivable that two men of the same general appearance could have been in the Gowan Avenue area on the morning of 26 April 1999.

Can any of the other sightings of 'suspicious' men have referred to this Mediterranean man, the man named Spiros? It would appear not because those who described complexion, other than those who reported sightings A, B and F, described a man who was pale and white. For witnesses to describe a man as Mediterranean the man must have been unmistakably dark skinned and not at all pale in complexion. Therefore it would seem the only witnesses who saw

Spiros were those who made sightings A and F, and possibly B. This indicates the Mediterranean man had left Gowan Avenue around 10:10 on the morning of the shooting. He may, therefore, have had nothing to do with Dando's murder.

Can any more sightings be attributed to the man named Robert? Sighting B was certainly not of Robert because of the differences in complexion. It is difficult to link sightings to this man because many people could be described in the same way as he. It is probable Robert had no involvement in the crime because he was seen to be jogging down Gowan Avenue around two hours before the murder. He was probably only on the avenue for a few minutes which explains why no one else saw a man wearing a suit and blue shirt.

It is also difficult to attribute more sightings to Daniel. This is because there seem to be no other sightings of a man of white, sallow complexion, with long hair and dark, loose fitting clothing, having been in the area at any time on that particular morning. This is not to say other witnesses did not see the killer, but it certainly is in keeping with the belief that the gunman entered the area quickly and left as swiftly as he had arrived.

Having linked numerous sightings to show some witnesses saw the same man, although numerous men were seen, we are still left with sightings we can not fit in with those for which names have been assigned. Some of the remaining sightings may be connected to Spiros, Robert and Daniel. However, there is insufficient information to say, with any degree of confidence, this is the case; theories cannot be constructed without sufficient facts.

There were numerous sightings, which were not at all similar to the others, and therefore cannot be linked to the murderer. Sighting G certainly does not fit in with any of the three men. This is because the man, whose description is provided in sighting G, had a different hair and suit colour to that of other sightings. Sighting I was of a man who was wearing a dark blue suit, which may or may not have been pinstriped. This man was also described as having worn glasses – a description which is unique. The man seen by the witness who reported sighting N, was wearing a body warmer. Clearly none of these can be linked with each other or, seemingly, any of the other sightings.

The descriptions were incredibly vague, with some witnesses being unable to provide an estimate of the age and height of the man they had seen. There is certainly insufficient information to link all, or even most, of the sightings due to the nature of the descriptions. Who is to say it is not possible for two men in the same area could be around 5'10, with dark hair and wearing a dark suit and be acting in a way that could later be viewed as suspicious?

Over the course of the operation, detectives received information leading to many of the sightings being disregarded as having involvement in the crime being investigated. During the first few days of the investigation an emphasis was placed upon a man seen speaking into a mobile phone near to the victim's home (sighting G). His loitering was considered to be very suspicious. This man, however, was eliminated from the enquiry, after many months, when it emerged he was a gasman who was working at the time. Therefore it is a known fact, more than one person was acting in a way which appeared to be suspicious in the area on the day of the murder. Is it possible other sightings could be unrelated to the crime?

This would depend upon how many different people were involved in the murder. For a significant amount of time the police incorporated all of the sightings into one scenario because it was easier to understand all of the sightings if they were connected together. They believed numerous witnesses had seen the same man although descriptions of a man who varied from the appearance of the person seen leaving Dando's garden had been provided. Discrepancies in the appearances of those described was accounted for by the suggestion of three different men being involved; the gunman, a lookout whose task was to ensure the gunman was not seen and a getaway driver which explained the sightings of Range Rovers.

If this was the case then it is difficult to eliminate sightings. However, this theory is easily destroyed. It relied too heavily on the view that every sighting was relevant. If only three men were involved this would only account for two men on Gowan Avenue, yet as was shown earlier the varying descriptions suggest there were more than two individuals reported to police. Also, the man seen in sighting Q left the area on a bus. If there was a getaway driver involved, why would this man, who the police considered to be the murderer, have to use a bus? As a result of Oxborough having related all of the sightings, which could not be eliminated, to the killer, unrealistic theories were created. As the police later took the view the murder was carried out by a lone gunman, then all the sightings, if they correspond to the killer, must all be the same man. This is clearly not the case.

Sightings M and N represent two different people; this is clear because both sightings were of a man wearing strikingly different clothing but they were both seen running across the same road at slightly different times. It is not possible they were the same man and therefore at least one of these men was not the gunman, despite the perceived suspicious actions observed.

Sighting N was certainly not a sighting of the fugitive. The sighting occurred at 11:38, at the earliest, and so between six and eight minutes had passed since the murder, yet the man was still on Gowan Avenue when he was first seen, before he ran quickly across Fulham Palace Road. The murderer had swiftly made his way down Gowan Avenue, and so it is unlikely in six to eight minutes he had only travelled as far as the end of the avenue. When studying sighting L it also seems, yet another man, who was uninvolved in the crime, was reported to the police. This is because the man was seen running on the opposite side of the road to that which the gunman had begun his escape.

The man reported in sighting I must have been uninvolved in the crime, if a lone gunman was responsible, because just minutes before the murder he was seen to be wearing a dark blue suit which does not resemble the description of the clothing worn by the man seen leaving the scene of the crime

Sightings O, P and Q were eventually believed by police to be sightings which were of a man (or men) who had no involvement in the circumstances which led to the death of Jill Dando. This is because of the variation in appearance between these sightings and the sightings from Gowan Avenue and areas immediately in its proximity. It is from one of these sightings (sighting Q) the E-fit of the killer, yet which the police produced, was based upon. Therefore the E-fit does not represent the killer, it is of someone who bore little resemblance in fact to the killer. However, it is important to discuss these sightings here as they were seen to be important pieces of information in the inquiry.

The descriptions of a man on Gowan Avenue on the day of the murder related to at least five, and probably more than five, men; Spiros, Robert, Daniel, the man with the body warmer and the man with the glasses and blue suit.

In addition to the sightings of men waiting, running and walking close to the scene, there were also reports of the sightings, listed earlier, of vehicles whose driver's were acting suspiciously. One vehicle, which was believed to be a blue Range Rover, drove away from the area at great speed approximately twenty minutes after the crime. Other vehicles, which were initially linked, were reported. Ironically these vehicles were considered to be separate vehicles because they looked too different. However, during George's trial all of the sightings reported by the prosecution witnesses were considered to be of the same man despite the fact they had different appearances.

Therefore, clearly a number of different individuals were acting suspiciously in the vicinity of the murder scene around the time and day of the murder. The police were wrong to assume the sightings were linked. By investigating men described by 'witnesses' who looked nothing like the man leaving the scene of the murder immediately following the murder, the police were wasting resources which were required elsewhere. During George's trial it was claimed to be *"inconceivable that there were two men in Gowan Avenue that morning, both of the same age height and general appearance ..."*[53]. However, as has been shown, there was more than one person acting suspicious and so suddenly the inconceivable becomes conceivable.

Those references of a man known as 'Trilby Man' were not listed above. This is because it is unlikely he was involved in the murder and there is no evidence to suggest this man was seen on the day of the crime. Nevertheless, it is important he is briefly discussed in this section, although police did not place much of an emphasis upon this man in their investigations.

The sightings of Trilby Man, a man seen in close proximity of Dando's home on three separate occasions in the weeks before her death, provided evidence suggesting the television presenter may have been stalked. There is no disputing the fact that on each occasion it was the same man who was seen, for it was the same witness who saw the man on each of the three occasions. It is possible that this man was interested in Dando although it is unlikely. If he had been staking out Dando's home he would have

---

[53] Orlando Pownall, of the prosecution counsel, speaking on 4 May 2001 during Barry George's trial.

known it was incredibly unlikely for the victim to have visited Gowan Avenue on that particular day. It was only by chance she happened to go there at all on 26 April 1999. Therefore it is unlikely this man was the killer.

The locations he was seen, suggest he was not interested in the victim. All of the sightings of this man were made in the Gowan Avenue area. However, none were particularly close to number 29 itself; on two days the man was standing at a spot where Dando's home could not even be seen. On the other day he was seen opposite the corner of Gowan Avenue and Munster Road near a school, and therefore was far from the presenter's house. When he was seen half an hour to three-quarters of an hour later, he was still in the same spot, indicating he had little or no interest in Dando's home. This is far from sufficient evidence to suggest he was stalking, or in any way interested, in the victim.

It is not as easy to link the different sightings of vehicles. This is because often it is only a registration plate, which makes them unique; two vehicles can look incredibly similar. Many people can own the same model of vehicle. There may be no connection between those reported to the police. Four of the sightings were believed to be of blue Range Rovers, which would suggest they could have possibly been linked. It later emerged one of the vehicles described as a dark blue Range Rover was really a Cherokee jeep and therefore this vehicle cannot be linked with the others seen on the morning of the murder. The Range Rover sighted in vehicle sighting 6, was eliminated from the investigation after it emerged the occupants had no involvement in the crime despite its suspicious movements.

In summary it is highly unlikely that many of the sightings of suspicious men and suspicious vehicles were in any way connected to the murder of Jill Dando. It is also probable that most of those 'eyewitnesses' who testified at George's trial had not seen anything of direct relevance to the case. Their evidence muddies the water and in no way helps determine who murdered Jill Dando.

Bibliography

Ainsworth, P. B. 2001. *Psychology, Law and Eyewitness Testimony.* - (New York: John Wiley and Sons, inc.).

Britton, P. 2001. *Picking Up the Pieces.* - (London: Transworld Publishers).

Conan Doyle, A. 1988. *Strange Studies From Life and Other Narratives: The Complete True Crime Writings of Sir Arthur Conan Doyle.* - (Bloomington: Gaslight Publications).

Cornish, W. R. 1968. *The Jury.* - (London: The Penguin Press).

Cutler, B. L., Penrod, S. and Fisher, R. P. 1994. Conceptual, practical and empirical issues associated with eyewitness identification test media. In D. E. Ross, J. D. Read and M. P. Togla (Eds.). *Adult Eyewitness Testimony: Current Trends and Development.* - (Cambridge: Cambridge University Press).

Cutler, B. L. and Penrod, S. D. 1995. *Mistaken Identification: The Eyewitness, Psychology and the Law.* - (Cambridge: Cambridge University Press).

Cutting Edge, 2002. *Did Barry George Kill Jill Dando?* 19 August 2002. Carlton TV.

Erzinçlioglu, Z. 2000. *Every Contact Leaves a Trace: Scientific Detection in the Twentieth Century.* - (London: Carlton Books Ltd).

Fleming, R. and Miller, H. 1995. *Scotland Yard: The True Life Story of the Metropolitan Police.* - (London: Penguin Books Ltd.).

Gallagher, R. 2002. *I'll Be Watching You: True Stories of Stalkers and Their Victims.* - (London: Virgin Books Ltd.).

Henderson, R. 2001. *Barry George and the Celebrity Effect: A Miscarriage of Justice in the Making.* - (London: Libertarian Alliance).

Houde, J. 1999. *Crime Lab: A Guide for Nonscientists.* - (Ventura: Calico Press).

Mansfield, M. 1994. *Presumed Guilty.* - (London: Reed Consumer Books Ltd).

McVicar, J. 2002. *Dead on Time: How and Why Barry George Executed Jill Dando.* - (London: Blake Publishing Ltd.).

Smith, D. J. 2002. *All About Jill: The Life and Death of Jill Dando.* - (London: Time Warner Books UK).

Smith, J. C. 1995. *Criminal Evidence.* - (London: Sweet and Maxwell).

Vrij, A. 2002. Deception in children: a literature review and implications for children's testimony. In H. L. Westcotts, G. M. Davies and H. C. Bull (Eds.). *Children's Testimony: A Handbook of Psychological Research and Forensic Practice.* - (Chichester: John Wiley and Sons Ltd.). pp. 175 – 194.

Printed in the United Kingdom
by Lightning Source UK Ltd.
108750UKS00001B/49-66